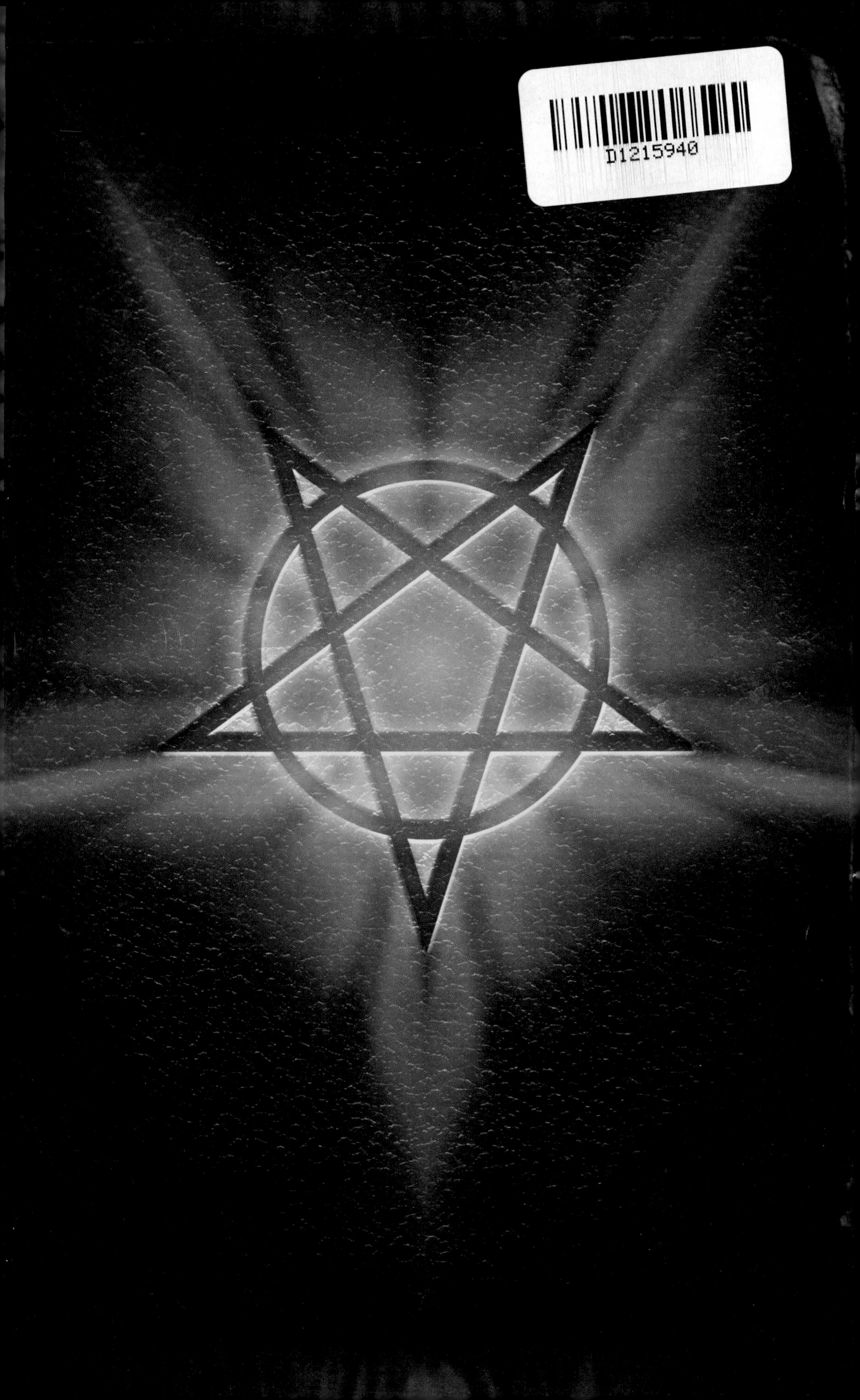

HELLSTROM
EVIL ORIGINS

WRITERS
GARY FRIEDRICH, CHRIS CLAREMONT, BILL MANTLO
& J.M. DeMATTEIS with DON PERLIN

PENCILERS
TOM SUTTON, JIM MOONEY, HERB TRIMPE,
SAL BUSCEMA, RUSS HEATH & DON PERLIN

INKERS
SYD SHORES, FRANK CHIARAMONTE, BOB McLEOD,
RUSS HEATH & PABLO MARCOS with JACK ABEL, KIM DeMULDER,
ANDY MUSHYNSKY & ALAN KUPPERBERG

COLORISTS
GEORGE ROUSSOS, LINDA LESSMANN, MARIE SEVERIN,
PETRA GOLDBERG, DIANE BUSCEMA & DON WARFIELD

LETTERERS
JOHN COSTANZA, CHARLOTTE JETTER, ART SIMEK
KAREN MANTLO, DIANA ALBERS & SHELLY LEFERMAN

ASSISTANT EDITORS
MARY JO DUFFY & ANN NOCENTI

EDITORS
ROY THOMAS, LEN WEIN, ARCHIE GOODWIN & AL MILGROM

FRONT COVER ARTISTS
GIL KANE & VERONICA GANDINI

COLLECTION EDITOR: JENNIFER GRÜNWALD
ASSISTANT MANAGING EDITOR: MAIA LOY
ASSISTANT MANAGING EDITOR: LISA MONTALBANO
ASSOCIATE MANAGER, DIGITAL ASSETS: JOE HOCHSTEIN
MASTERWORKS EDITOR: CORY SEDLMEIER
SENIOR EDITOR, SPECIAL PROJECTS: MARK D. BEAZLEY
VP PRODUCTION & SPECIAL PROJECTS: JEFF YOUNGQUIST
RESEARCH & LAYOUT: JEPH YORK
COLOR & ART RESTORATION: MICHAEL KELLEHER & KELLUSTRATION,
TOM MULLIN, COLORTEK, DIGIKORE, & JERRON QUALITY COLOR
BOOK DESIGNERS: JAY BOWEN with RODOLFO MURAGUCHI
SVP PRINT, SALES & MARKETING: DAVID GABRIEL
EDITOR IN CHIEF: C.B. CEBULSKI

HELLSTROM: EVIL ORIGINS. Contains material originally published in magazine form as GHOST RIDER (1973) #1-2, MARVEL SPOTLIGHT (1971) #12-13 and #24, SON OF SATAN (1976) #8, and DEFENDERS (1972) #92 and #120-121. First printing 2020. ISBN 978-1-302-92516-1. Published by MARVEL WORLDWIDE, INC., a subsidiary of MARVEL ENTERTAINMENT, LLC. OFFICE OF PUBLICATION: 1290 Avenue of the Americas, New York, NY 10104. © 2020 MARVEL No similarity between any of the names, characters, persons, and/or institutions in this magazine with those of any living or dead person or institution is intended, and any such similarity which may exist is purely coincidental. **Printed in the U.S.A.** KEVIN FEIGE, Chief Creative Officer; DAN BUCKLEY, President, Marvel Entertainment; JOHN NEE, Publisher; JOE QUESADA, EVP & Creative Director; TOM BREVOORT, SVP of Publishing; DAVID BOGART, Associate Publisher & SVP of Talent Affairs; Publishing & Partnership; DAVID GABRIEL, VP of Print & Digital Publishing; JEFF YOUNGQUIST, VP of Production & Special Projects; DAN CARR, Executive Director of Publishing Technology; ALEX MORALES, Director of Publishing Operations; DAN EDINGTON, Managing Editor; SUSAN CRESPI, Production Manager; STAN LEE, Chairman Emeritus. For information regarding advertising in Marvel Comics or on Marvel.com, please contact Vit DeBellis, Custom Solutions & Integrated Advertising Manager, at vdebellis@marvel.com. For Marvel subscription inquiries, please call 888-511-5480. **Manufactured between 6/19/2020 and 7/21/2020 by LSC COMMUNICATIONS INC., KENDALLVILLE, IN, USA.**

10 9 8 7 6 5 4 3 2 1

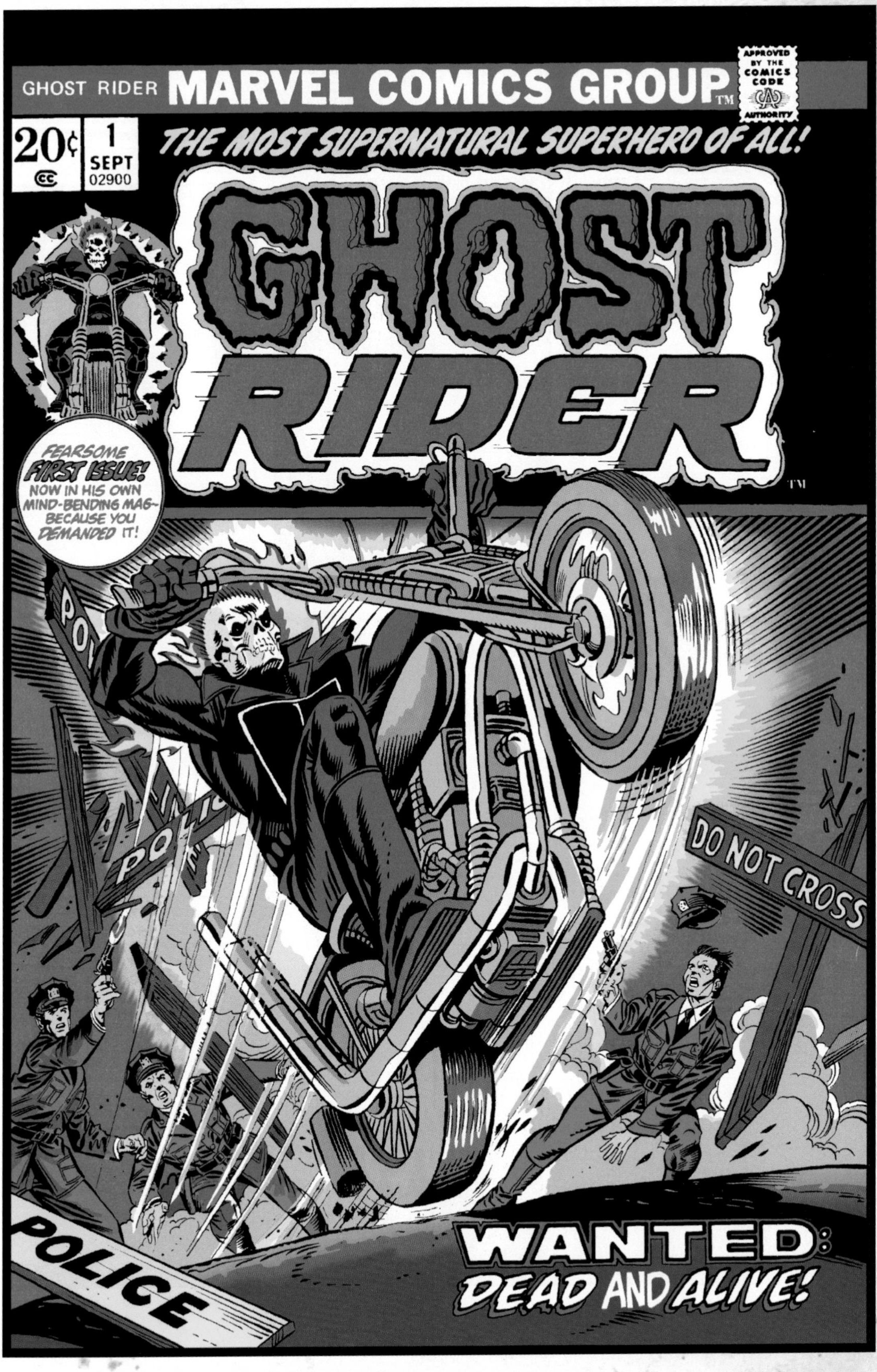
GHOST RIDER
MARVEL COMICS GROUP
APPROVED BY THE COMICS CODE AUTHORITY
20¢
1
SEPT
02900
THE MOST SUPERNATURAL SUPERHERO OF ALL!
GHOST RIDER
FEARSOME FIRST ISSUE! NOW IN HIS OWN MIND-BENDING MAG-- BECAUSE YOU DEMANDED IT!
DO NOT CROSS
POLICE
WANTED: DEAD AND ALIVE!

STAN LEE PRESENTS: THE GHOST RIDER! ™

| GARY FRIEDRICH, WRITER | TOM SUTTON, ARTIST | SYD SHORES, INKER | JOHN COSTANZA, LETTERER | GEORGE ROUSSOS, COLORIST | ROY THOMAS, EDITOR |

EARLY MORNING! THE FIRST RAYS OF DAWN ARE TOO WEAK TO CUT THROUGH THE HEAVY FOG WHICH ENSHROUDS A TINY CEMETERY IN NEW ENGLAND--

VICTORIA HELLSTROM
BORN MARCH 4, 1928
DIED AUG. 21, 1953

A HAND! IT REACHES DOWNWARD THROUGH THE SWIRLING MISTS AND PLACES A GOLD CROSS UPON A GRAVE--

HELLSTROM
BORN MARCH 4, 1928
DIED AUG. 21, 1953

A MAN! HE STANDS BY THE GRAVE AND STARES AT THE WEATHER-BEATEN TOMBSTONE--

--REMEMBERING HIS MOTHER, AND WONDERING IF HE WILL EVER FACE AGAIN--

"A WOMAN POSSESSED!"

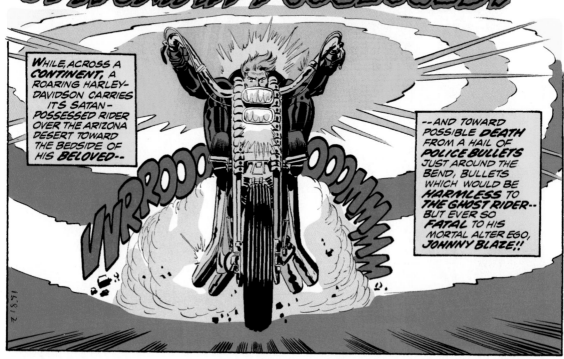

WHILE, ACROSS A CONTINENT, A ROARING HARLEY-DAVIDSON CARRIES ITS SATAN-POSSESSED RIDER OVER THE ARIZONA DESERT TOWARD THE BEDSIDE OF HIS BELOVED--

VVRROOOOOOOOMMM

--AND TOWARD POSSIBLE DEATH FROM A HAIL OF POLICE BULLETS JUST AROUND THE BEND, BULLETS WHICH WOULD BE HARMLESS TO THE GHOST RIDER-- BUT EVER SO FATAL TO HIS MORTAL ALTER EGO, JOHNNY BLAZE!!

4

BUT THE POLICE ARE NOT ON HIS MIND -- NOR IS HIS CONSTANT BATTLE TO AVOID THE LOSS OF HIS SOUL TO *SATAN!* ON THIS MORNING, *JOHNNY BLAZE* THINKS ONLY OF THE GIRL NAMED *ROXANNE* -- THE GIRL HE *LOVES* -- THE GIRL WHO AT THIS VERY MOMENT MAY LIE *DYING!*

HIS PULSE *POUNDS* AS HE REMEMBERS THE DEADLY *COPPERHEADS* WHICH BIT HER IN THE MIDST OF A RITUAL CONDUCTED BY THE MAD INDIAN WITCH-DOCTOR CALLED * *SNAKE-DANCE* --

*MARVEL SPOTLIGHT #9. --ROY.

AND BITTER *TEARS* STING HIS EYES AS HE RECALLS THE PHYSICIAN'S FATEFUL *WORDS* --

IF WE DON'T GET *SERUM* -- THERE'S NO WAY SHE CAN *LIVE!*

THEN, BANNED FROM HER *BEDSIDE,* HE RECALLS BEING CHASED INTO THE DESERT BY POLICE -- AND TRAPPED THERE BY THE TREACHEROUS *WITCH-WOMAN* -- *

*MARVEL SPOTLIGHT #11! --ROY AGAIN!

-- A DESPERATE DAUGHTER OF THE DEVIL WHO NEARLY *DESTROYED* HIM BEFORE *FAILING* HER MASTER AND HURLING HERSELF TO A FIERY DEATH ON THE DESERT FLOOR!

SUDDENLY, THE PAST EXPLODES INTO *OBLIVION* -- AND THE *PRESENT* COMES RUSHING TOWARD HIM LIKE THE *GRIM REAPER* ON A JET-PROPELLED CYCLE -- A *ROADBLOCK* -- THE *LAW* --

GOING *WAY* TOO FAST TO *STOP!*

ONLY CHANCE IS TO *CRASH* IT -- AND EVEN THAT'S A *LONG ONE!*

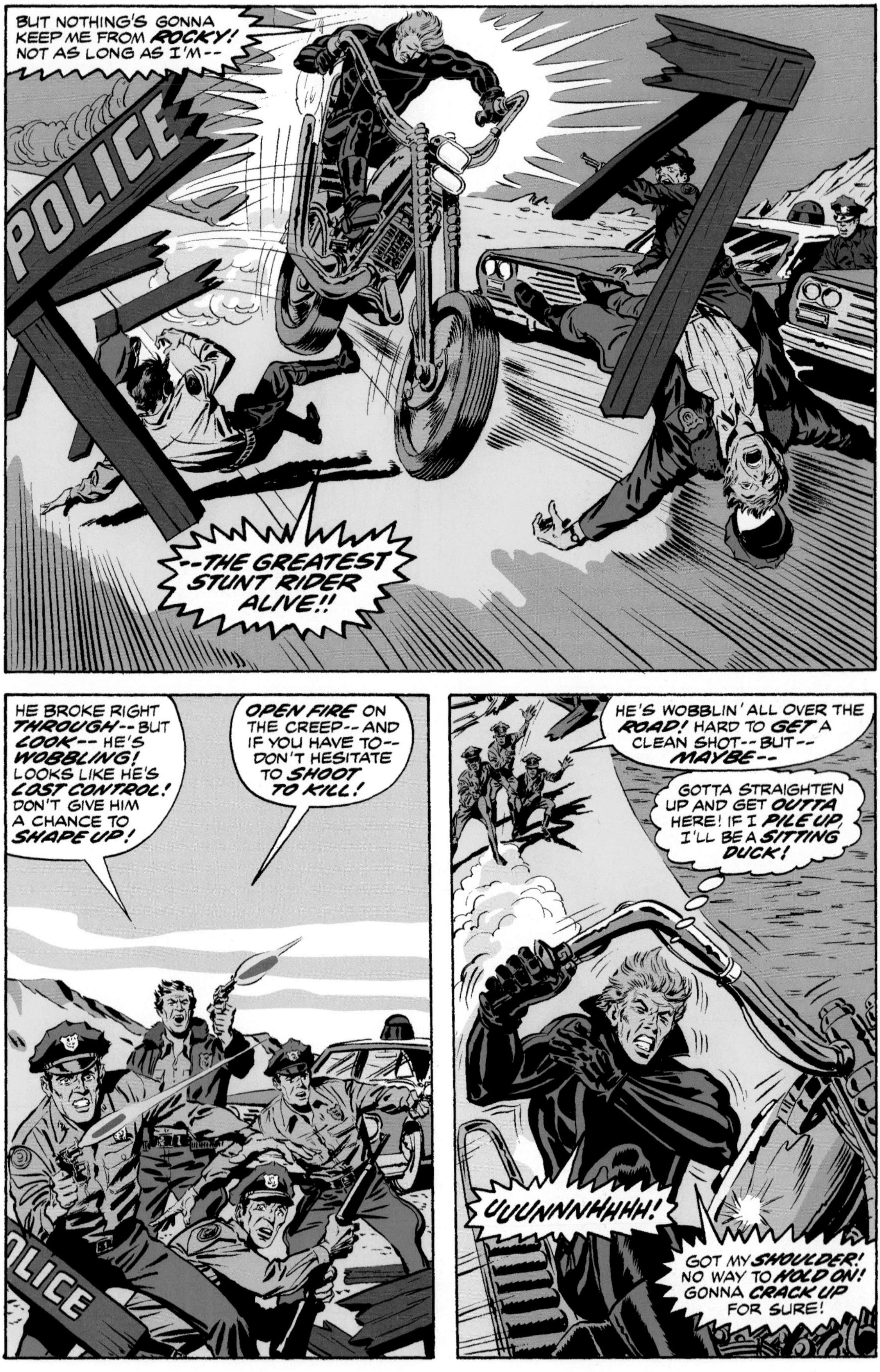
BUT NOTHING'S GONNA KEEP ME FROM ROCKY! NOT AS LONG AS I'M--
POLICE
--THE GREATEST STUNT RIDER ALIVE!!
HE BROKE RIGHT THROUGH-- BUT LOOK-- HE'S WOBBLING! LOOKS LIKE HE'S LOST CONTROL! DON'T GIVE HIM A CHANCE TO SHAPE UP!
OPEN FIRE ON THE CREEP-- AND IF YOU HAVE TO-- DON'T HESITATE TO SHOOT TO KILL!
LICE
HE'S WOBBLIN' ALL OVER THE ROAD! HARD TO GET A CLEAN SHOT-- BUT-- MAYBE--
GOTTA STRAIGHTEN UP AND GET OUTTA HERE! IF I PILE UP, I'LL BE A SITTING DUCK!
UUUNNNHHHH!
GOT MY SHOULDER! NO WAY TO HOLD ON! GONNA CRACK UP FOR SURE!

HAND...FROZEN TO THE *THROTTLE*--AND--*WIDE OPEN!*

GETTING *DIZZY*--STARTING TO VEER OFF THE *ROAD!* OH, MAN-- THIS IS *IT!!*

WHROOM!

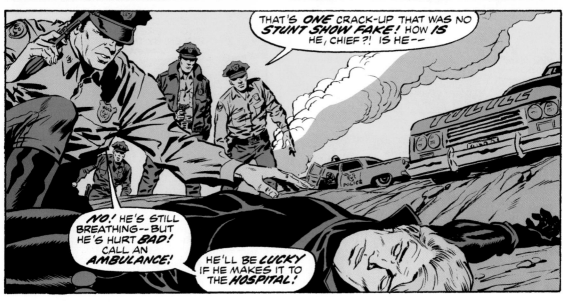

THAT'S *ONE* CRACK-UP THAT WAS NO *STUNT SHOW FAKE!* HOW *IS* HE, CHIEF?! IS HE--

NO! HE'S STILL BREATHING--BUT HE'S HURT *BAD!* CALL AN *AMBULANCE!*

HE'LL BE *LUCKY* IF HE MAKES IT TO THE *HOSPITAL!*

SEVERAL MILES AWAY FROM THE CRASH SITE, YET *ANOTHER* TRAGEDY IS UNFOLDING ON A SHABBY *INDIAN RESERVATION* AS AN OLD OLD APACHE MEDICINE MAN WHO ONCE CALLED HIMSELF *SNAKE-DANCE* DISCOVERS--

U.S. GOV INDIA RESER

THIS IS HOW I *FOUND* HER, SAM-- STARING AT THE *CEILING,* HER EYES *OPEN* BUT *UNSEEING!*

WELL, WHAT THE DEVIL'S *WRONG* WITH HER?! DOES SHE HAVE A *FEVER?!*

NO! I HAVE SEEN IT *BEFORE* -- MANY *YEARS* AGO! IT IS THE WORK OF A *DEMON!*

DON'T START THAT MUMBO-JUMBO AGAIN! THIS IS NO TIME FOR *FOLK-LORE!* CALL A *DOCTOR!*

THERE *IS* NO DOCTOR-- FOR A SOUL *POSSESSED!*

SHE DOESN'T EVEN KNOW WE'RE *HERE!* AND SHE'S SO *COLD*--

I MAY BE AN *OLD FOOL*-- BUT THIS I HAVE WITNESSED *BEFORE!* YOU MUST *BELIEVE* ME, MY SON--

-- WHEN THE EYES GROW *WIDE*-- AND THE SKIN BECOMES LIKE NEW-FALLEN SNOW-- A *DEVIL* IS RESPONSIBLE!

THAT IS ONLY LINDA'S *BODY* WE SEE LYING THERE! HER SOUL IS *GONE*-- STOLEN BY THE FORCES OF *DARKNESS!*

AND THERE IS NOTHING-- *NOTHING*-- WE CAN DO TO *SAVE* HER!

MORNING, ROCKY! BROUGHT BY SOME FLOWERS TO CHEER YOU *UP!*

BART! THAT'S VERY *SWEET* OF YOU! IT'S GOOD TO SEE A *FAMILIAR FACE!*

GUESS I HAD A *CLOSE CALL--* BUT I FEEL *FINE* THIS MORNING!

GLAD TO *HEAR* IT! WE CAN USE YOU BACK AT THE *SHOW--* SINCE *BLAZE* HASN'T BEEN *SHOWING UP* LATELY!

BUT-- HE WAS WITH *ME* LAST NIGHT, BART! HE SAVED MY *LIFE!*

SO I *HEARD--* AN' IM GLAD HE *DID!* AN' MAYBE I'M ONLY *BART SLADE,* MR. HIGH-AND-MIGHTY JOHNNY BLAZE'S *ROAD MANAGER--*

--BUT I'M ALSO WORRIED ABOUT THE *CYCLE SHOW!*

IF YOUR FLAME-FACED BOY FRIEND DOESN'T START *RIDING--* IT'S GONNA GO *BROKE!*

AND IF *THAT* HAPPENS, *ALL* OF US START COLLECTING UNEMPLOYMENT!

SO JOHNNY BETTER STOP THIS *VANISHING ACT* OF HIS AND--

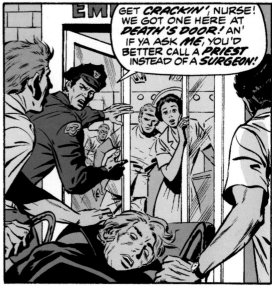

GET *CRACKIN',* NURSE! WE GOT ONE HERE AT *DEATH'S DOOR!* AN' IF YA ASK *ME,* YOU'D BETTER CALL A *PRIEST* INSTEAD OF A *SURGEON!*

MY DAUGHTER--MY PRECIOUS LITTLE ONE! IT IS TRUE! THERE IS NO WAY TO HELP HER!

MAYBE NOT! BUT I LOVE HER TOO--AND I'M SURE GONNA TRY!

NO! WE MUST STAY WITH HER--UNTIL THE DEMON LETS HER SOUL REST!

YOU STAY WITH HER, OLD MAN! I'VE GOT ANOTHER IDEA!

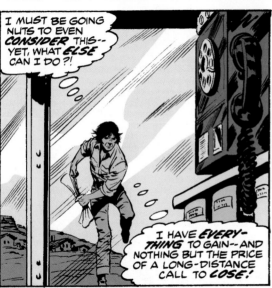

I MUST BE GOING NUTS TO EVEN CONSIDER THIS-- YET, WHAT ELSE CAN I DO?!

I HAVE EVERY-THING TO GAIN--AND NOTHING BUT THE PRICE OF A LONG-DISTANCE CALL TO LOSE!

THAT'S RIGHT, OPERATOR-- PERSON-TO-PERSON-- MR. DAIMON HELLSTROM-- IN BOSTON!

AND WOULD YOU PLEASE HURRY? THIS IS AN EMERGENCY!

WHA--?! OH, THE PHONE! I MUST HAVE DOZED OFF! PERHAPS IT'S A CUSTOMER! I COULD CERTAINLY USE ONE!

RRING!

YES-- THIS IS DAIMON HELLSTROM! MAY I BE OF SOME SERVICE TO YOU?!

MY AD IN THE NEWSPAPER-- YES, I HAVE PLACED THAT AD ACROSS THE COUNTRY-- AND I DO SPECIALIZE IN EXPELLING DEMONS!

10

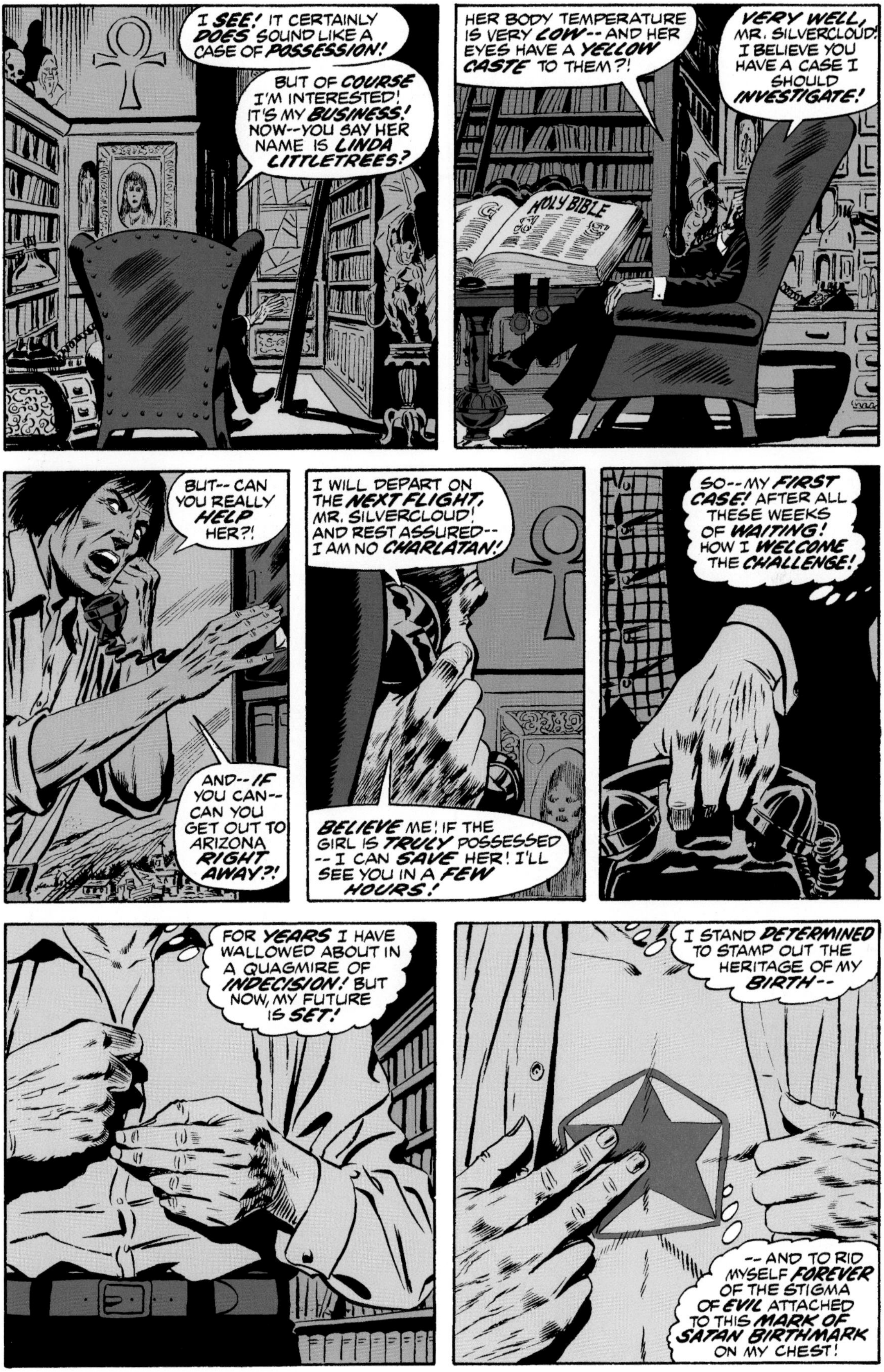

I SEE! IT CERTAINLY DOES SOUND LIKE A CASE OF POSSESSION!
BUT OF COURSE I'M INTERESTED! IT'S MY BUSINESS! NOW--YOU SAY HER NAME IS LINDA LITTLETREES?
HER BODY TEMPERATURE IS VERY LOW--AND HER EYES HAVE A YELLOW CASTE TO THEM?!
VERY WELL, MR. SILVERCLOUD! I BELIEVE YOU HAVE A CASE I SHOULD INVESTIGATE!
HOLY BIBLE
BUT-- CAN YOU REALLY HELP HER?!
AND--IF YOU CAN--CAN YOU GET OUT TO ARIZONA RIGHT AWAY?!
I WILL DEPART ON THE NEXT FLIGHT, MR. SILVERCLOUD! AND REST ASSURED--I AM NO CHARLATAN!
BELIEVE ME! IF THE GIRL IS TRULY POSSESSED--I CAN SAVE HER! I'LL SEE YOU IN A FEW HOURS!
SO--MY FIRST CASE! AFTER ALL THESE WEEKS OF WAITING! HOW I WELCOME THE CHALLENGE!
FOR YEARS I HAVE WALLOWED ABOUT IN A QUAGMIRE OF INDECISION! BUT NOW, MY FUTURE IS SET!
I STAND DETERMINED TO STAMP OUT THE HERITAGE OF MY BIRTH--
--AND TO RID MYSELF FOREVER OF THE STIGMA OF EVIL ATTACHED TO THIS MARK OF SATAN BIRTHMARK ON MY CHEST!

EXCUSE ME-- MISS SIMPSON?! *MISS ROXANNE SIMPSON?!*

YES! THAT'S ME! WHAT IS IT, OFFICER?!

IS IT--*JOHNNY?!* OH, LORD, HAS SOMETHING *HAPPENED* TO JOHNNY?!

I'M AFRAID SO, MISS! HE'S BEEN IN AN *ACCIDENT!* HE'S IN *EMERGENCY* RIGHT NOW!

SEEMS HE LED OUR BOYS QUITE A *CHASE* LAST NIGHT! THEN THIS MORNING, HE TRIED TO RUN A *ROADBLOCK!*

WE HAD TO *SHOOT* HIM--THEN HIS *BIKE* CRASHED --AND, WELL-- HE'S IN *BAD SHAPE!*

YOU *FOOL!* CAN'T YOU SEE SHE'S IN NO *CONDITION* FOR A SHOCK LIKE THAT?!

NO! IT'S NOT *TRUE!* TELL ME IT'S NOT *SO!*

SORRY! I'M JUST TRYIN' TO DO MY *JOB!*

WELL YOU'VE *DONE* IT, COPPER-- SO GET *OUT* OF HERE! YOU'VE DONE *ENOUGH* DAMAGE FOR ONE DAY!

STOP IT, BART! HE'S ONLY DOING WHAT HE *HAD* TO! WE HAVE TO WORRY ABOUT JOHNNY!

YEAH, *SURE,* BABY! GUESS I FLEW OFF THE *HANDLE* 'CAUSE I WAS SO *SHOOK* BY THE NEWS!

SORRY, OFFICER! YOU CAN GO NOW, THOUGH! I'LL TAKE CARE OF *HER!*

OKAY, AND FOR THE *RECORD--* I HOPE HE *PULLS THROUGH!* HE'S THE GREATEST STUNT BIKER *ALIVE!*

AND *WHATEVER* HE DID--I'M SURE HE HAD A GOOD *REASON--* IF HE JUST LIVES TO *TELL* US ABOUT IT!

AND, ELSEWHERE...

I'M TYING HER TO MAKE SURE NOTHING **HAPPENS** BEFORE **HELLSTROM** GETS HERE!

I HAVE TO GET TO **WORK!** BUT **CALL** ME IF ANYTHING AT ALL COMES **UP!**

I WILL **WATCH OVER** HER-- BUT IT IS ONLY A **DEATH VIGIL!** THERE IS **NO** MAGIC TO **CURE** HER!

THE TIRED OLD MAN STARES PITIFULLY AT THE SHELL OF WHAT ONCE WAS HIS **DAUGHTER** AS SAM SILVERCLOUD TAKES HIS **LEAVE!** BUT THE AGING EYES ARE **TIRED**-- AND THEY FAIL TO NOTICE A SUDDEN **GLIMMER** IN **HER** PUPILS AS THE DOOR SLAMS SHUT **BEHIND** SAM--

THEN, SLOWLY BUT SURELY, THE LACK OF SLEEP TAKES ITS **TOLL!** AND, AS SNAKE DANCE DRIFTS INTO **FITFUL SLUMBER**--

AWAKE, LINDA **LITTLETREE!** AWAKE AND SERVE YOUR **MASTER!**

I TOLD YOU YOU WOULD HAVE A **SECOND CHANCE** TO SERVE ME *-- AND THE MOMENT HAS **ARRIVED!**

I **HEAR,** MASTER! AND I WILL **OBEY!** YOU HAVE ONLY TO **ASK**-- AND I WILL **SERVE!**

*IT HAPPENED **LAST ISH!**-- ROY.

GOOD! THEN I MUST ASK THE USE OF YOUR **BODY!** MY SOUL WILL **POSSESS** IT-- WHILE **YOURS** RESTS PEACEFULLY IN **LIMBO**--

--UNTIL SUCH TIME AS I CAN **CAPTURE** THE SOUL OF **JOHNNY BLAZE!** WHAT SAY YOU, MY **SERVANT?!** DO YOU **AGREE** TO THIS?!

13

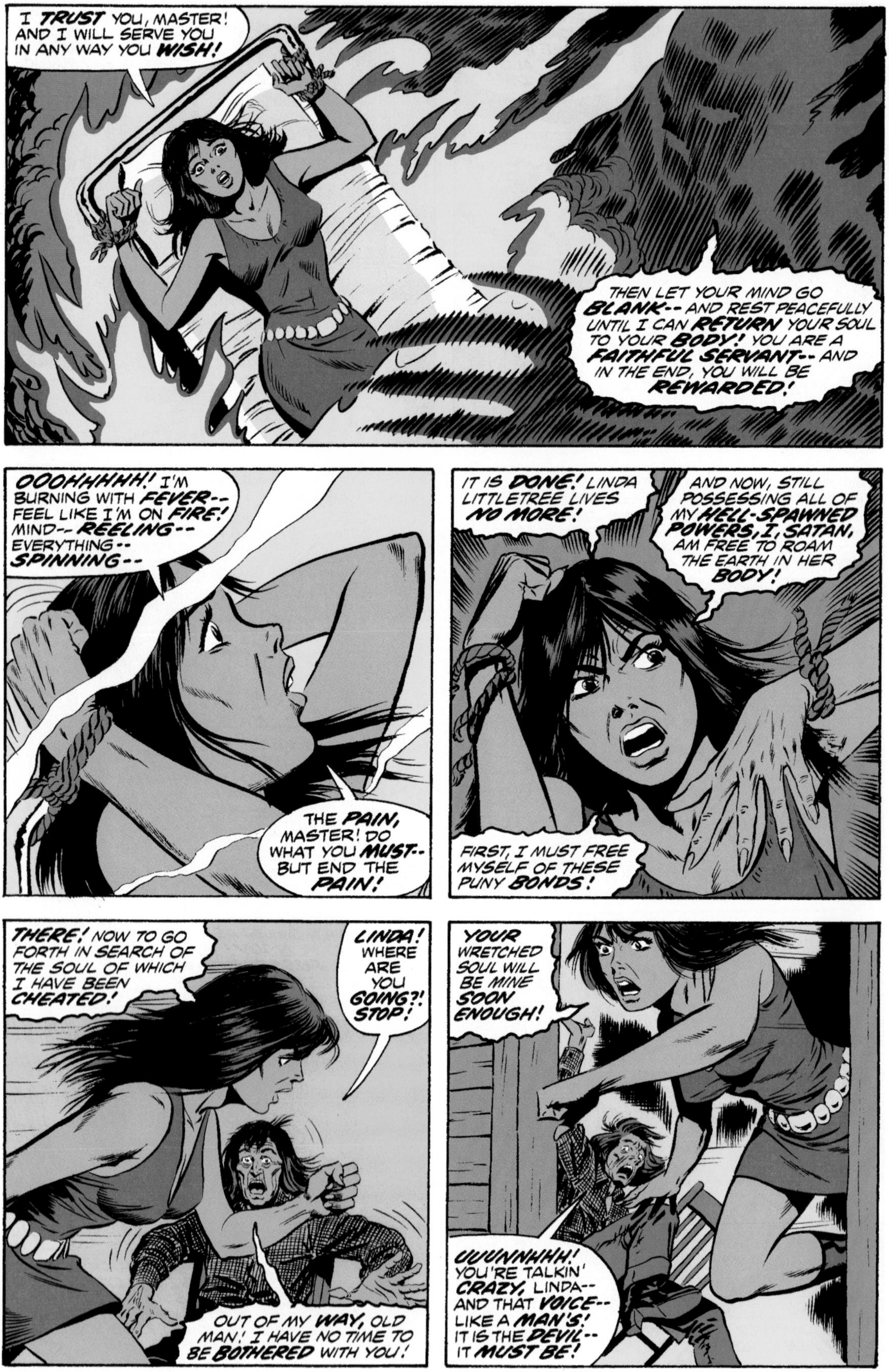

I TRUST YOU, MASTER! AND I WILL SERVE YOU IN ANY WAY YOU WISH!
THEN LET YOUR MIND GO BLANK-- AND REST PEACEFULLY UNTIL I CAN RETURN YOUR SOUL TO YOUR BODY! YOU ARE A FAITHFUL SERVANT-- AND IN THE END, YOU WILL BE REWARDED!
OOOHHHHH! I'M BURNING WITH FEVER-- FEEL LIKE I'M ON FIRE! MIND-- REELING-- EVERYTHING-- SPINNING--
THE PAIN, MASTER! DO WHAT YOU MUST-- BUT END THE PAIN!
IT IS DONE! LINDA LITTLETREE LIVES NO MORE!
AND NOW, STILL POSSESSING ALL OF MY HELL-SPAWNED POWERS, I, SATAN, AM FREE TO ROAM THE EARTH IN HER BODY!
FIRST, I MUST FREE MYSELF OF THESE PUNY BONDS!
THERE! NOW TO GO FORTH IN SEARCH OF THE SOUL OF WHICH I HAVE BEEN CHEATED!
LINDA! WHERE ARE YOU GOING?! STOP!
OUT OF MY WAY, OLD MAN! I HAVE NO TIME TO BE BOTHERED WITH YOU!
YOUR WRETCHED SOUL WILL BE MINE SOON ENOUGH!
UUUNNHHH! YOU'RE TALKIN' CRAZY, LINDA-- AND THAT VOICE-- LIKE A MAN'S! IT IS THE DEVIL-- IT MUST BE!

OOOHHHH! HEAD'S *SPLITTING*-- FEELS LIKE I'VE BROKEN EVERY BONE IN MY *BODY!*

LORD, I'M IN THE *HOSPITAL!* BUT *WHY?!* HOW DID-- THE *CRASH*-- EARLY *THIS MORNING!*

RELAX, MR. BLAZE! YOU'VE BEEN *BADLY INJURED*, BUT YOU'LL *PULL THROUGH!* HE'S *CONSCIOUS*, DOCTOR!

THAT'S A *GOOD SIGN*, BUT HE'S STILL *VERY CRITICAL!* KEEP HIM AS QUIET AS POSSIBLE!

YOU *HEARD* THE DOCTOR, MR. BLAZE! TAKE IT EASY AND TRY TO *SLEEP!* IT'S ALMOST *DARK*, ANYWAY!

DARK?! BUT IT *CAN'T* BE! WHAT WILL *HAPPEN* TO ME?!

I'M GOING TO KEEP A *NURSE* OUTSIDE HIS *DOOR* ALL NIGHT, JUST IN CASE!

TOO WOOZY FROM THE PAIN-KILLERS TO *THINK* CLEARLY-- BUT I *MUST!*

AT LEAST THEY'RE GOING TO LEAVE ME *ALONE* IN THE *ROOM!* THAT'S A *BREAK* FOR ME-- IN CASE--

SLEEP WELL, JOHNNY! I'LL CHECK IN ON YOU FIRST THING IN THE *MORNING!*

HOW *CAN* I SLEEP?! THE *SUN'S* GONE DOWN! IT'S ALMOST *NIGHT!*

WILL I *CHANGE?!* OR DID THE ACCIDENT PUT A *STOP* TO IT?!

AND IF I *DO* CHANGE, WHAT KIND OF EFFECT WILL THE *INJURIES* HAVE ON-- *THE GHOST RIDER?!*

15

AGGGHH!

IT'S BEGINNING!

NO WAY TO STOP IT NOW!

EVIDENTLY *NOTHING* CAN CHANGE IT! THE TRANSFORMATION OCCURS EVERY NIGHT-- NO MATTER *WHAT!*

AND NOW, ONCE AGAIN-- I AM-- *THE GHOST RIDER!!*

BUT MY *INJURIES--?!* THEY SEEM TO BE *HEALED!* I'M IN *PERFECT HEALTH* AGAIN!

EVIDENTLY, WHAT HAPPENS TO *JOHNNY BLAZE--* HAS NO *EFFECT* ON THE GHOST RIDER!

WHAT DO I *DO,* THOUGH?! I CAN'T STAY *HERE--* LET THE DOCTORS FIND ME LIKE THIS!

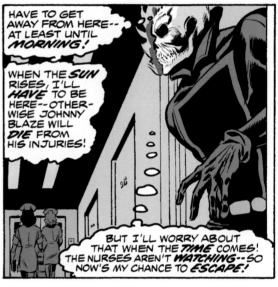

HAVE TO GET AWAY FROM HERE-- AT LEAST UNTIL *MORNING!*

WHEN THE *SUN* RISES, I'LL *HAVE* TO BE HERE-- OTHERWISE JOHNNY BLAZE WILL *DIE* FROM HIS INJURIES!

BUT I'LL WORRY ABOUT THAT WHEN THE *TIME* COMES! THE NURSES AREN'T *WATCHING--* SO NOW'S MY CHANCE TO *ESCAPE!*

MADE IT-- THANKS TO THE DESERTED *SERVICE ENTRANCE!*

BUT NOW THAT I'M *OUT--* WHERE DO I *GO?!* UNLESS-- OH, *NO!* I COMPLETELY *FORGOT!*

HOSPIT PARKIN

ASK NO *QUESTIONS,* MORTAL! MERELY TAKE ME TO *COPPERHEAD CANYON!* I AM TO JUMP IT TONIGHT-- ON A *MOTORCYCLE!*

WHAT IN BLAZES--?! OH, YEAH-- YOU MUST BE JOHNNY BLAZE-- IN YER *GHOST GET-UP!* GET IN AN' I'LL *TAKE* YA-- BUT COOL IT WITH THAT *SPOOKY VOICE,* HUH?!

HOSPITAL

TAXI

IF I DON'T *ARRIVE* IN TIME-- *BART* IS LIABLE TO ATTEMPT IT! AND I MUST NOT LET THAT *HAPPEN!*

SO JOHNNY BLAZE HAS BEEN *HURT*-- AND IS IN THE *HOSPITAL*!

SO MUCH THE *BETTER*! IN HIS *WEAKENED STATE*-- HE WILL BE LESS APT TO *RESIST* ME!

I'M A FRIEND OF *MR. BLAZE*! WHAT ROOM IS HE IN?!

FORMATION

ROOM 210-- BUT HE ISN'T ALLOWED *VISITORS*!

A GOOD THING I REMEMBERED TO DISGUISE MY *VOICE*! THE RASPY TONES OF *SATAN* COMING FROM A *GIRL* MIGHT HAVE PROVED *DISASTROUS*!

ALERT SECURITY! JOHNNY BLAZE HAS *DISAPPEARED*!

WHAT?! THEN I MUST *LEAVE* THIS PLACE! I HAVE NO TIME FOR THE FOOLISH QUESTIONS OF *MORTALS*!

HAS ANYONE HERE *SEEN* HIM?! I DON'T KNOW HOW HE COULD HAVE *ESCAPED*!

THAT *GIRL* OVER THERE WAS *ASKING* FOR HIM, DOCTOR!

MISS! I'D LIKE TO ASK YOU-- *WHAT GIRL*?! THERE'S NO ONE *THERE*!

SHE WAS STANDING THERE A *SECOND* AGO!

THIS IS NO *JOKING* MATTER, MISS AMES! THE MAN IS *CRITICALLY* INJURED--

--AND YET HE MANAGED TO *LEAVE* THE HOSPITAL SOMEHOW! NOW YOU GIVE ME A *DISAPPEARING GIRL*! I DON'T KNOW WHAT THIS IS ALL *ABOUT*--

--BUT *BELIEVE* ME, I INTEND TO *FIND OUT*! AFTER YOU'VE CALLED THE *POLICE*, OF COURSE!

LOOK AT THE *CROWD!* *FANTASTIC!!*

AS SOON AS I JUMP THE *CANYON*-- *BLAZE* WILL BE *FINISHED!* ALL THE GLORY WILL BE *MINE!* I'LL NEVER TAKE A BACK SEAT TO HIM *AGAIN!*

THIS IS *CRAZY,* BART! THIS JUMP WOULD HAVE BEEN RISKY FOR *JOHNNY!*

FOR A RIDER WITH NO MORE EXPERIENCE THAN *YOU*-- IT'S *SUICIDE!*

YOU'RE *WRONG,* ROCKY! AND I'M GOING TO *PROVE* IT TO YOU!

I'VE *ALWAYS* BEEN AS GOOD AS BLAZE-- EVEN *BETTER!* NOW I CAN PROVE THAT'S THE *TRUTH!*

BESIDES, THE SHOW IS *DYING* BECAUSE THE STAR'S NEVER *AROUND!* IF I *MAKE* THIS JUMP-- I CAN *CHANGE* ALL THAT!

AND I'M *GONNA* MAKE IT-- FOR THE SHOW-- FOR YOU-- FOR *US!*

JUST *BELIEVE* IN ME-- AND I'M AS GOOD AS ON THE *OTHER SIDE!*

YOU'RE *WONDERFUL,* BART! BUT PLEASE-- BE *CAREFUL!*

AND THERE HE GOES, LADIES AND GENTLEMEN! A MERE STAND-IN FOR JOHNNY BLAZE IS GOING TO ATTEMPT TO MAKE CYCLING HISTORY--

--OR, AS MANY OF US FEAR, GET HIMSELF KILLED IN THE ATTEMPT!

"THIS IS *HOWARD GIFFORD* REPORTING, LADIES AND GENTLEMEN, AND I DON'T THINK THE WORLD OF SPORTS HAS EVER BEFORE KNOWN A MOMENT LIKE *THIS!* A VIRTUALLY UNKNOWN CYCLIST NAMED *BART SLADE* IS ABOUT TO ATTEMPT WHAT *EVIL KNIEVEL* AND *JOHNNY BLAZE* HAVE ONLY *TALKED* ABOUT--

"THE CROWD IS WRAPPED IN A SILENT SHROUD OF BOTH EAGER ANTICIPATION AND *DEADLY DREAD* AS SLADE'S CYCLE ROARS TOWARD THE RAMP HE HOPES WILL CATAPAULT HIM *ACROSS* THIS VAST CANYON AND ONTO THE FRONT PAGE OF EVERY NEWSPAPER IN THE *WORLD*--

"NOW A ROAR GOES UP AS HE HITS THE RAMP AND STARTS UPWARD AT MORE THAN A *HUNDRED MILES-PER-HOUR!*

"NO ONE *KNOWS* WHY JOHNNY BLAZE DIDN'T *SHOW UP* FOR THIS JUMP AS SCHEDULED--BUT AT THIS MOMENT, I DARE SAY NO ONE *CARES!*

"HE'S HALFWAY UP THE RAMP NOW, STILL ACCELERATING AND LOOKING VERY *STABLE*-- ON HIS WAY TO *FAME* OR *DISASTER!*

SPEED *GOOD*-- TRAJECTORY LOOKS *PERFECT!* I'M GOING TO *MAKE* IT!

I *HAVE* TO MAKE IT! IT'S ALL I'VE EVER *LIVED* FOR!

"HOLD YOUR BREATHS ALONG WITH THE MULTI- TUDINOUS THRONG *GATHERED* HERE, AMERICA! HE'S AT THE EDGE OF THE RAMP AND ABOUT TO GO HURTLING THROUGH *SPACE!* IN A FRACTION OF A *SECOND*, WE'LL ALL KNOW IF THE REWARD OF THIS YOUNG MAN'S COURAGE IS *GLORY*--OR *DEATH!!*

"HE'S AIRBORNE!

HE'S *UP*-- LOOKS LIKE HE'S GOT THE SPEED TO *MAKE IT!*

READ MARVEL

OH, GOD-- I'M *TOO LATE!* ALL I CAN DO IS *WATCH*-- AND *PRAY!*

"HE LOOKS *STRONG* AT THE APEX OF HIS *TRAJECTORY!* NOW HE'S STARTING *DOWN*--

PLEASE, GOD! LET HIM MAKE IT-- PLEASE LET HIM MAKE THIS JUMP *SAFELY!*

"HE'S COMING *FAST*--BUT IT LOOKS LIKE HE'S GOING TO *MAKE* IT! HE APPEARS TO HAVE THE NECESSARY *DISTANCE*--

"YES! YES! YES! HE *IS* GOING TO MAKE IT! HE'S ON A STRAIGHT PATH FOR THE *FAR RAMP!* HISTORY IS ABOUT TO BE *MADE!*

NO *SWEAT!* I'VE *DONE* IT!

JUST HOLD HER *STEADY,* AND-- A *WIND GUST*--!!

NOOOO!

20

"OH, NO! THE *WIND* SEEMS TO HAVE CAUGHT HIM! GOD *HELP* HIM! HE'S GOING TO SMASH INTO--"

KER-WHOOM!

"*MY GOD!* YOU'LL HAVE TO *FORGIVE* ME, LADIES AND GENTLEMEN! LIKE THE *CROWD* HERE -- *SHOCK* HAS TEMPORARILY STILLED MY *VOICE!* NEVER IN MY *CAREER* HAVE I WITNESSED SO *GHASTLY* -- SO *GROTESQUE* -- SO *HORRIBLE* A TRAGEDY!"

THE WIND BLEW HIM *OFF COURSE* -- SMASHED HIM SMACK INTO THE *CANYON WALL!*

NOOO! IT CAN'T BE! FIRST *JOHNNY* -- NOW *THIS!*

CONTROL YOUR-SELF, WOMAN! WE WILL GRIEVE TOGETHER -- *LATER!*

GO *AWAY!* I WON'T *ANSWER* ANY--

JOHNNY!

YES! BUT DON'T ASK *ME* ANY QUESTIONS *EITHER!* THERE'S NO *TIME* FOR IT NOW! JUST COME *WITH* ME!

HEY! I THOUGHT BLAZE WAS IN THE *HOSPITAL* -- BUT *THERE HE IS!*

HE MUST'VE *ESCAPED!* COME ON AND *GRAB* HIM! DON'T GIVE 'EM A CHANCE TO *GET AWAY!*

SHE COULD HAVE PICKED A BETTER TIME TO *FAINT* -- BUT IF THIS *TRUCK* WILL RUN -- WE CAN STILL *MAKE* IT!

THE POLICE HAVE *SPOTTED* ME -- BUT I HAVE A GOOD ENOUGH JUMP TO *LOSE* THEM -- IF THE POWERS THAT BE *WILL* IT -- AND THE OWNER LEFT HIS *KEYS* IN THE VEHICLE!

AT LAST-- A LITTLE *LUCK* COMES MY WAY! NOT ONLY WERE THE *KEYS* IN IT-- IT ALSO HAS *FOUR-WHEEL DRIVE!*

WITH *THAT,* I'LL BE ABLE TO *LOSE* THE POLICE SOMEWHERE OUT IN THE *DESERT!*

BUT THAT WON'T *HELP* MUCH-- NOT WHEN *MORNING* DAWNS-- AND I BECOME A *CRITICALLY-INJURED JOHNNY BLAZE* AGAIN!

UNLESS I CAN BOTH LOSE THE POLICE AND FIND MY WAY TO A *HOSPITAL* BY SUNRISE-- I'M AS GOOD AS *DEAD!*

A RUNDOWN *INDIAN SHACK!* I'M NOT GOING TO GET *RICH* OFF THIS ASSIGNMENT!

HELLO-- I AM *DAIMON HELLSTROM!* I BELIEVE SOMEONE *SENT* FOR ME-- SOMETHING ABOUT A YOUNG GIRL BEING *POSSESSED!*

YES! I AM THE GIRL'S *FATHER!* BUT YOU HAVE ARRIVED *TOO LATE!*

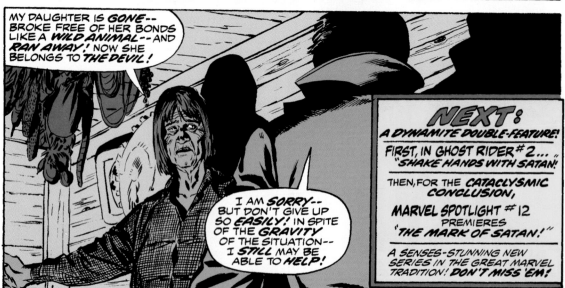

MY DAUGHTER IS *GONE*-- BROKE FREE OF HER BONDS LIKE A *WILD ANIMAL*-- AND *RAN AWAY!* NOW SHE BELONGS TO *THE DEVIL!*

I AM *SORRY*-- BUT DON'T GIVE UP SO *EASILY!* IN SPITE OF THE *GRAVITY* OF THE SITUATION-- I *STILL* MAY BE ABLE TO *HELP!*

NEXT:
A DYNAMITE DOUBLE-FEATURE!
FIRST, IN GHOST RIDER #2... *"SHAKE HANDS WITH SATAN!"*
THEN, FOR THE *CATACLYSMIC CONCLUSION,*
MARVEL SPOTLIGHT #12 PREMIERES *"THE MARK OF SATAN!"*
A SENSES-STUNNING NEW SERIES IN THE GREAT MARVEL TRADITION! *DON'T MISS 'EM!*

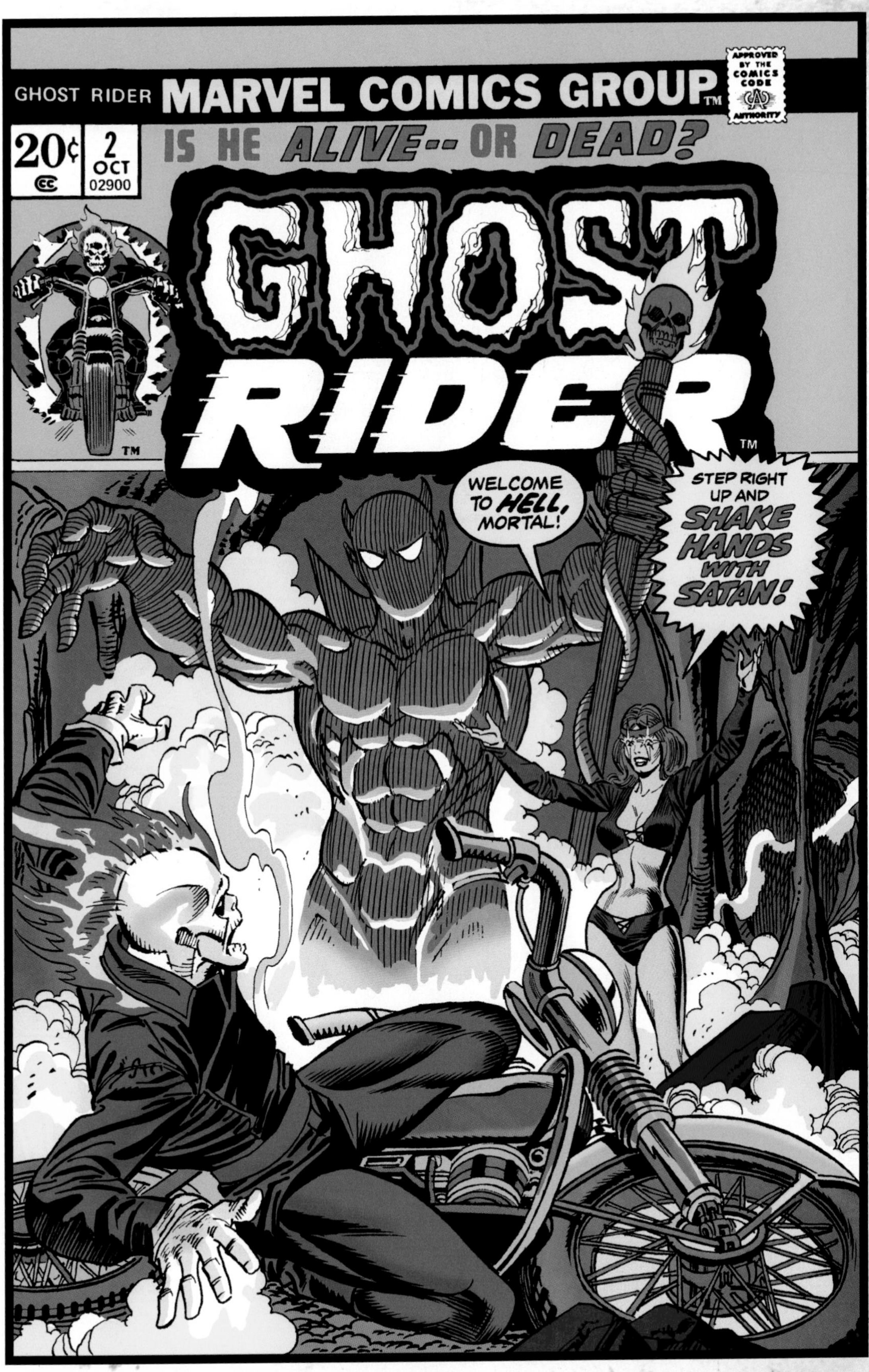
GHOST RIDER
MARVEL COMICS GROUP
APPROVED BY THE COMICS CODE AUTHORITY
20¢
2 OCT 02900
IS HE ALIVE-- OR DEAD?
GHOST RIDER
WELCOME TO HELL, MORTAL!
STEP RIGHT UP AND SHAKE HANDS WITH SATAN!

STAN LEE PRESENTS: **THE GHOST RIDER!** ™

NIGHT--A RARE RAINSTORM DRENCHES THE *DESERT!*

JOHNNY BLAZE-- *THE GHOST RIDER*--

--SQUINTS TO SEE THE ROAD THROUGH A WINDSHIELD TURNED *OPAQUE* BY THE TORRENT OF WATER RUSHING OVER IT!

AND AS HE STRUGGLES TO MAINTAIN *CONTROL*--HIS SOUL IS RIPPED APART BY A NAGGING *DECISION* HE MUST MAKE--

--TO *CONTINUE* HIS FLIGHT FROM *JUSTICE* AND *DIE* AT SUNRISE-- OR TO *SURRENDER* HIMSELF TO THE PURSUING *POLICE!*

SUDDENLY, AS HE RECALLS THE HORRIBLE DEATH OF *BART SLADE* WHILE ATTEMPTING A JUMP HE HIMSELF SHOULD HAVE MADE *-- HE REALIZES THERE IS A *THIRD CHOICE!*

THOUGH THE VERY *THOUGHT* MAKES HIS BLOOD RUN *COLD*--HE KNOWS HE CAN *END* HIS RUNNING AND--

* IT HAPPENED LAST ISH!-- R.T.

SHAKE HANDS WITH SATAN!

WRITTEN BY	DRAWN BY	INKED BY	COLORED BY	LETTERED BY	EDITED BY
GARY FRIEDRICH	JIM MOONEY	SYD SHORES	L. LESSMANN	C. JETTER	ROY THOMAS

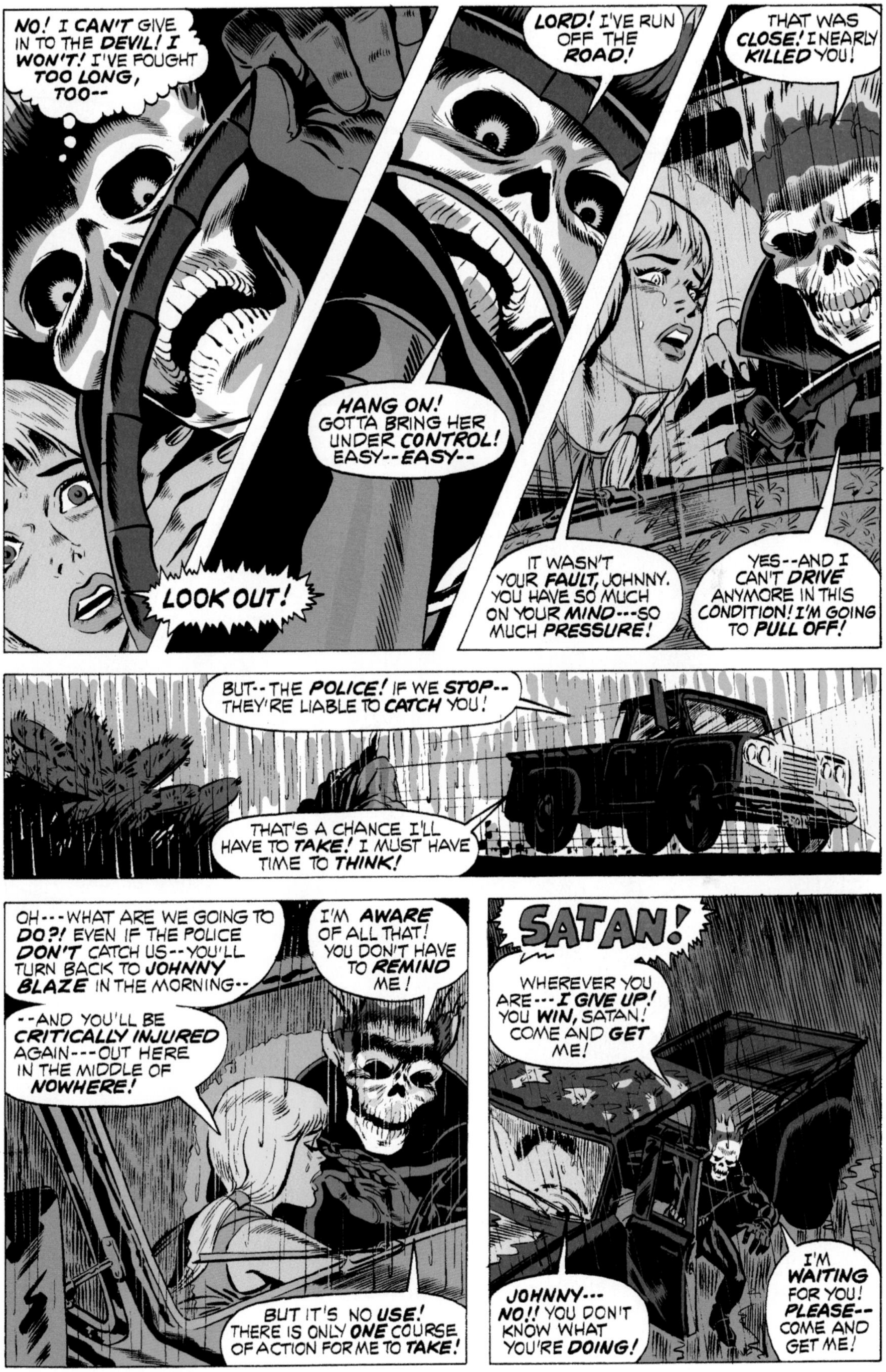
NO! I CAN'T GIVE IN TO THE DEVIL! I WON'T! I'VE FOUGHT TOO LONG, TOO--
LOOK OUT!
HANG ON! GOTTA BRING HER UNDER CONTROL! EASY--EASY--
LORD! I'VE RUN OFF THE ROAD!
THAT WAS CLOSE! I NEARLY KILLED YOU!
IT WASN'T YOUR FAULT, JOHNNY. YOU HAVE SO MUCH ON YOUR MIND---SO MUCH PRESSURE!
YES--AND I CAN'T DRIVE ANYMORE IN THIS CONDITION! I'M GOING TO PULL OFF!
BUT--THE POLICE! IF WE STOP--THEY'RE LIABLE TO CATCH YOU!
THAT'S A CHANCE I'LL HAVE TO TAKE! I MUST HAVE TIME TO THINK!
OH---WHAT ARE WE GOING TO DO?! EVEN IF THE POLICE DON'T CATCH US--YOU'LL TURN BACK TO JOHNNY BLAZE IN THE MORNING--
--AND YOU'LL BE CRITICALLY INJURED AGAIN---OUT HERE IN THE MIDDLE OF NOWHERE!
I'M AWARE OF ALL THAT! YOU DON'T HAVE TO REMIND ME!
BUT IT'S NO USE! THERE IS ONLY ONE COURSE OF ACTION FOR ME TO TAKE!
SATAN!
WHEREVER YOU ARE---I GIVE UP! YOU WIN, SATAN! COME AND GET ME!
JOHNNY---NO!! YOU DON'T KNOW WHAT YOU'RE DOING!
I'M WAITING FOR YOU! PLEASE--COME AND GET ME!

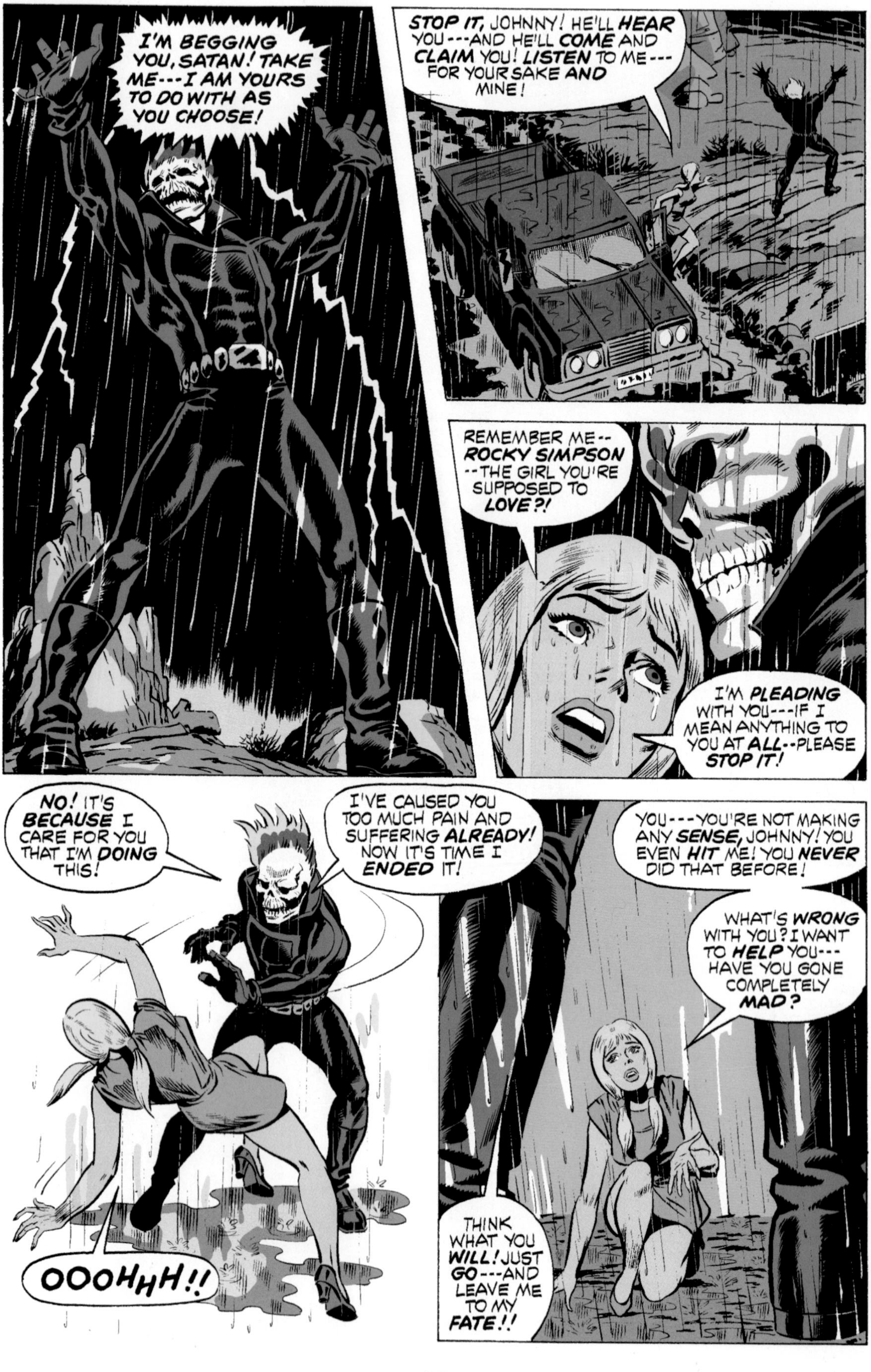
I'M BEGGING YOU, SATAN! TAKE ME---I AM YOURS TO DO WITH AS YOU CHOOSE!
STOP IT, JOHNNY! HE'LL HEAR YOU---AND HE'LL COME AND CLAIM YOU! LISTEN TO ME---FOR YOUR SAKE AND MINE!
REMEMBER ME--ROCKY SIMPSON--THE GIRL YOU'RE SUPPOSED TO LOVE?!
I'M PLEADING WITH YOU---IF I MEAN ANYTHING TO YOU AT ALL--PLEASE STOP IT!
NO! IT'S BECAUSE I CARE FOR YOU THAT I'M DOING THIS!
I'VE CAUSED YOU TOO MUCH PAIN AND SUFFERING ALREADY! NOW IT'S TIME I ENDED IT!
OOOHHH!!
YOU---YOU'RE NOT MAKING ANY SENSE, JOHNNY! YOU EVEN HIT ME! YOU NEVER DID THAT BEFORE!
WHAT'S WRONG WITH YOU? I WANT TO HELP YOU---HAVE YOU GONE COMPLETELY MAD?
THINK WHAT YOU WILL! JUST GO---AND LEAVE ME TO MY FATE!!

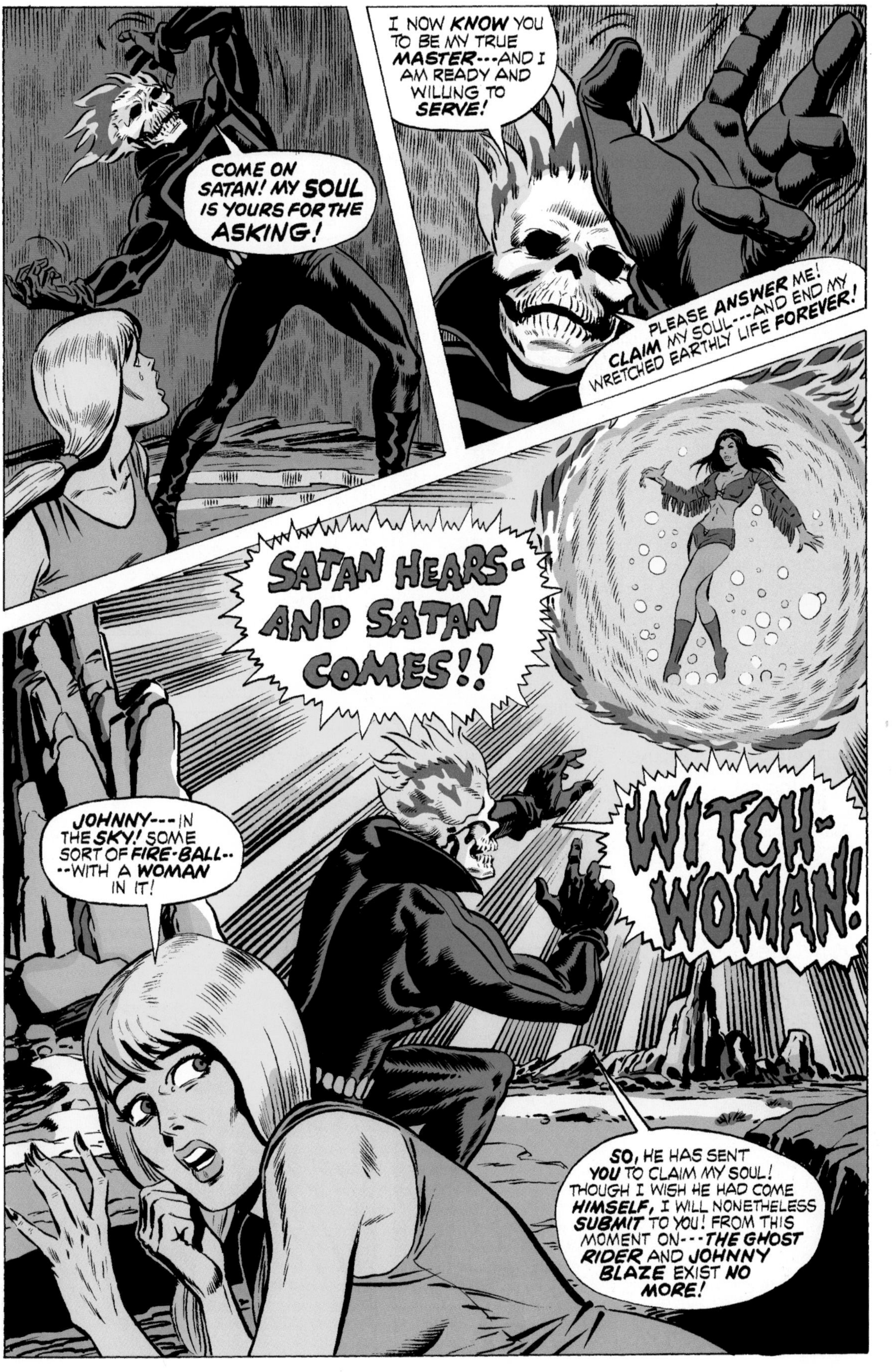
COME ON SATAN! MY SOUL IS YOURS FOR THE ASKING!
I NOW KNOW YOU TO BE MY TRUE MASTER---AND I AM READY AND WILLING TO SERVE!
PLEASE ANSWER ME! CLAIM MY SOUL---AND END MY WRETCHED EARTHLY LIFE FOREVER!
SATAN HEARS- AND SATAN COMES!!
JOHNNY---IN THE SKY! SOME SORT OF FIRE-BALL-- --WITH A WOMAN IN IT!
WITCH-WOMAN!
SO, HE HAS SENT YOU TO CLAIM MY SOUL! THOUGH I WISH HE HAD COME HIMSELF, I WILL NONETHELESS SUBMIT TO YOU! FROM THIS MOMENT ON---THE GHOST RIDER AND JOHNNY BLAZE EXIST NO MORE!

MEANWHILE, MILES AWAY ON THE RUNDOWN *APACHE RESERVATION* ONCE DOMINATED BY THE SINISTER *SNAKE-DANCE*, A STRANGE *VISITOR* HAS ARRIVED AT THE INN WHICH THE NOW-DOMICILE WITCH DOCTOR LIVES---

--A VISITOR WHOSE PRESENCE WILL HAVE *FAR-REACHING EFFECTS* ON THE LIVES OF EVERYONE HE *TOUCHES*, INCLUDING THE SEEMINGLY DOOMED *GHOST RIDER!*

YOUR POSSESSED DAUGHTER HAS *ESCAPED?!* WHEN ---*HOW?!*

I SENT FOR YOU, *DAIMON HELLSTROM*, AND *YOU* WILL ANSWER *MY QUESTIONS*, IF YOU DON'T MIND!

WAIT, SAM! SHE IS MY DAUGHTER AND YOUR *FIANCEE*! WE BOTH HAVE AN *EQUAL* INTEREST IN HER!

I AM AFRAID I *LET* HER ESCAPE, SIR!

SHE ISN'T *HERSELF*, MR. HELLSTROM --LIKE I TOLD YOU ON THE *PHONE!*

YOU'RE SUPPOSED TO BE AN *EXORCIST*--- A MAN WHO CAN *CAST OUT DEMONS!* AND THAT'S WHAT LINDA *NEEDS!*

I UNDERSTAND---AND I *MAY* BE ABLE TO HELP HER-- -- BUT NOT *NOW!* SHE ISN'T *HERE*--- AND *DARKNESS* IS FALLING! THEREFORE, THERE IS NOTHING I CAN DO UNTIL *TOMORROW!*

HOWEVER, IF I AM TO HELP HER TOMORROW--- OR *ANY* TIME, YOU MUST GRANT ME A *FAVOR!*

THIS WILL DOUBTLESS SOUND SOMEWHAT *BIZZARE* TO YOU---

---BUT IT IS OF THE *UTMOST IMPORTANCE* THAT YOU FOLLOW MY INSTRUCTIONS *EXPLICITLY!*

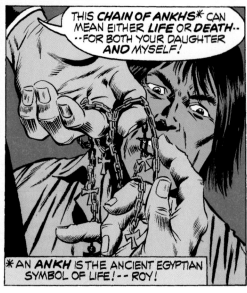

THIS *CHAIN OF ANKHS* CAN MEAN EITHER *LIFE* OR *DEATH*-- --FOR BOTH YOUR DAUGHTER AND MYSELF!

* AN *ANKH* IS THE ANCIENT EGYPTIAN SYMBOL OF *LIFE!* -- ROY!

"YOU MUST WRAP MY **WRISTS** IN THE CHAIN--- AND LOCK IT **SECURELY!** THEN YOU MUST LOCK ME IN A SMALL **ROOM!**

"AND NO MATTER WHAT I **SAY**---HOW MUCH I **BEG** AND **PLEAD**--- YOU MUST NOT RELEASE ME UNTIL **MORNING!**"

I DON'T **UNDERSTAND,** BUT I WILL DO AS YOU **ASK!**

I HOPE YOU WILL BE **COMFORTABLE** HERE - IF YOU **NEED** ANYTHING--- SIMPLY **CALL** ME!

NO! YOU MUSTN'T GIVE ANYTHING---**DO** ANYTHING FOR ME!

MERELY LEAVE ---LOCKING THE DOOR **BEHIND** YOU! AND DO NOT **ENTER** AGAIN UNTIL **SUNRISE** ---NO MATTER **WHAT!**

IF THAT'S THE WAY YOU **WANT** IT! SEE YOU FOR **BREAKFAST!**

CLICK!

WEIRD, MAN--- DEFINITELY, INCREDIBLY, **WEIRD!**

HOLY FATHER IN HEAVEN---ONCE MORE I ASK YOU TO SEE ME **THROUGH** THE NIGHTLY ORDEAL WHICH IS ABOUT TO **DESCEND** UPON ME!

AND GIVE THOSE WHO ARE MY HOSTS THE **STRENGTH** TO RESIST THE TERRIBLE TEMPTATIONS I AM DOOMED TO USE **AGAINST** THEM!

PLEASE, LORD---SEE ME THROUGH THIS **NIGHT** THAT I MAY RISE ON THE MORROW TO DO **YOUR** WORK---

---RATHER THAN **RELEASING** ME WHEN I AM NOT **MYSELF,** TO DO THE EVIL WORK OF MY **FATHER!**

29

SO, JOHNNY BLAZE---WE MEET *AGAIN*, JUST AS I *PROMISED!*＊ AND ALSO AS I VOWED---THIS TIME I AM THE *VICTOR!*

EVEN *MORE SO* THAN I HAD *ANTICIPATED!* YOUR COMPANION IS VERY *LOVELY*---

＊ *MARVEL SPOTLIGHT* #11!--ROY.

--SO LOVELY, IN FACT, I BELIEVE SHE WOULD BE A MOST PLEASING *GIFT* FOR THE MASTER!

LEAVE ROCKY *OUT* OF IT! THIS IS BETWEEN THE *DEVIL* AND *ME!*

SILENCE, FOOL! DO YOU NOT REALIZE THAT THE SITUATION IS NO LONGER IN YOUR *HANDS?!*

YOU HAVE *SURRENDERED* YOUR SOUL TO THE MASTER-- AND I AM CERTAIN *SHE* WOULD WANT TO DO *LIKEWISE*---TO BE WITH *YOU!*

FORGET IT! THE OFFER I MADE WAS FOR *MY* SOUL---NO ONE *ELSE'S!* I WILL *GO* WITH YOU---BUT ROCKY *STAYS!*

AS I HAVE ALREADY *STATED*--- THE CHOICE IS NOT *YOURS!*

SO YOU *SAY*---BUT IT WILL TAKE MORE THAN THE WORDS OF A *FEMALE* TO MAKE ME A BELIEVER!

EVEN IN A SITUATION SUCH AS *THIS* MALE CHAUVINISM REARS ITS *UGLY HEAD!* BUT TO NO *AVAIL*---

LOOK INTO MY *EYES,* JOHNNY BLAZE--- AND LET THE POWER OF *SATAN* DRAIN THE *RESISTANCE* FROM YOUR BODY!

NEVER! THOUGH MY EYES ARE IRRESISTIBLY *DRAWN* TO YOURS-- MY WALL OF FLAME BURNS *HIGH* ENOUGH THAT I *CANNOT* RETURN YOUR *STARE OF DEATH!*

BRRROOOOMM!

CYCLES ---PROBABLY THE *POLICE!* THIS IS THE *END,* ROCKY---ONE WAY OR THE *OTHER!*

THEN IT WILL BE *MY* WAY--- FOR NO MERE HUMANS ARE A MATCH FOR *WITCH-WOMAN!*

THE HOUR IS *LATE*, SAM--- AND YET, SOMEHOW, I CANNOT *SLEEP!*

I *TELL* YOU, SOME TERRIBLE *EVIL* HAS INVADED THIS HOUSE---AND THE MAN *HELLSTROM* IS A *PART* OF IT!

HOW *CAN* HE BE?! HIS SPECIALTY IS *COMBATING* EVIL---CASTING OUT *DEMONS*---NOT *CREATING* IT!

IT'S SO LATE--- NEARLY *MIDNIGHT!* AND STILL, NOTHING HAS *HAPPENED!*

BUT IT HAS HAPPENED THIS WAY *BEFORE*--- STRIKING WHEN I LEAST *EXPECT* IT!

I MUST STAY *AWAKE*--- *ALERT!* I CANNOT LET DOWN MY *GUARD!*

PERHAPS IF I GO TO THE *WINDOW* ---LOOK TO THE *HEAVENS*---AND *PRAY*---

LET ME OUT!

YOU MUST LET ME *TALK* TO YOU! IT IS *URGENT!*

IGNORE WHAT I TOLD YOU EARLIER! I MUST *SPEAK* TO YOU--- OR YOUR DAUGHTER WILL *DIE!*

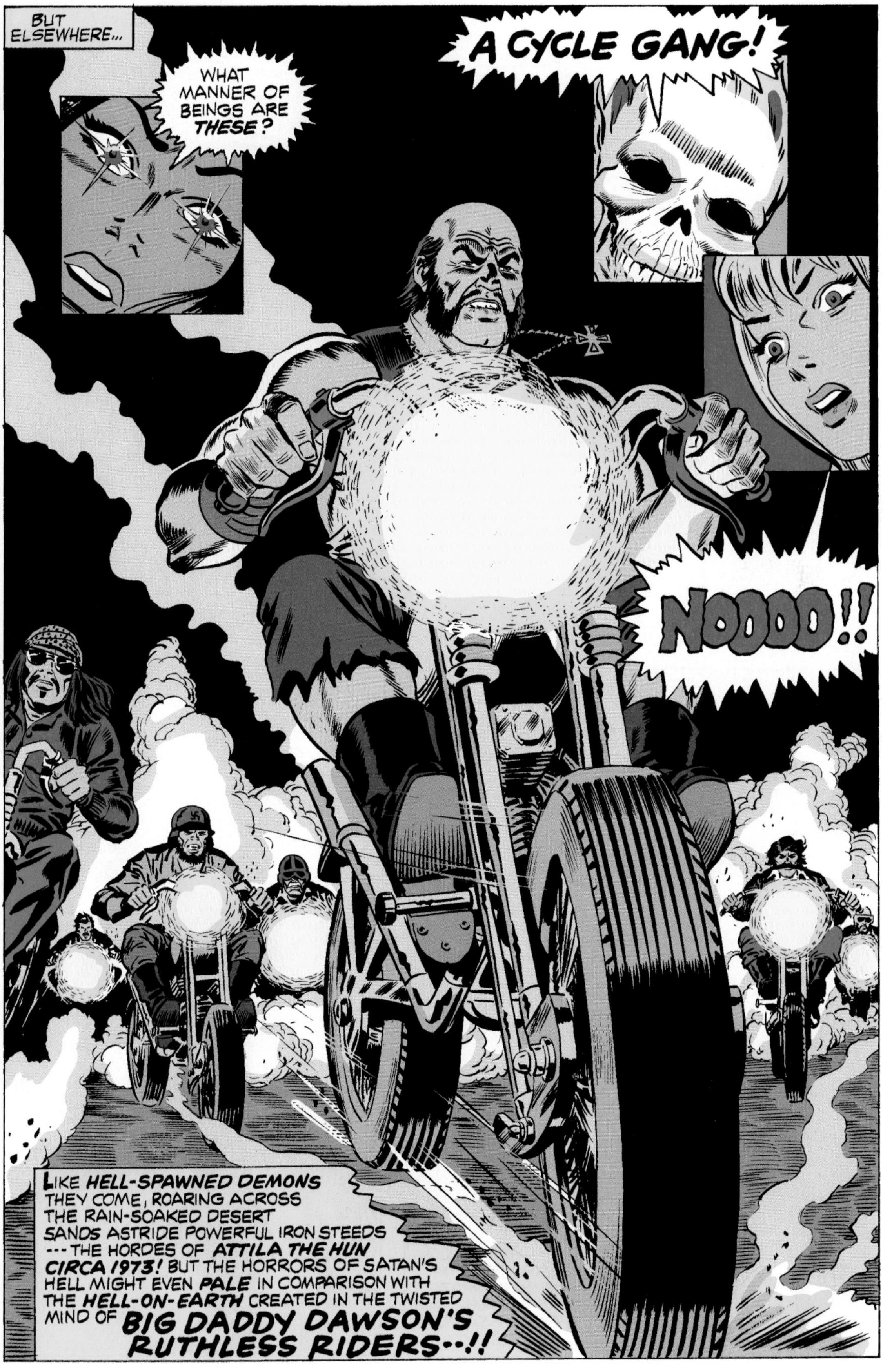
BUT ELSEWHERE...
WHAT MANNER OF BEINGS ARE THESE?
A CYCLE GANG!
NOOOO!!
LIKE HELL-SPAWNED DEMONS THEY COME, ROARING ACROSS THE RAIN-SOAKED DESERT SANDS ASTRIDE POWERFUL IRON STEEDS --- THE HORDES OF ATTILA THE HUN CIRCA 1973! BUT THE HORRORS OF SATAN'S HELL MIGHT EVEN PALE IN COMPARISON WITH THE HELL-ON-EARTH CREATED IN THE TWISTED MIND OF BIG DADDY DAWSON'S RUTHLESS RIDERS--!!

CIRCLE 'EM, BOYS! LET'S SEE HOW TOUGH THIS *GHOST RIDER* REALLY *IS*!

NOT TOUGH ENOUGH THAT A GOOD *CHAIN WHIPPIN'* WON'T BREAK 'IM!

JOHNNY-- STOP THEM! GOD KNOWS *WHAT* THEY'LL *DO* TO US!

ONE MAN--STOP US? LADY-- *DREAM ON*!

HE CAN'T HOPE TO STOP ME-- *BIG DADDY DAWSON*, EVEN WITH HIS *HALLOWEEN MASK*!

HE'S GOT ME *THERE*! CAN'T USE MY *FIRE* POWERS!

--THAT WOULD EXPOSE TO THE *PUBLIC* WHAT I REALLY *AM*--A PAWN OF *SATAN* BY NIGHT!

WELL, *COME ON*, HERO! *YOU'RE* THE BIG DUDE *BIKER*!

EITHER *LIVE UP* TO YOUR *REP*---OR I'M GONNA GRIND YOU INTO A *BLOODY PULP*!

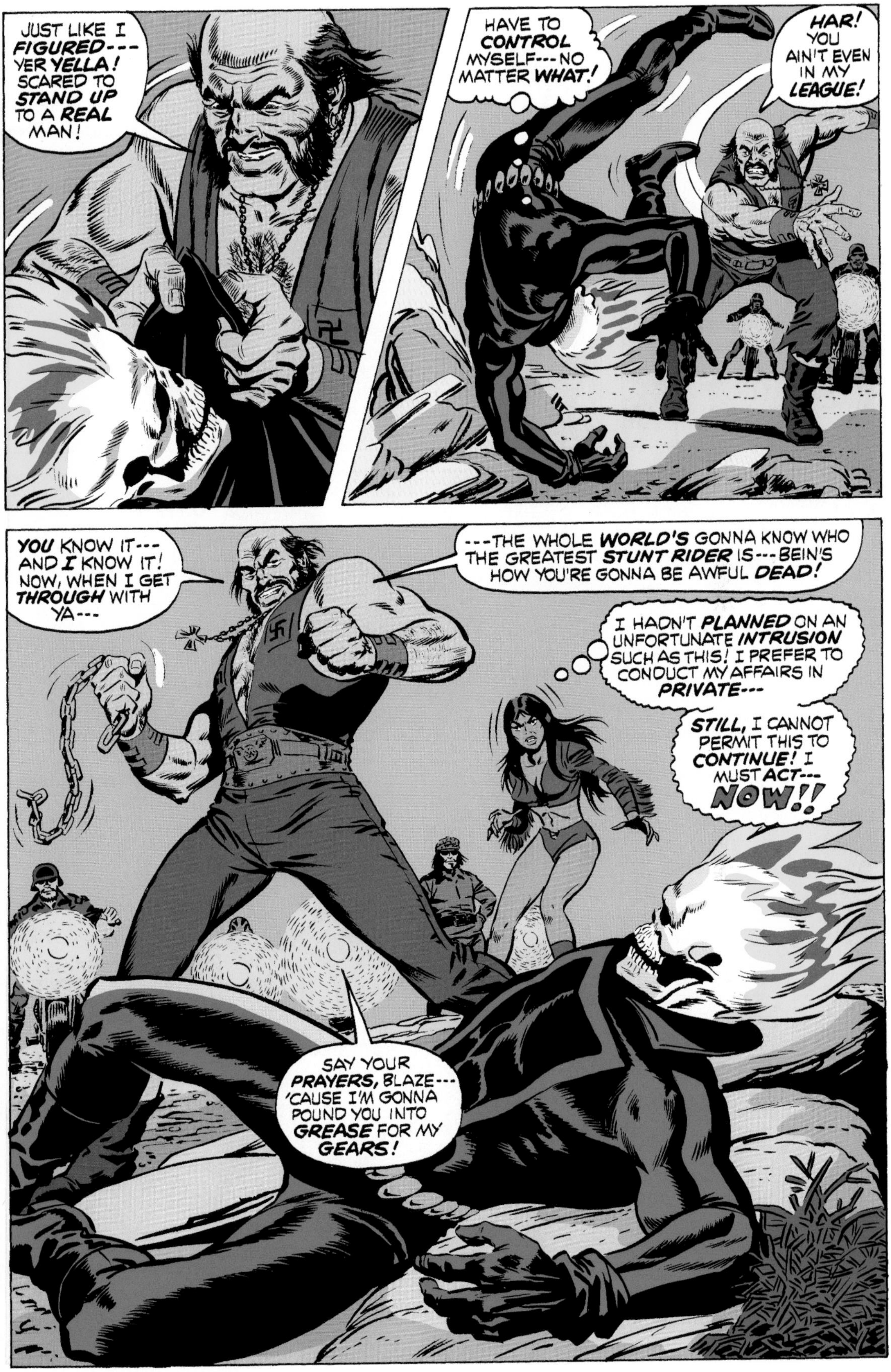
JUST LIKE I FIGURED--- YER YELLA! SCARED TO STAND UP TO A REAL MAN!
HAVE TO CONTROL MYSELF---NO MATTER WHAT!
HAR! YOU AIN'T EVEN IN MY LEAGUE!
YOU KNOW IT--- AND I KNOW IT! NOW, WHEN I GET THROUGH WITH YA---
---THE WHOLE WORLD'S GONNA KNOW WHO THE GREATEST STUNT RIDER IS---BEIN'S HOW YOU'RE GONNA BE AWFUL DEAD!
I HADN'T PLANNED ON AN UNFORTUNATE INTRUSION SUCH AS THIS! I PREFER TO CONDUCT MY AFFAIRS IN PRIVATE---
STILL, I CANNOT PERMIT THIS TO CONTINUE! I MUST ACT--- NOW!!
SAY YOUR PRAYERS, BLAZE--- 'CAUSE I'M GONNA POUND YOU INTO GREASE FOR MY GEARS!

ENOUGH OF THIS PETTY MORTAL INTERFERENCE WITH THE WORKINGS OF SATAN!

SNAP

COME, JOHNNY BLAZE--- TO THE NETHER WORLD-- YOUR HOME FOR ETERNITY!

NO---WAIT! I CANNOT LEAVE WITHOUT---

POOF!

HEY---WHAT'S GOIN' ON?! WHAT KINDA STUNT IS THAT?!

WELL---WHEREVER HE WENT--

--DIG THE GOODIES HE LEFT BEHIND!

NOOOOO! STAY AWAY FROM ME! JOHNNY-- HELP ME!!

FACE IT, LITTLE LADY--- YER GUTLESS ROMEO DONE SPLIT WITH ANOTHER CHICK!

BUT THAT'S HIS LOSS---AND YOUR GAIN! AFTER ALL, NOW YOU GOT YOUR- SELF A REAL MAN TO TAKE CARE 'A YA!

TRUST ME--- BIG DADDY'S GONNA MAKE YA FORGET THAT CREEP EVER LIVED!

WHILE, ELSEWHERE--

36

HE SAYS HE CAN *HELP* LINDA! I'M GONNA LET HIM *OUT!*

NO, SAM! YOU *MUSTN'T!*

I *HAVE* TO! I *LOVE* HER--- AND IF HE *CAN* HELP---

THEN LET WHAT YOU ARE ABOUT TO DO BE ON *YOUR HEAD* FOREVER!

FREE!!

YOU---YOU'VE *CHANGED!* THAT *COSTUME*---THE STRANGE BIRTH-MARK ON YOUR *CHEST!*

VERY *OBSERVANT* OF YOU, MORTAL--- AND VERY *FOOLISH* OF YOU TO *RELEASE* ME!

BUT---*LINDA!* YOU SAID YOU'D *HELP* HER IF I FREED YOU!

I LIED FOOL-- AND NOW--- I MUST BE *GONE!*

STOP *ME?!* YOU'D DO AS WELL TO TRY AND CATCH THE *WIND,* FOOLS!

SNAKE DANCE--GET YOUR *RIFLE!* HE MUST BE *STOPPED!*

*TO LEARN THE *STUNNING SECRET* OF DAIMON HELLSTROM DON'T MISS *MARVEL SPOTLIGHT #12,* ON SALE NOW!---ROY!

FAREWELL, FOOLS-- AND MAY YOUR NAMES BE FOR-EVER ETCHED IN THE LEGENDS OF *INFAMY* FOR THE DEED YOU HAVE PER-FORMED THIS NIGHT.*

THROUGH A SWIRLING VORTEX OF *LIGHT* AND *DARK*, THE GHOST RIDER AND WITCH-WOMAN ARE BORNE AT BLINDING SPEEDS ON THE WINGS OF A *SINISTER SPELL* TO THE BONE-CHILLING NETHERWORLD GLIMPSED ONCE *BEFORE* BY THE SATAN-CURSED *JOHNNY BLAZE* --- A WORLD OF INTENSE HEAT, BUBBLING POOLS OF MOLTEN LAVA AND *DEADLY DEMONS* --- A WORLD KNOWN TO WORSHIPPING MORTALS ON EARTH AS --- *HELL!!!*

WELCOME TO MY *WORLD*, JOHNNY BLAZE --- A WORLD SOON TO BE *YOURS*, AS WELL!

SPARE ME THE *TOURIST GUIDE SPEECH!* *I KNOW* WHERE I AM --- BUT I AM NOT YET A *WILLING RESIDENT!*

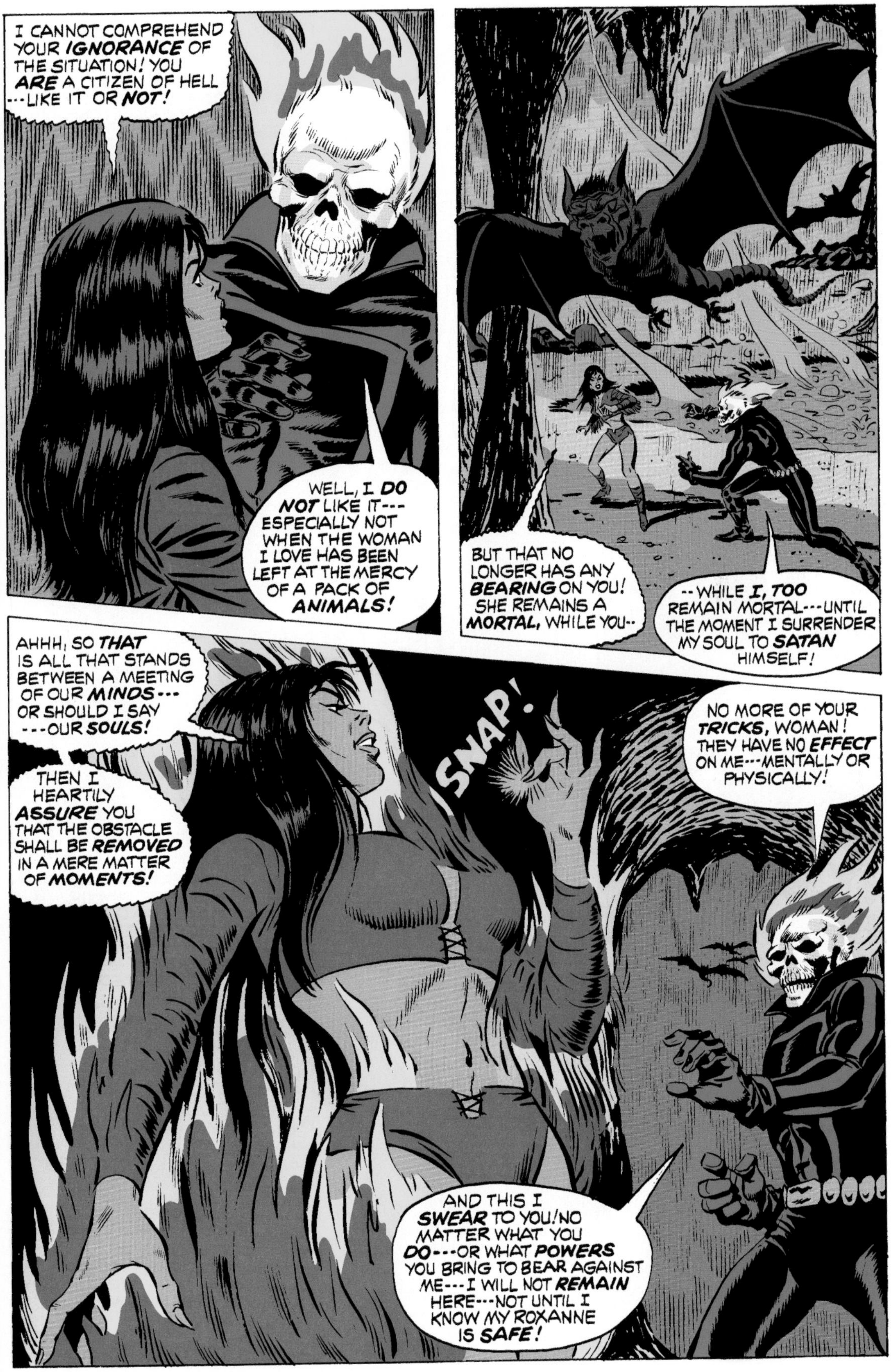
I CANNOT COMPREHEND YOUR IGNORANCE OF THE SITUATION! YOU ARE A CITIZEN OF HELL ---LIKE IT OR NOT!
WELL, I DO NOT LIKE IT--- ESPECIALLY NOT WHEN THE WOMAN I LOVE HAS BEEN LEFT AT THE MERCY OF A PACK OF ANIMALS!
BUT THAT NO LONGER HAS ANY BEARING ON YOU! SHE REMAINS A MORTAL, WHILE YOU--
--WHILE I, TOO REMAIN MORTAL---UNTIL THE MOMENT I SURRENDER MY SOUL TO SATAN HIMSELF!
AHHH, SO THAT IS ALL THAT STANDS BETWEEN A MEETING OF OUR MINDS--- OR SHOULD I SAY ---OUR SOULS!
THEN I HEARTILY ASSURE YOU THAT THE OBSTACLE SHALL BE REMOVED IN A MERE MATTER OF MOMENTS!
SNAP!
NO MORE OF YOUR TRICKS, WOMAN! THEY HAVE NO EFFECT ON ME---MENTALLY OR PHYSICALLY!
AND THIS I SWEAR TO YOU! NO MATTER WHAT YOU DO---OR WHAT POWERS YOU BRING TO BEAR AGAINST ME--- I WILL NOT REMAIN HERE---NOT UNTIL I KNOW MY ROXANNE IS SAFE!

WHAT MANNER OF TRICKERY IS **THIS**?! DO YOU SEEK TO **SHOCK** ME BY APPEARING TO **BURN TO DEATH** BEFORE MY VERY **EYES**?!

NO!

WHAT YOU HAVE SEEN WAS NO **TRICK**, JOHNNY BLAZE---IT WAS MERELY THE TRANSFORMATION OF MY **OWN** SOUL BACK INTO MY OWN **BODY**!

YOU SEE THE **WITCH-WOMAN** WAS MERELY **ME**---DISGUISED WITHIN HER BODY TO EASE MY MOVEMENTS IN THE **MORTAL WORLD**!

YOU--SATAN!! I SHOULD HAVE **KNOWN**!

BUT NOW, AS ONCE MORE I **FACE** YOU, IT ALL COMES **BACK** TO ME!

HOW WELL I REMEMBER WHEN **LAST** WE MET HERE IN YOUR **DOMAIN**---AND I WAS FORCED TO DUEL TO THE **DEATH** WITH **CRASH SIMPSON**---THE MAN WHO **REARED** ME---

---WITH THE LIFE OF HIS DAUGHTER ROXANNE, THE WOMAN I LOVE, AT **STAKE**!*

WHAT A **CHOICE** YOU LEFT FOR ME---EITHER LET **THEM** DIE---OR SURRENDER MY **OWN LIFE** TO YOU!

*****MARVEL SPOTLIGHT #8!**--RELENTLESS ROY.**

40

AND NOW WE FACE EACH OTHER *AGAIN*---AND ONCE MORE *ROXANNE* STANDS BETWEEN YOU AND YOUR GOAL OF ENSLAVING MY *SOUL!*

"BUT I WAS *SPARED* THAT AGONIZING CHOICE WHEN CRASH BROKE *FREE* OF YOUR SPELL AND SACRIFICED HIS LIFE TO SAVE *MINE!* THEN I WAS *RESCUED* FROM HELL BY THE *MYSTERIOUS MESSENGER*---

WRONG, JOHNNY BLAZE! THIS TIME IT IS *DIFFERENT!* THERE WILL BE *NO* MESSENGER TO SAVE YOU!

THIS TIME--- YOUR SOUL WILL BE *MINE!*

AFTER HIM, MY LOYAL SERVANTS! BUT DO NOT *SLAY* HIM --- MERELY *DELIVER* HIM UNTO ME···*ALIVE!*

NEVER! THE PURITY OF ROXANNE HAS *THUS FAR* SPARED ME FROM YOUR EVIL WRATH---AND SO SHALL IT SPARE ME *ONCE MORE!*

THUS, THOUGH WITHOUT ROXANNE AT HIS SIDE AS A LIVING *REPELLANT* TO THE POWERS OF SATAN, HIS ALL-CONSUMING *LOVE* FOR HER SPURS HIM TO BATTLE WITH EVERY FIBRE OF STRENGTH IN HIS BODY AS HE FACES THE *HORRIBLE HORDES OF HELL*---IN A BATTLE TO THE *DEATH!!*

IN AN ENDLESS *DELUGE*, THEY COME AT HIM, DEMONS WHICH WALK, CRAWL, FLY AND SPEW FORTH SIZZLING STREAMS OF FIRE ON *FETID BREATHS*---

---AND STILL, EVEN AGAINST UNBELIEVABLY HOPELESS ODDS, HE *FIGHTS ON*----

---UNTIL, AT LAST, HE IS *BURIED* IN THE SEA OF THE DEVIL'S *LEGIONS*---PINNED HELPLESSLY TO THE FLOOR OF *HADES* TO AWAIT HIS *FATE*!

IT IS NOW ENDED *FOREVER*, JOHNNY BLAZE! I NOW COMMAND THE *SACRED SWORD OF SATAN* TO PIERCE YOUR HEART--

--MAKING YOU FOREVER MY *PRISONER*! LET THE SWORD *FALL*!

STOP!

BEFORE YOU CLAIM ANOTHER *LIFE*, SATAN---YOU FIRST MUST ANSWER TO *ME*!

NO-- *NOT YOU*-- *NOT YOU!!*

THE CATACLYSMIC CONCLUSION APPEARS IN

MARVEL SPOTLIGHT

ON SALE NOW! DON'T DARE MISS IT!!!

42

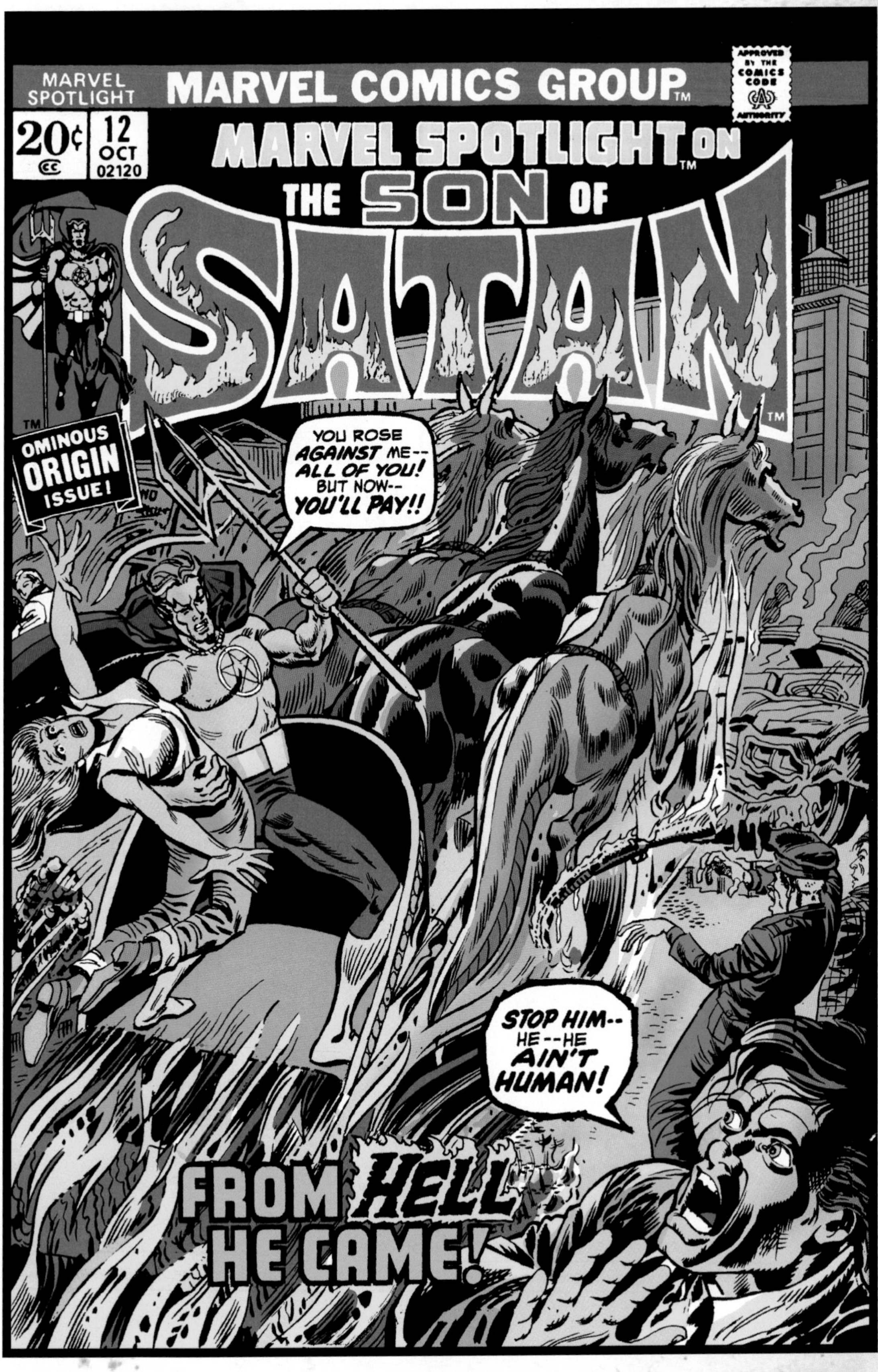
MARVEL SPOTLIGHT
MARVEL COMICS GROUP
APPROVED BY THE COMICS CODE AUTHORITY
20¢
12 OCT 02120
MARVEL SPOTLIGHT ON THE SON OF SATAN
OMINOUS ORIGIN ISSUE!
YOU ROSE AGAINST ME-- ALL OF YOU! BUT NOW-- YOU'LL PAY!!
STOP HIM-- HE--HE AIN'T HUMAN!
FROM HELL HE CAME!

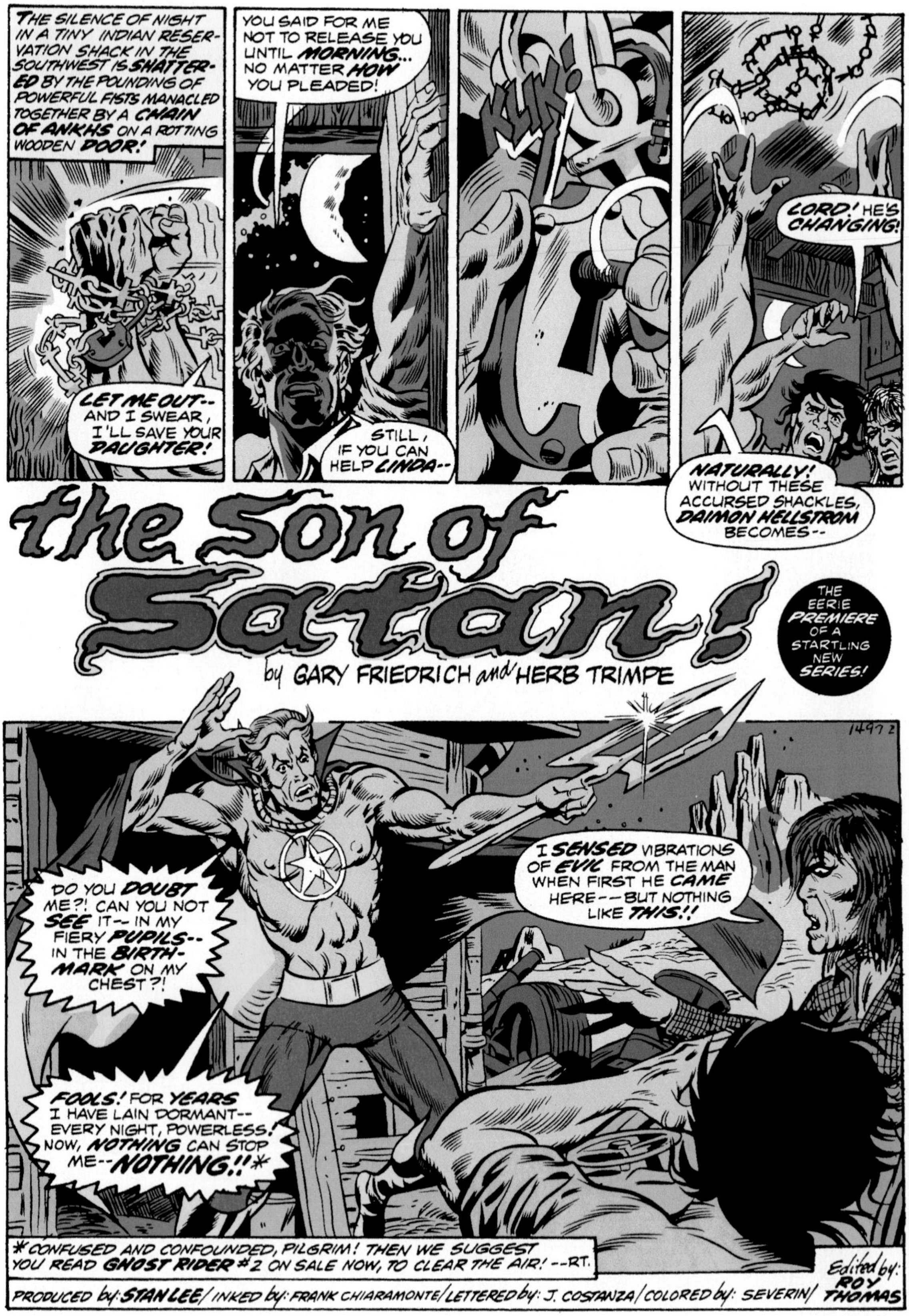
THE SILENCE OF NIGHT IN A TINY INDIAN RESERVATION SHACK IN THE SOUTHWEST IS SHATTERED BY THE POUNDING OF POWERFUL FISTS MANACLED TOGETHER BY A CHAIN OF ANKHS ON A ROTTING WOODEN DOOR!
LET ME OUT-- AND I SWEAR, I'LL SAVE YOUR DAUGHTER!
YOU SAID FOR ME NOT TO RELEASE YOU UNTIL MORNING... NO MATTER HOW YOU PLEADED!
STILL, IF YOU CAN HELP LINDA--
KLIK!
LORD! HE'S CHANGING!
NATURALLY! WITHOUT THESE ACCURSED SHACKLES, DAIMON HELLSTROM BECOMES--
the Son of Satan!
by GARY FRIEDRICH and HERB TRIMPE
THE EERIE PREMIERE OF A STARTLING NEW SERIES!
DO YOU DOUBT ME?! CAN YOU NOT SEE IT-- IN MY FIERY PUPILS-- IN THE BIRTHMARK ON MY CHEST?!
I SENSED VIBRATIONS OF EVIL FROM THE MAN WHEN FIRST HE CAME HERE--BUT NOTHING LIKE THIS!!
FOOLS! FOR YEARS I HAVE LAIN DORMANT-- EVERY NIGHT, POWERLESS! NOW, NOTHING CAN STOP ME--NOTHING!!*
*CONFUSED AND CONFOUNDED, PILGRIM! THEN WE SUGGEST YOU READ GHOST RIDER #2 ON SALE NOW, TO CLEAR THE AIR! --RT.
Edited by: ROY THOMAS
PRODUCED by: STAN LEE/ INKED by: FRANK CHIARAMONTE/ LETTERED by: J. COSTANZA/ COLORED by: SEVERIN/

YOU SEE, I AM A MAN DOMINATED BY *TWO CHARACTERS!* IN THE *DAYLIGHT HOURS* -- I AM THE PUNY, RELIGIOUS WEAKLING *DAIMON HELLSTROM,* SWORN ENEMY OF MY FATHER!

BUT BY *NIGHT,* MY TRUE AND *RIGHTFUL HERITAGE* TAKES CONTROL -- AND I BECOME MY FATHER'S *SON!*

FOR FAR *TOO LONG,* HAS HELLSTROM KEPT ME AT *BAY* -- BUT NOW, ALL THAT IS *ENDED* -- THANKS TO *YOU!*

IT IS BEYOND *BELIEF* -- YET SOMEHOW, I SENSE HE SPEAKS THE *TRUTH!* YOU MUST *STOP* HIM, SAM SILVERCLOUD -- *NOW!*

I DON'T GET ANY OF THIS -- BUT IF HE'S NOT GONNA HELP *LINDA,* I AIM TO *NAIL* 'IM!

ARE YOU *MAD?!* *STAND BACK!*

YOU *REFUSE?* THEN PERHAPS THE *ELEMENTAL TRIDENT* WILL PERSUADE YOU TO CHANGE YOUR *MINDS!*

WITH BUT A *MOTION* OF IT -- AND THE SLIGHTEST *MENTAL SUGGESTION* -- THE VERY EARTH YOU *WALK* ON IS AT MY *COMMAND!*

ZZAAK!

CONSIDER YOURSELVES *FORTUNATE!* HAD I NOT BEEN IN NEED OF *INFORMATION* FROM YOU --

-- IT WOULD HAVE BEEN *NOTHING* FOR ME TO DESTROY YOUR *ENTIRE VILLAGE* -- AND YOURSELVES ALONG *WITH* IT!

NOW TELL ME OF THIS *GIRL*-- THIS *LINDA* YOU SPEAK OF-- THE ONE YOU SAY IS *POSSESSED!*

NOTHING DOING! EVEN IF I *KNEW* WHERE SHE WAS-- I WOULDN'T *TELL* YOU!

BUT YOU *MUST!* IF WHAT YOU SAID IS *TRUE*-- MY FATHER, THE *DEVIL* HIMSELF, MAY HAVE TAKEN CONTROL OF HER BODY!

AND IF SUCH IS THE *CASE*-- I WILL STOP AT *NOTHING* TO *FIND* HER!

SPEAK-- OR I SHALL UNLEASH ALL THE POWER OF THE *MOLTEN EARTH'S CORE UPON* YOU!

DO YOUR *THING!* I'M NOT *TALKIN'!*

WITH BUT A *WAVE* OF THE GLEAMING TRIDENT, THE DESERT FLOOR SHIMMERS SLIGHTLY, THEN SURGES VIOLENTLY *UPWARD* AS IF THE ENTIRE *PLANET* IS ABOUT TO EXPLODE FROM *WITHIN!*

GO ON AND *KILL* US! GET IT *OVER* WITH!

NO!

I AM *SATAN'S SON,* AND I WILL NOT BE *DENIED* THAT WHICH I *DESIRE!*

46

CEASE!

ONCE MORE I HAVE SPARED YOU --BUT I PROMISE IT WILL BE MY *LAST* SUCH ACT OF *GENEROSITY!*

THEN STOP MOUTHING OFF AND *DO US IN!* I THINK THE OLD MAN'S *ALREADY* HAD IT!

NEVER HAVE I ENCOUNTERED SUCH *STUBBORNESS* --NOR SUCH TOTAL DISREGARD FOR ONE'S OWN *LIFE!*

BUT I WARN YOU, MY PATIENCE WEARS *THIN!* I MUST HAVE *INFORMATION*-- AND YOU MUST *GIVE* IT TO ME!

I *UNDERSTAND* YOU FEAR I WILL *HARM* THE GIRL-- BUT I PROMISE YOU I WILL *NOT!*

IT IS NOT *SHE* I SEEK-- BUT, RATHER, HE WHO *POSSESSES* HER--SATAN, HE WHO *SIRED* ME! NOW, FOR THE *LAST* TIME-- WHERE *IS* SHE, SILVER CLOUD??

"ALL RIGHT, I'LL TELL YOU ALL I *KNOW*-- WHICH ISN'T *MUCH*-- IF YOU PROMISE LINDA WON'T BE *HARMED!*

"AS I TOLD YOU WHEN YOU WERE *HELLSTROM,* SHE SEEMED TO BE *POSSESSED!* WE DIDN'T KNOW WHAT TO DO-- UNTIL I SAW YOUR AD IN THE *PAPER!*

"THOUGH I DON'T *BELIEVE* IN DEMONS OR *EXORCISM*-- OR AT LEAST I DIDN'T UNTIL *NOW*-- I WAS DESPERATE! SO I CALLED YOU AND ASKED YOU TO COME AND *HELP* HER IF YOU COULD!

"THERE WAS SOMETHING IN YOUR VOICE WHICH ALMOST *CONSOLED* ME--MADE ME FEEL YOU *WOULD* SAVE HER! BUT WHEN I RETURNED TO THE SHACK, SHE WAS *GONE*--VANISHED INTO THE *DESERT* AFTER KNOCKING HER FATHER ASIDE LIKE SOME *WILD ANIMAL!* AND I *SWEAR,* THAT'S ALL I CAN *TELL* YOU!"

47

YOU'D BEST BE SPEAKING THE **TRUTH**--

--FOR IF YOU'VE **LIED**, I SWEAR YOU WILL DIE A **THOUSAND DEATHS** FOR IT!

BUT THAT IS SOMETHING ONLY **TIME** CAN ANSWER-- AND TIME IS MOST **PRECIOUS** TO ME!

I HAVE ONLY UNTIL DAYLIGHT TO **FIND** HER-- AND THRU HER--MY **FATHER!** I'D BEST BE **STARTING!**

WITH A WAVE OF THE **ELEMENTAL TRIDENT** AND AN ALMOST INAUDIBLY MUTTERED **CHANT**, DARK STORM CLOUDS APPEAR ON A HORIZON WHICH ONLY MOMENTS BEFORE STOOD SPARKLING WITH **STARS**--

LIGHTNING FLASHES ALL AROUND, STREAKING EARTHWARD LIKE DEADLY SPEARS OF **ELECTRICITY**, STRIKING WITHIN **INCHES** OF THE WILDLY-GESTURING MAN WHO HAS **SUMMONED** IT!

AND WHILE THE TWO INDIANS **COWER** IN THE WAKE OF THE STORM'S DREADFUL **FURY**, DAIMON HELLSTROM STARES DIRECTLY INTO ITS **EYE**--

--UNFLINCHING, UNAFRAID, ALMOST **REVELING** IN ITS NEAR-TORNADIC **TERROR**--

--AS IF WAITING IN BARELY-CONTROLLED **ANTICIPATION** OF THAT WHICH IS YET TO **COME!**

THEN, A BLINDING BOLT OF LIGHTNING WHICH ILLUMINATES THE MIDNIGHT SKY LIKE A BLAZING SUN AT *HIGH NOON* -- AN EAR-SPLITTING CLAP OF *THUNDER* WHICH SHAKES THE EARTH TO ITS VERY CORE! AND IN ITS *WAKE*, CHARGING OUT OF THE BLACKNESS LIKE THE FIRE-SPAWNED WRAITH IT *IS* -- *THE DEMON-DRAWN CHARIOT OF SATAN* APPEARS.!!!

TO ME, FAITHFUL STEEDS! I HAVE NEED TO *TRAVEL* WHERE ONLY YOU CAN *TAKE* ME!

NOW, FOOLS--I TAKE MY *LEAVE!* BUT REMEMBER WELL WHAT YOU HAVE *SEEN* THIS NIGHT--

--AND LIVE IN MORTAL FEAR OF MY *RETURN,* SHOULD I FIND YOU HAVE *DECEIVED* ME! NOW, MY STEEDS-- *AWAAAYYY!*

THEN, BORNE ON A VORTEX OF SWIRLING WIND AND FLAMES, THE UNEARTHLY CHARIOT FADES INTO THE *NIGHT--*

WHAT KIND OF MADNESS *IS* THIS? DID YOU PUT SOMETHING IN MY *FOOD,* OLD MAN-- SOMETHING TO *CAUSE* THESE HALLUCINATIONS?!

YOU ARE NOT HAVING *VISIONS,* SAM SILVERCLOUD! YOU HAVE WITNESSED A *MIRACLE* OF SORTS!

A *MIRACLE*-- OR PERHAPS A *CURSE!*

HOW *SWEET* IS THE SENSATION-- HURTLING THROUGH THE AIR-- THE TORRID *HELL-WINDS* IN MY FACE!

IT HAS BEEN FAR *TOO LONG* SINCE I HAVE KNOWN SUCH *EXULTATION!* NEVER AGAIN CAN I ALLOW MYSELF TO *HUNGER* FOR THIS FEELING! IT MUST BE MINE *FOREVER!*

IT IS *TRUE!* I RUB MY EYES-- AND STILL I *SEE* IT!

YOU SEE IT--BECAUSE IT IS *THERE!* I CAN *FEEL* THE EVIL *AROUND* US--

--AND I FEAR WE HAVE UNLEASHED SOMETHING MORE *TERRIBLE* THAN THE WORLD HAS EVER *KNOWN!*

WHILE, SEVERAL MILES AWAY IN A *REMOTE AREA* OF THE DESERT, ROXANNE SIMPSON FINDS HERSELF LEFT TO THE MERCY OF A RAMPAGING *CYCLE GANG*--

--FOLLOWING THE SUDDEN, INEXPLICABLE *DISAPPEARANCE* OF JOHNNY BLAZE--*THE GHOST RIDER*--AND THE MYSTERIOUS *WITCH-WOMAN*--!*

*IT ALL HAPPENED IN *GHOST RIDER #2!*-- HIT-'EM-OVER-THE-HEAD-WITH-IT-ROY.

AND DON'T I *DIG* IT, ANIMAL! IF I CAN'T HAVE *BLAZE*-- GUESS I'LL HAVE TO SETTLE FOR HIS *MOMMA!*

I DON'T KNOW HOW THEY *DONE* IT, BIG DADDY-- BUT AT LEAST THEY LEFT *THIS* LITTLE HONEY BEHIND!

NOW ALL YOU DUDES KEEP YER PAWS *OFF*, 'CAUSE SHE'S STRICTLY *PRIVATE PROPERTY*--

--*MY* PRIVATE PROPERTY, SINCE HER HE-MAN DONE WENT AND *SPLIT* ON HER!

NO! STAY *AWAY* FROM ME! JOHNNY WILL *KILL* YOU IF YOU *TOUCH* ME!

DREAM ON, LADY! HE SPLIT WITH ANOTHER *CHICK,* SO WHY NOT JUST TURN ON TO *ME?!*

ZAK!

TOUCH THE GIRL AND I SWEAR YOU WILL DIE!!

51

WHAT THE DEVIL'S *GOIN' ON?* LIGHTNING ON A *CLEAR NIGHT--* NUTTY VOICES FROM OUTTA *NOWHERE?!*

IF THIS IS SOME MORE OF YOUR CHEAP *TRICKS,* BLAZE, THEY AIN'T GONNA- WHO ARE *YOU?!*

WHO I AM IS *NO* CONCERN OF *YOURS!* I ONLY WISH TO QUESTION THE *GIRL!*

OH, YA *DO,* HUH?! WELL I'M GETTIN' ME A GUT-*FULL* OF *COSTUMED CRAZIES* HORNIN' IN ON MY *BUSINESS!*

AND I'M THINKIN' IT'S TIME I PUT ME A *STOP* TO IT!

I *WARN* YOU-- STAND BACK AND ALLOW ME TO *SPEAK* WITH HER--AND YOU WON'T BE *HARMED!*

HEAR *THAT,* BOSS? HE'S GOT A *TATTOO--* AND HE THINKS HE'S GONNA *HURT* US!

I *HEARD* 'IM-- AN' WE'RE GONNA *DO* SOMETHIN' ABOUT IT! *GET* 'IM, BOYS--MAKE 'IM *EAT* THAT CREEPY CAPE-- PULVERIZE THE CRUMB!

CRETINS! KNOW YOU NOT THAT THE *SON OF SATAN* HAS THE STRENGTH OF A *HUNDRED MEN*?!

RUTHLESS RIDERS

SON OF SATAN??

YOU MUST BE SMACK FROM THE *LOONEY BIN*, BUD!

BUT-- CRAZY OR *NOT*-- *CRUSHER CROWDER* DON'T SHOW NO MERCY TO *NOBODY*, ONCE BIG DADDY'S PUT THE *FINGER* ON 'EM!

FOOL! YOU ARE LITTLE MORE THAN A *FLY* TO ME!

WHUH WHOM!

NOW, WHAT *SAY* YOU?! WILL YOU STAND ASIDE AND LET ME *SPEAK* WITH THE GIRL--

-- OR MUST I *FURTHER* CONVINCE YOU OF MY OBVIOUS MENTAL AND PHYSICAL *SUPERIORITY*?

NEITHER ONE, CURLY! 'CAUSE NO MATTER HOW *STRONG* YOU ARE-- OR HOW MANY *MAGIC TRICKS* YOU CAN PULL--

--I GOT ME A LITTLE *EQUALIZER* HERE! IT'S CALLED A *HEATER*-- AND YOU MAKE ANOTHER MOVE-- I'LL USE IT TO BLOW YOUR HEAD INTO THE *NEXT COUNTY*!

STILL YOU FAIL TO RECOGNIZE MY *IDENTITY* -- FAIL TO GRASP THE EXTENT OF MY *POWERS?!* I HAVE NO *QUARREL* WITH YOU--

--NOR YOU WITH *ME!* SO WHY NOT STAND *ASIDE--?!*

THIS IS YOUR *LAST CHANCE,* CURLY! EITHER *BUTT OUT* -- OR GET *DEAD!* NOBODY HORNS IN ON *MY* TERRITORY!

ENOUGH OF THIS IDLE *BANTERING!* LET THE *SACRED SCEPTRE* PUT AN *END* TO THIS!

IN A SPACE OF TIME FAR TOO *INFINITE* TO BE *MEASURED* BY MAN, HIS WRIST FLICKS *FORWARD*-- AND A GLEAMING TARGET HURTLES TOWARD ITS STARTLED *TARGET!*

WHAT IN *BLAZES--?!* HE THREW IT AND *NAILED* ME-- SO FAST I DIDN'T EVEN HAVE TIME TO PULL THE *TRIGGER!*

NOR WILL YOU HAVE FURTHER *OPPORTUNITY* TO DO SO!

ALL THE HEAT OF *HELL ITSELF* IS MINE TO *COMMAND* -- AND I CHOSE TO COMMAND IT *NOW!*

SOME KIND'A *RAYS*-- SHOOTIN' FROM HIS *FINGERTIPS!*

THE GUN-- LOOKIT THE GUN, MAN! IT'S *MELTIN'!* WHOEVER THIS DUDE IS-- HE'S FOR *REAL!*

YOU STAY IF YA **WANT**, BIG DADDY-- BUT WE'RE **SPLITTIN'**! THAT DUDE'S MADE A **BELIEVER** OF US!

IF YOU ARE **WISE**-- YOU WILL DEPART **WITH** THEM! SURELY YOU WOULD NOT WISH TO CONTINUE A JOUST WITH--

--THE SON OF SATAN!!

NOW, AT LAST WE CAN **TALK**, MY DEAR! YOU ARE VERY **BEAUTIFUL**--

--AND I **PITY** THE FACT I HAVEN'T TIME TO **LINGER** WITH YOU-- AND PERHAPS WHISPER WORDS OF **LOVE** INTO YOUR EAR!

YOUR GOLDEN HAIR IS MOST **INTRIGUING**-- SO SOFT, SO SHIMMERING IN THE PALE **MOONLIGHT**!

ONLY **RARELY** HAVE I BEHELD SUCH **LOVLIENESS** BUT FOR NOW, A MERE **TOUCH** IS ALL TIME **ALLOWS** ME--

--THEN TO **BUSINESS**! I FEEL YOU HAVE RECENTLY BEEN IN CONTACT WITH MY **FATHER**!

OOOHHH!

SPEAK, WOMAN! I CAN SENSE HIS RECENT **PRESENCE** HERE! WHERE **IS** HE? WHERE IS **SATAN**?!

I-- I DON'T **KNOW**! I **SWEAR** IT! HE WASN'T **HERE**-- ONLY THAT **WOMAN**!

SHE WAS AN **INDIAN**-- CALLED HERSELF **WITCH-WOMAN**--AND SHE DIS-APPEARED WITH **JOHNNY**!

WITCH-WOMAN? THAT IS ONE OF THE MANY FORMS **HE** USES! BUT, IF HE HAS THE **SOUL** HE SOUGHT-- I **KNOW** WHERE HE HAS TAKEN IT!

55

WITH CALLOUS DISREGARD FOR ANYTHING SAVE HIS OWN PERSONAL *QUEST*, HE LEAVES ROCKY SIMPSON ALONE IN THE *DESERT* *-- AND MAKES HIS WAY TO A SECLUDED SPOT ON A *HIGH PLATEAU!*

* TO FIND OUT WHAT *HAPPENS* TO HER, DON'T MISS *GHOST RIDER #3!* -- PLUG-HAPPY ROY.

SOON HE FINDS IT, A HUGE SMOULDERING CAVERN WHICH SEEMINGLY LEADS TO THE VERY *BOWELS* OF THE EARTH-- THE *GATEWAY TO HELL..!*

THEN HE BEGINS WINDING HIS WAY *DOWNWARD,* THROUGH TUNNEL AFTER TUNNEL FILLED WITH THE FETID STENCH OF SIMMERING *LAVA--*

--UNTIL, AT *LAST,* HE REACHES THE *THRONE ROOM* OF HIS FATHER'S UNDER-WORLD *KINGDOM,* A VAST NOTCH AT THE EARTH'S CENTER FILLED WITH A *MILLION HORRORS*-- HORRORS WHICH FILL THE STOMACH OF EVEN *SATAN'S SON* WITH DISGUST AND *REVULSION--*

FATHER-- I AM HERE!!

DAIMON-- MY SO-CALLED SON-- OR SHOULD I SAY SON OF MY *FLESH*-- BUT NOT OF MY *SPIRIT?!*

STILL, I BID YOU *WELCOME!* YOU ARE JUST IN TIME TO WITNESS A MOST SACRED *RITUAL!*

BEHOLD, DAIMON-- TWO LOST SOULS ABOUT TO BECOME MY *ETERNAL SERVANTS!*

THE FEMALE, ONE *LINDA LITTLETREE,* IS OF LITTLE *CONSEQUENCE*-- BUT THE MAN, *JOHNNY BLAZE,* IS ONE I HAVE SOUGHT *RELENTLESSLY!* AND NOW-- HE IS ABOUT TO BECOME *MINE!*

YET ANOTHER SIGN OF YOUR MENTAL *DETERIORATION*, MY FATHER! PERHAPS EVEN *THE DEVIL* GROWS *OLD*, EH?

MIND YOUR *TONGUE*, LAD-- LEST I FORGET OUR UNFORTUNATE *RELATIONSHIP* AND TOSS YOU TO MY EVER-STARVING *DEMONS*!

AH, THE TRUTH IS *PAINFUL* TO YOU-- THAT YOU NOW SEEK *MALE* SERVANTS RATHER THAN BEAUTIFUL *WOMEN*!

YES, AGE *IS* CREEPING UP ON YOU-- TO THINK YOU NOW SEEK *RAW POWER* RATHER THAN FULLFILL-MENT OF YOUR UNQUENCHABLE *LUST*!

ENOUGH! I WILL NOT *HEAR* THIS BLASPHEMY IN THE CONFINES OF MY OWN *DOMAIN*!

BUT YOU *MUST* HEAR THEM, FATHER-- OR HAVE YOU FORGOTTEN THAT I POSSES THE *SACRED TRIDENT*--

--MADE OF *NETHERAN-IUM*, THE ONE SUBSTANCE WHICH CAN *SAP* YOU OF YOUR *POWERS*?!

NO! KEEP THAT THING *AWAY* FROM ME!

WHAT MANNER OF SON HAVE I *SIRED*-- FIRST TO BLASPHEM-- THEN TO *THREATEN* HIS OWN FATHER?!

TRUE, YOUR TRIDENT RENDERS ME *PERSON-ALLY* HELPLESS AGAINST YOU-- BUT IT HAS NO EFFECT ON MY *MINDLESS MINIONS*!

ATTACK! ATTACK AND DESTROY HIM!

LIKE A **LIMITLESS ARMY** THEY COME AT HIM BY THE **HUNDREDS!** AND THOUGH HE FIGHTS **BRAVELY,** FOR EVERY DEMON HE **SMITES,** TWO MORE CHARGE FORWARD TO TAKE ITS **PLACE!**

STILL, IN SPITE OF THE OVERWHELMING ODDS **AGAINST** HIM, HE FIGHTS ON, RENDING FLESH WITH THE SACRED TRIDENT, CRUSHING BONES WITH THE FURY OF HIS **FISTS!** YES, THOUGH THE BATTLE SEEMS LOST BEFORE IT HAS BEGUN, HE FIGHTS EVER **ONWARD** -- FOR THIS IS NO **ORDINARY WARRIOR** -- NAY, HE IS, AFTER ALL, **THE SON OF SATAN!!**

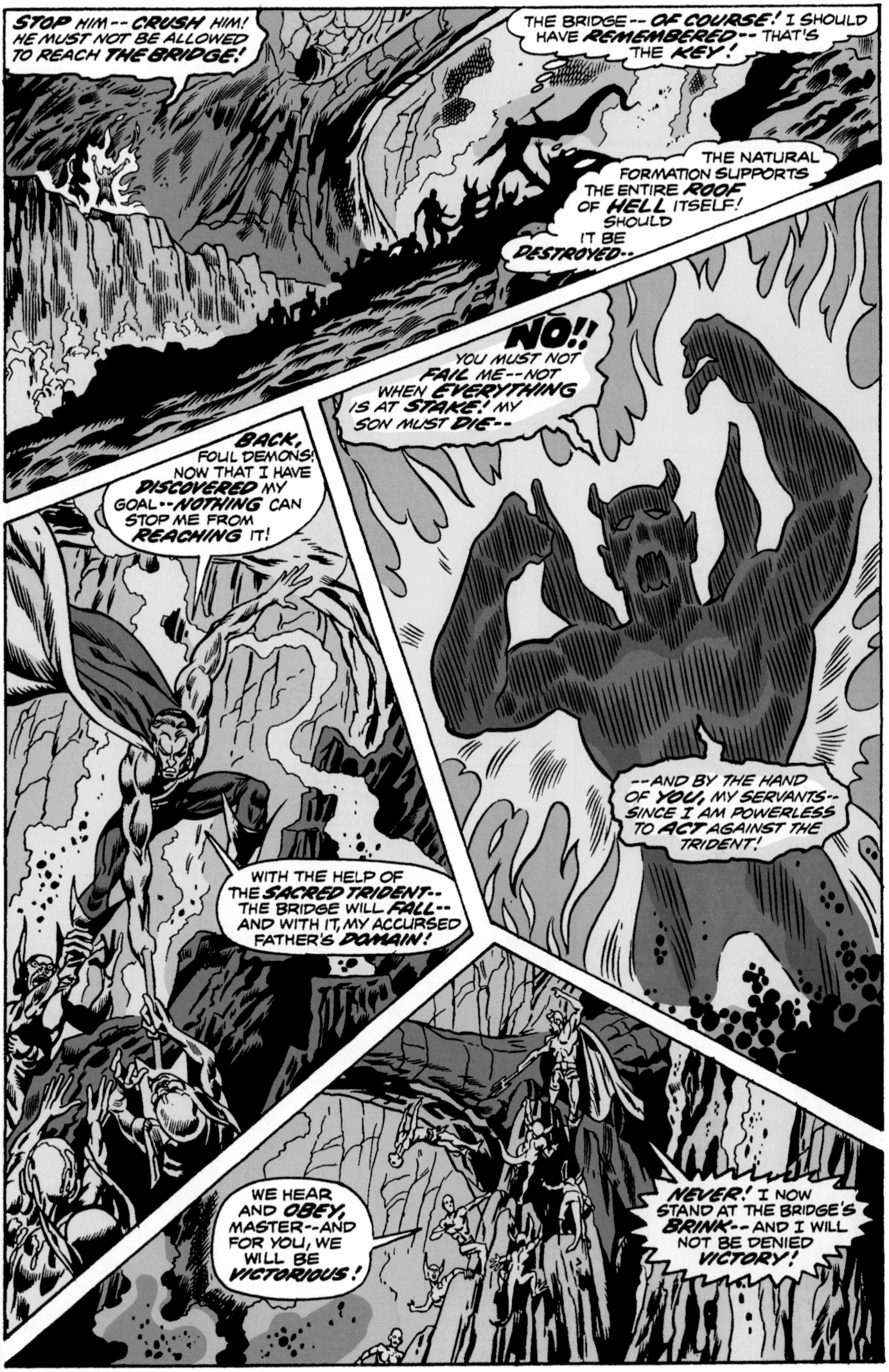
STOP HIM -- CRUSH HIM! HE MUST NOT BE ALLOWED TO REACH THE BRIDGE!
THE BRIDGE -- OF COURSE! I SHOULD HAVE REMEMBERED -- THAT'S THE KEY!
THE NATURAL FORMATION SUPPORTS THE ENTIRE ROOF OF HELL ITSELF! SHOULD IT BE DESTROYED--
NO!! YOU MUST NOT FAIL ME--NOT WHEN EVERYTHING IS AT STAKE! MY SON MUST DIE--
BACK, FOUL DEMONS! NOW THAT I HAVE DISCOVERED MY GOAL--NOTHING CAN STOP ME FROM REACHING IT!
--AND BY THE HAND OF YOU, MY SERVANTS-- SINCE I AM POWERLESS TO ACT AGAINST THE TRIDENT!
WITH THE HELP OF THE SACRED TRIDENT-- THE BRIDGE WILL FALL-- AND WITH IT, MY ACCURSED FATHER'S DOMAIN!
WE HEAR AND OBEY, MASTER--AND FOR YOU, WE WILL BE VICTORIOUS!
NEVER! I NOW STAND AT THE BRIDGE'S BRINK-- AND I WILL NOT BE DENIED VICTORY!

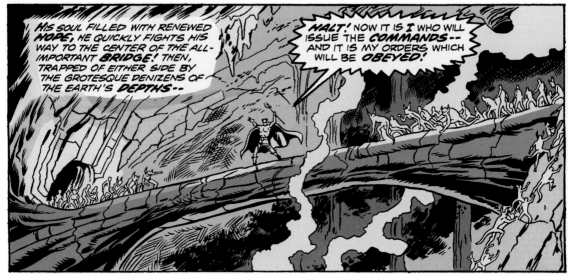

HIS SOUL FILLED WITH RENEWED *HOPE,* HE QUICKLY FIGHTS HIS WAY TO THE CENTER OF THE ALL-IMPORTANT *BRIDGE!* THEN, TRAPPED OF EITHER SIDE BY THE GROTESQUE DENIZENS OF THE EARTH'S *DEPTHS*--

HALT! NOW IT IS *I* WHO WILL ISSUE THE *COMMANDS*-- AND IT IS MY ORDERS WHICH WILL BE *OBEYED!*

I AM SORELY TEMPTED TO *DESTROY* THIS HORRID PLACE-- AND MYSELF ALONG *WITH* IT!

SO MAKE NO FURTHER MOVE *TOWARD* ME-- LEST I BE TEMPTED TO MAKE A *HASTY DECISION!*

FOR THE *MOMENT,* I AM AT YOUR *MERCY*-- YET I AM *PROUD!* YOU ARE *TRULY* MY SON!

STILL MERE PRIDE DOES NOT SLAVE MY *ANGER*-- AT WHAT YOU HAVE *DONE!*

SO TELL ME, *QUICKLY,* WHAT IT IS YOU *WANT* OF ME!

FOR *NOW,* MERELY THE LIVES OF YOUR TWO *HOSTAGES* -- THAT AND SAFE PASSAGE BACK TO THE *SURFACE!*

I KNEW IT! YOU SEEK ONLY TO *DEPRIVE* ME OF THAT I SEEK *MOST*-- BUT SO BE IT! I HAVE NO *CHOICE!*

BE WARNED, THOUGH YOU BE MY *FLESH*--YOU WILL NOT BE *FORGIVEN!* ON THIS DAY, I *DISOWN* YOU--AND I WILL NOT REST UNTIL YOU GROVEL AT MY *FEET!*

WE ARE **SAFE** NOW! MY FATHER CANNOT STRIKE SO LONG AS I HOLD THE **TRIDENT**!

AND HOLD IT I WILL--UNTIL I GAIN THE FINAL, ULTIMATE **REVENGE**--FOR WHAT HE DID TO MY **MOTHER** AND **SISTER***!

* MORE ON THE MOTHER **NEXT ISH**! AND AS FOR HIS SULTRY SISTER **SATANA**, YOU CAN GET A FLEETING GLIMPSE OF HER IN OUR GIANT-SIZE **VAMPIRE TALES #2**, NOW ON SALE! --ROY

BUT IF YOU **ARE** HIS SON--WHY DID YOU SAVE **US**?!

ONLY TO **SPITE** HIM, I ASSURE YOU! THERE WERE NO **NOBLE** MOTIVES INVOLVED!

I EXIST ONLY TO **DESTROY** HIM--AND ONE DAY SOON, I **WILL**!

RUUMMMMBLLLEEEEERRROOAAR!

THAT **RUMBLING**-- LIKE THE BEGINNINGS OF AN **EARTHQUAKE**!

TAKE COVER! EVIDENTLY HE HAS DECIDED TO DESTOY ME **INDIRECTLY**-- BY MEANS OF A **VOLCANO**!

WHROOM

NOW WHERE ARE YOUR THREATS--YOUR HOLLOW ECHOES OF **VICTORY**?! HOW IRONIC THAT YOU MUST **DIE** TO LEARN THAT SATAN IS EVER **ALL-POWERFUL**!

HUG THIS **BOULDER**-- MAKE YOUR BODY A PART OF IT! IT WILL **PROTECT** US UNTIL I CAN **THINK** OF A METHOD OF **ESCAPE**!

IF I CAN THINK OF ONE! OTHERWISE--THIS IS THE **END**! HE HAS **WON**--AND I AM **VANQUISHED**!

WAIT! OF COURSE THERE IS HOPE-- AS ALWAYS THERE MUST BE!

CLOSE YOUR EYES-- AND DO NOT STARE INTO THE STORM-- WHILE I SUMMON THE MEANS TO OUR ESCAPE!

ONCE MORE THE HEAVENS OPEN WITH A THUNDROUS ROAR AND BLINDING FLASHES OF LIGHTNING! THEN, IN THE STORM'S WAKE, THE DEMON-DRAWN CHARIOT APPEARS.!!

THEN, IN LESS THAN AN INSTANT, THE FIERY VEHICLE STREAKS ACROSS THE SKY IN A FLAMING STREAK, CARRYING ITS HUMAN CARGO OUT OF HARM'S WAY--

--WHILE, FAR BELOW, THE SATAN-SPAWNED DEATH-TRAP CEASES TO SPEW FORTH ITS DEADLY SPRAY OF LAVA, LEAVING IN ITS PLACE A USELESS, SIMMERING CRATER!

THERE-- THAT BARREN SPOT--IS WHERE I WILL TAKE MY LEAVE OF YOU!

THERE IS A PLACE TO WHICH I MUST RETURN BY MORNING--

--SO THERE IS NO TIME FOR ME TO DEPOSIT YOU ELSE- WHERE!

I AM SORRY I ACCUSED YOU OF HUMANITARIANISM! TRULY YOUR HEART IS AS COLD AS THAT OF YOUR FATHER!

THINK WHAT YOU MUST! IT IS OF LITTLE CONSEQUENCE TO ME! YOU ARE STILL ALIVE-- AND THAT MUCH YOU OWE ME!

THOUGH I CANNOT TELL THEM, I WILL RETURN LATER AS DAIMON HELLSTROM! PERHAPS HE WAS RIGHT ABOUT ME-- BUT THERE ARE SO MANY QUESTIONS TO BE ANSWERED--SO MANY!!

AND WE'LL ANSWER A LOT OF THEM NEXT ISH WITH: "THE BIRTH OF SATAN'S SON!" (THAT MEANS AN ORIGIN, FRANTIC ONE, SO DON'T DARE MISS IT!)

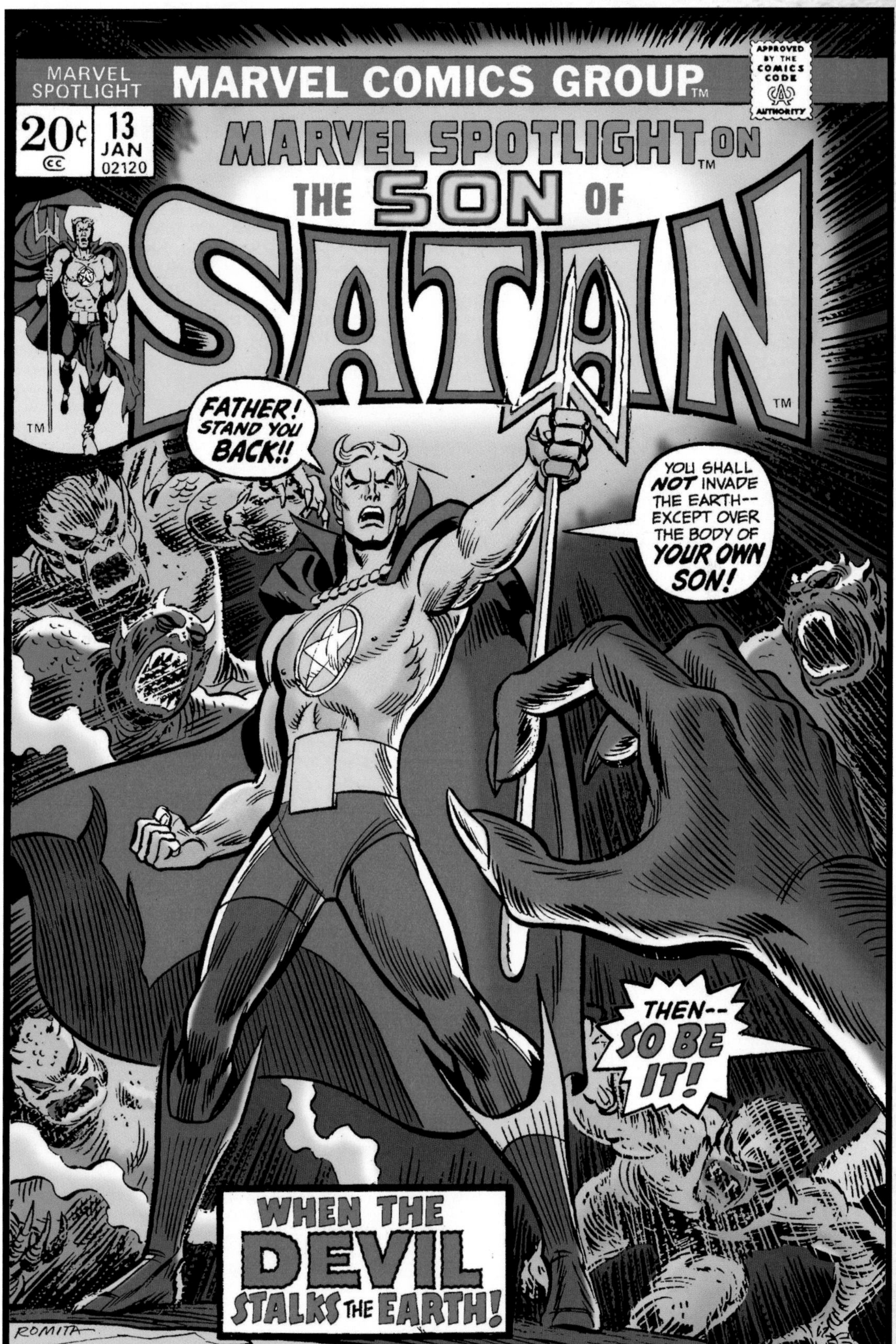
MARVEL SPOTLIGHT
MARVEL COMICS GROUP
APPROVED BY THE COMICS CODE AUTHORITY
20¢
13 JAN 02120
MARVEL SPOTLIGHT ON
THE SON OF SATAN
FATHER! STAND YOU BACK!!
YOU SHALL NOT INVADE THE EARTH-- EXCEPT OVER THE BODY OF YOUR OWN SON!
THEN-- SO BE IT!
WHEN THE DEVIL STALKS THE EARTH!
ROMITA

STAN LEE PRESENTS: SON OF SATAN™

WHEN SATAN STALKED THE EARTH!

HEAR ME, YOU WHO ARE SATAN'S SON-- MY SON--

--THIS ONE TIME YOU HAVE *BESTED* ME--BUT FOR THAT PALTRY VICTORY-- YOU WILL PAY WITH YOUR *LIFE!*

THE INVISIBLE BUT EVER-PRESENT SPECTER OF SATAN HANGS HEAVY OVER THE HEAD OF DAIMON HELLSTROM AS HIS FIERY, DEMON-DRAWN CHARIOT STREAKS ACROSS THE PRE-DAWN NEW ENGLAND SKY! HE IS HOMEWARD BOUND, THIS OFFSPRING OF THE DEVIL-- BUT AS HE SPEEDS ON, HE CANNOT HELP BUT WONDER IF THERE CAN EVER BE AN ESCAPE FROM HIS DEADLY BIRTHRIGHT!!

GARY FRIEDRICH WRITER	HERB TRIMPE ARTIST	FRANK CHIARAMONTE INKER
ARTIE SIMEK LETTERING	PETRA GOLDBERG COLORING	ROY THOMAS EDITOR

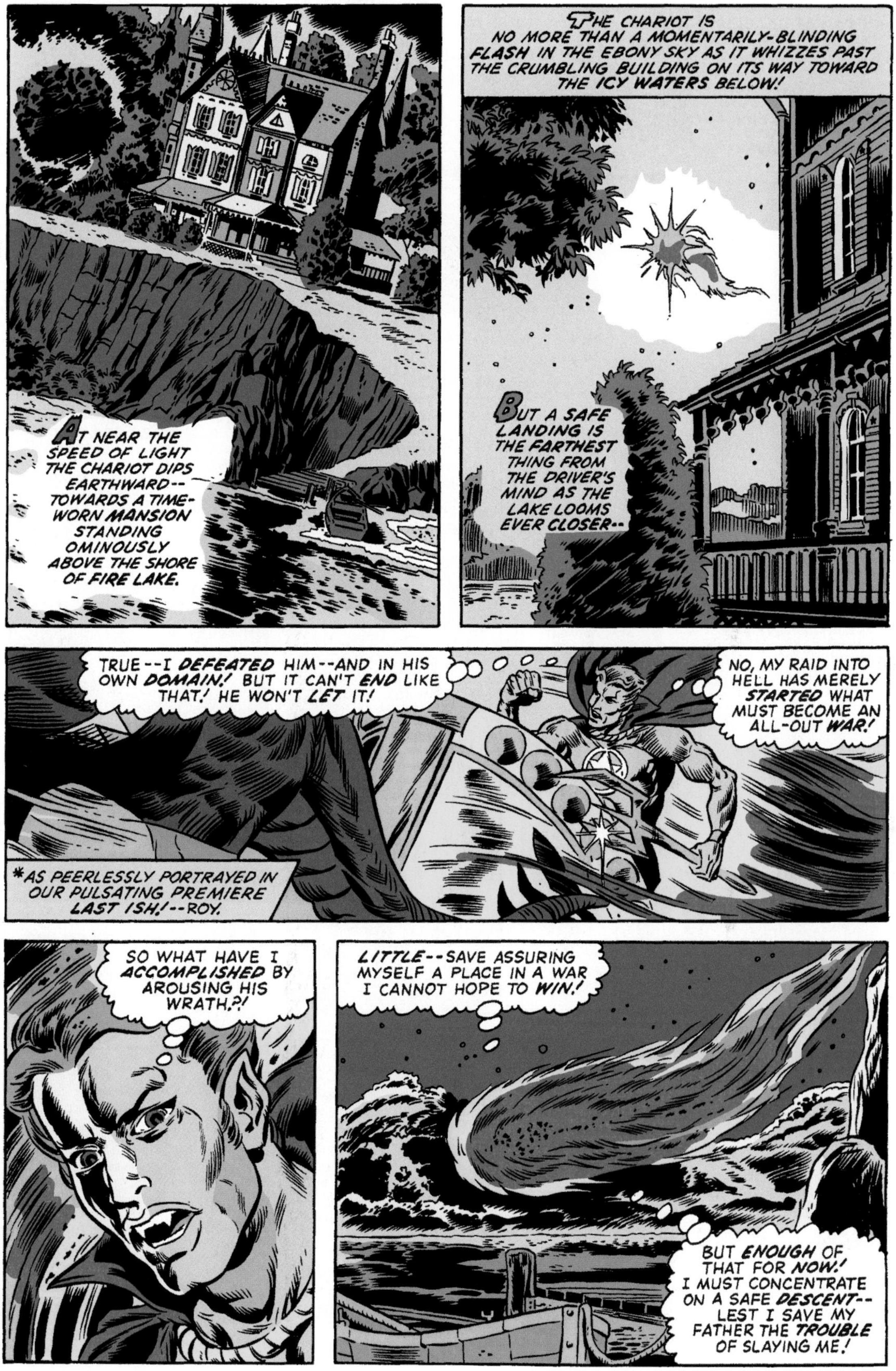
AT NEAR THE SPEED OF LIGHT THE CHARIOT DIPS EARTHWARD-- TOWARDS A TIME-WORN MANSION STANDING OMINOUSLY ABOVE THE SHORE OF FIRE LAKE.
THE CHARIOT IS NO MORE THAN A MOMENTARILY-BLINDING FLASH IN THE EBONY SKY AS IT WHIZZES PAST THE CRUMBLING BUILDING ON ITS WAY TOWARD THE ICY WATERS BELOW!
BUT A SAFE LANDING IS THE FARTHEST THING FROM THE DRIVER'S MIND AS THE LAKE LOOMS EVER CLOSER--
TRUE--I DEFEATED HIM--AND IN HIS OWN DOMAIN! BUT IT CAN'T END LIKE THAT! HE WON'T LET IT!
NO, MY RAID INTO HELL HAS MERELY STARTED WHAT MUST BECOME AN ALL-OUT WAR!
*AS PEERLESSLY PORTRAYED IN OUR PULSATING PREMIERE LAST ISH!--ROY.
SO WHAT HAVE I ACCOMPLISHED BY AROUSING HIS WRATH?!
LITTLE--SAVE ASSURING MYSELF A PLACE IN A WAR I CANNOT HOPE TO WIN!
BUT ENOUGH OF THAT FOR NOW! I MUST CONCENTRATE ON A SAFE DESCENT-- LEST I SAVE MY FATHER THE TROUBLE OF SLAYING ME!

IT NEVER CEASES TO *AMAZE* ME THAT I HAVE THE POWER TO *WITHSTAND* SUCH AN IMPACT!

YET I *KNOW* MY CHARIOT AND I WILL DISAPPEAR BENEATH THE WAVES IN AN *INSTANT*--

--AND I WILL EMERGE TOTALLY *UNSCATHED!*

HEY, JACKIE-- LOOK AT *THAT!*

WHAT *WAS* IT-- A *SHOOTING STAR.?!*

I AINT *SURE*-- BUT IT'S HIGH TIME I TOOK YOU *HOME!* MAN, NO *WONDER* THEY CALL THIS *FIRE LAKE!*

WITH A *DAZZLING* DISPLAY OF FLAMES AND FOAM, THE CHARIOT CRASHES INTO THE WATER AND IS *GONE* IN LESS THAN A SECOND--

FLLIZZZAT!!

--COMING TO REST IN AN UNDERGROUND *CAVERN* FATHOMS BELOW AND LEAVING TWO ASTONISHED TEENAGERS TO BELIEVE THEY HAVE SEEN NOTHING MORE THAN ONE OF NATURE'S *PHENOMENONS!*

MOMENTS LATER, HIS *UNEARTHLY STEEDS* UNBRIDLED AND FED, THE MAN CALLED *DAIMON HELLSTROM* MOUNTS THE STAIRS OF THE PLACE HE CALLS *HOME*--

--*ONLY* TO BE GREETED BY A DANK, FETID SCENT WHICH CHILLS HIS HEART AND AWAKENS HIS WEARY SENSES!

MY *FATHER* HAS BEEN HERE--OR IS *STILL* HERE!

DOES HE INTEND FOR MY *DEATH* TO COME SO *SOON?!*

THE TUNNEL TO *HELL*-- IN THE *CELLAR!* COULD HE HAVE BROKEN THE *SEAL?!*

FOR *TWO YEARS* IT HAS HELD HIM AT *BAY,* BUT NOW--I MUST *CHECK!*

DIE, *TRAITOR!* THE MASTER *DEMANDS* IT!

MY *SCEPTER*-- BUT PERHAPS I'LL NOT *NEED* IT, IF SATAN MERELY SENDS HIS *LACKEYS* FOR ME!

MY FATHER *UNDERESTIMATES* ME! FOR THOUGH THE ELEMENT OF SURPRISE IS *YOURS*--

--THE *POWER* OF SATAN STILL BELONGS TO *ME!*

AND IT WILL TAKE FAR MORE THAN THE PITIFUL LIKES OF DEMONS LIKE *YOU*--

--TO *OVERCOME* WHAT I INHERITED AT *BIRTH!*

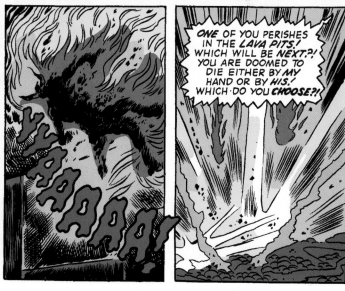

ONE OF YOU PERISHES IN THE *LAVA PITS!* WHICH WILL BE *NEXT?!* YOU ARE DOOMED TO DIE EITHER BY *MY* HAND OR BY *HIS!* WHICH DO YOU *CHOOSE?!*

SO, YOU CHOSE TO *RUN*-- MISERABLE WRETCHES THAT YOU ARE.! BUT THERE CAN *BE* NO ESCAPE FOR YOU!

WHUMP!

SINCE YOU *MUST* DIE, IT IS FAR BETTER THAT YOU DIE BY *MY* HAND--THAT SATAN MAY KNOW HIS SON IS TRULY HIS *EQUAL!*

WHAT.?! YOU DARE CONFRONT ME WITH MY OWN *SCEPTER.?!* WHAT A PITIFUL *FOOL* YOU ARE!

GRROWR!

DO YOU NOT REALIZE IT HAS NO *EFFECT* ON ME.?!

THE *NETHERANIUM* IN ITS POINTS WEAKEN ONLY YOUR *MASTER!* TO ME--IT IS USEFUL ONLY AS A *WEAPON*--

--WITH WHICH TO SLAY MY *ENEMIES!*

BACK WITH YOU-- BACK TO THE BUBBLING DEPTHS FROM WHENCE YOU CAME!

PERHAPS YOUR FAILURE TO **CONQUER** ME WILL DISSUADE MY FATHER FROM SUCH FOOLISH VENTURES IN THE **FUTURE!**

NOW I'LL SEAL AWAY THE **SCEPTER** --WHERE HE CAN NEVER **FIND** IT!

FOR IF EVER HE **SHOULD**-- THE ONLY POWER I **WIELD** OVER HIM WOULD INSTANTLY **DISAPPEAR!**

AH, I AM WEARY FROM THE **BATTLE**-- BUT MY MIND WON'T ALLOW ME TO **REST!**

IS THERE NO WAY I CAN KNOW **PEACE**-- UNTIL SATAN IS **DESTROYED.?!**

MY MOTHER'S **DIARY**--PERHAPS BY **READING** IT AGAIN, I CAN FIND A **WAY**--THE MEANS TO GAIN MY **REVENGE!**

BUT WHERE TO **START**--? I SUPPOSE THERE'S ONLY **ONE PLACE**-- THE **BEGINNING!**

"**THOUGH** IT WILL BE **PAINFUL,** YOU MUST KNOW THESE THINGS, MY **SON**--

"--AND THEN YOU MUST **FIGHT** YOUR FATHER, WITH ALL YOUR **STRENGTH!**

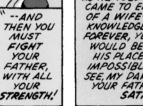

"AS HE TOLD ME, HE FIRST CAME TO EARTH IN SEARCH OF A WIFE--SECURE IN THE KNOWLEDGE HE WOULD LIVE FOREVER, YET AFRAID THERE WOULD BE NONE TO TAKE HIS PLACE SHOULD THE IMPOSSIBLE OCCUR! YOU SEE, MY DARLING DAIMON, YOUR FATHER WAS--IS-- SATAN!!"

"WHY HE CHOSE MY HOME TOWN, I'LL NEVER KNOW-- BUT I ASSUME HE LIKED THE SECLUSION AROUND FIRE LAKE. HE SOMEHOW CONJURED UP THE GHASTLY MANSION I CAME TO KNOW AS HOME!

"THEN, WITH A BASE OF OPERATIONS ESTABLISHED, HE CHANGED HIS FORM TO THAT OF THE MOST HANDSOME MAN ANY EARTHLY WOMAN HAD EVER SEEN!

"IN SPITE OF THE EVIL ESSENCE WHICH ALWAYS SEEMED TO BLAZE IN HIS EYES, HE WAS THE PERFECT MAN TO CAPTURE THE INNOCENT HEART OF A SHY, LONELY YOUNG GIRL LIKE MYSELF--

"I SHALL NEVER FORGET THE FIRST TIME I SAW HIM! I WAS TERRIFIED-- YET SOMEHOW MESMERIZED BY HIS PRESENCE--

YOU ARE LOVELY! COME-- TAKE MY HAND-- WALK WITH ME!

BUT-- BUT I DON'T EVEN KNOW YOU! I--

THAT IS UNIMPORTANT! ALL THAT MATTERS IS THAT WE ARE HERE-- TOGETHER!

"WE SPENT THE REST OF THE DAY ROAMING THE FORESTS-- TALKING-- TOUCHING! AND WHEN AT LAST SUNSET CAME, I WAS NO LONGER ABLE TO RESIST HIM! I WAS HIS FOR THE MERE ASKING--

"I AM SO *SORRY*, MY DARLING SON. IF ONLY I'D HAD THE SLIGHTEST *INKLING* AS TO HIS IDENTITY-- BUT I *DIDN'T!* I WAS A NAIVE YOUNG WOMAN IN SEARCH OF *ROMANCE*, MAY THE LORD FORGIVE ME--"

"WE WERE MARRIED AND MOVED IMMEDIATELY INTO THE HOUSE IN WHICH YOU WERE *BORN* LITTLE MORE THAN A YEAR *LATER*--"

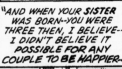

"AND WHEN YOUR *SISTER* WAS BORN--YOU WERE THREE THEN, I BELIEVE-- I DIDN'T BELIEVE IT POSSIBLE FOR ANY COUPLE TO BE HAPPIER--"

"YOUR FATHER BEGAN TO TAKE EXTENDED *TRIPS* FREQUENTLY AFTER THAT! BUT I HAD YOU CHILDREN, AND I ASSUMED HE WAS AWAY ON BUSINESS--"

"SO I IGNORED IT FOR SEVERAL YEARS MORE! UNTIL THAT HORRIBLE TIME I WENT TO THE *CELLAR* --LOOKING FOR YOUR FATHER AND SISTER--"

MY GOD! WHAT'S HAPPENED TO THE *CAT?!* WHAT ARE YOU *DOING?!*

SHE'S MERELY OBEYING MY *ORDERS*, VICTORIA! SHE *KNOWS* THE TRUTH-- AND I SUPPOSE IT'S TIME YOU LEARNED IT, *TOO!*

I'M *LEAVING,* DADDY! I DON'T WANT TO SEE HER FACE WHEN YOU *TELL* HER!

WHAT DOES SHE *MEAN?!* WHAT'S THIS ALL *ABOUT?!*

I'VE MEANT TO TELL YOU FOR *YEARS* NOW--BUT I THINK THE BEST WAY IS TO *SHOW* YOU!

WATCH--AND THEN YOU'LL FINALLY KNOW *WHO* YOU MARRIED!

NOW DO YOU SEE?! YOU'RE THE BRIDE OF--

--*SATAN!*

EEEEEEEEE!

"I DON'T HAVE ANY *IDEA* HOW LONG IT WAS BEFORE I STOPPED *SCREAMING!* BUT WHEN I DID, I WAS LOCKED AWAY IN A *PADDED CELL* SOMEWHERE, UNABLE TO TALK OR REALLY EVEN *THINK,* UNTIL A FEW HOURS BEFORE THE *DEATH* I KNEW WAS APPROACHING--

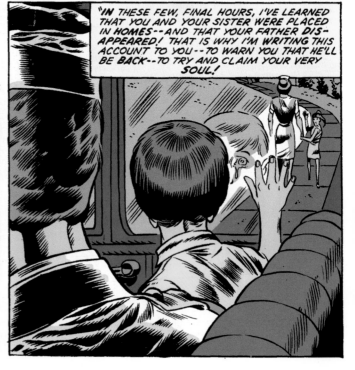

"*IN* THESE FEW, FINAL HOURS, I'VE LEARNED THAT YOU AND YOUR SISTER WERE PLACED IN *HOMES*--AND THAT YOUR FATHER DISAPPEARED! THAT IS WHY I'M *WRITING* THIS ACCOUNT TO YOU--TO WARN YOU THAT HE'LL BE *BACK*--TO TRY AND CLAIM YOUR VERY *SOUL!*

"AND THE *ANKH* CHAIN--REMEMBER? I GAVE IT TO YOU THE LAST TIME YOU *VISITED!* GUARD IT WITH YOUR *LIFE*--FOR IT IS THE ONLY THING WHICH CAN *SAVE* YOU FROM HIM--THE ONLY THING!"

AH, THERE'S NOTHING IN THE *DIARY*--BUT MAYBE IF I KEEP SEARCHING THE PAST! WHAT'S *THERE*, THOUGH? I GREW UP AS NORMALLY AS AN ORPHAN *CAN*, NEVER HEARING A *WORD* FROM MY SISTER OR FATHER!

"*THEN* I MADE MY *DECISION*-- I'D ENTER A *MONESTARY* AND BECOME A *PRIEST!* I SPENT MORE THAN *THREE YEARS* THERE, AND WAS ON MY WAY TO BEING *ORDAINED*--THAT'S WHEN I GOT THE NOTE ABOUT MY *INHERITANCE!*

"*I* TOOK A *LEAVE* AND WENT HOME, TO THE HOUSE MOTHER AND FATHER HAD LEFT FOR ME TO INHERIT ON MY *TWENTY-FIRST BIRTHDAY!* AND THERE I FOUND IT--THE *DIARY* THAT WAS TO TURN MY LIFE AROUND!

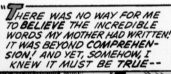

"*THERE* WAS NO WAY FOR ME TO *BELIEVE* THE INCREDIBLE WORDS MY MOTHER HAD WRITTEN! IT WAS BEYOND *COMPREHENSION!* AND YET, SOMEHOW, I KNEW IT MUST BE *TRUE*--

"*AND* IN THAT ONE, HORRIFYING MOMENT, I, *DAIMON HELLSTROM*, MAN OF GOD AND PEACE, LEARNED THE TRUE MEANING OF THE WORD *HATE!!!*

"AS I SAT THERE, RAGING-- SEETHING INSIDE, I HEARD A VOICE! AND I KNEW WHO IT WAS--MY FATHER! BUT FILLED WITH HATRED AS I WAS, I SOMEHOW COULDN'T RESIST HIS TEMPTATIONS--

DAIMON--LISTEN TO ME! FOLLOW MY VOICE--COME WITH ME!

DO NOT TRY TO RESIST! FOR NOT ONLY AM I YOUR FATHER--I AM ALSO YOUR MASTER! SO TAKE OFF THE CHAIN--AND COME!

"IT WAS INSANE! I KNEW I SHOULD IGNORE HIM--BUT IT WASN'T POSSIBLE! SO, LIKE A FOOL, I REMOVED MY ONLY MEANS OF PROTECTION, AND OBEYED HIM-- THOUGH I THINK THAT EVEN THEN, IN MY SUBCONSCIOUS, I WAS PLOTTING AGAINST HIM!

"DOWN, DOWN INTO THE ENDLESS CAVERNS BELOW THE MANSION HE LED ME--

"UNTIL, AT LAST, I FACED A SOLID WALL WHICH SUDDENLY OPENED AS IF BY MAGIC! I STOOD FROZEN FOR A MOMENT--THEN HIS VOICE BECKONED ME INSIDE--AND I FOLLOWED INTO THE DARKNESS, THOUGH THE HOT, FETID AIR FROM WITHIN MADE ME NAUSEOUS--

"I MUST HAVE WALKED FOR MILES, ALWAYS FOLLOWING AND OBEYING HIS BOOMING VOICE! BUT, STRANGELY, I NEVER GREW TIRED! INSTEAD, I ACTUALLY SEEMED TO GAIN STRENGTH AS I PLODDED ALONG! THEN, I CAME INTO A HUGE, BRIGHTLY-LIT OPENING, AND IN THAT MOMENT, I KNEW I HAD REACHED --

--THE GATEWAY TO HELL!!

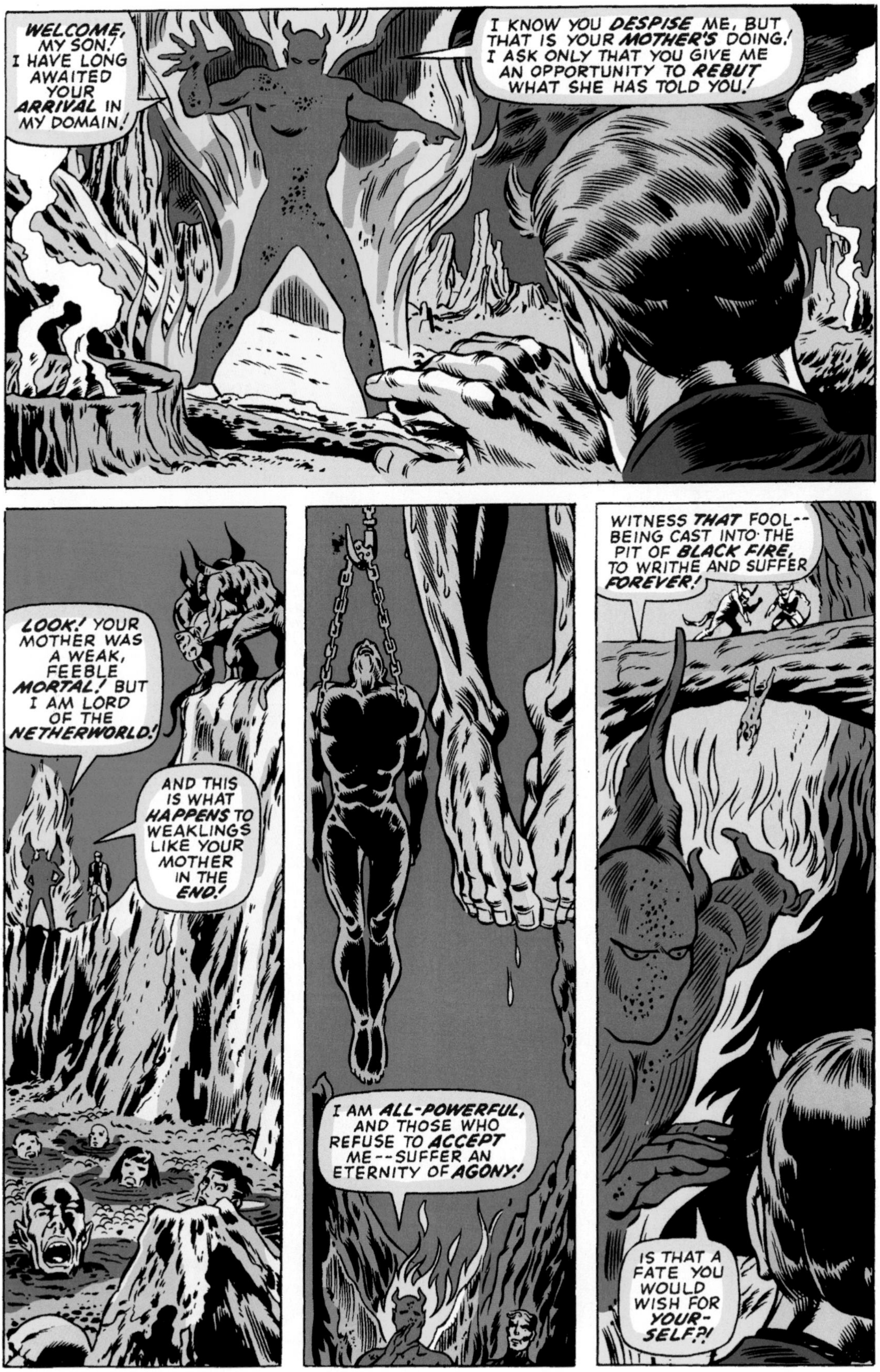
WELCOME, MY SON! I HAVE LONG AWAITED YOUR ARRIVAL IN MY DOMAIN!
I KNOW YOU DESPISE ME, BUT THAT IS YOUR MOTHER'S DOING! I ASK ONLY THAT YOU GIVE ME AN OPPORTUNITY TO REBUT WHAT SHE HAS TOLD YOU!
LOOK! YOUR MOTHER WAS A WEAK, FEEBLE MORTAL! BUT I AM LORD OF THE NETHERWORLD!
AND THIS IS WHAT HAPPENS TO WEAKLINGS LIKE YOUR MOTHER IN THE END!
I AM ALL-POWERFUL, AND THOSE WHO REFUSE TO ACCEPT ME--SUFFER AN ETERNITY OF AGONY!
WITNESS THAT FOOL--BEING CAST INTO THE PIT OF BLACK FIRE, TO WRITHE AND SUFFER FOREVER!
IS THAT A FATE YOU WOULD WISH FOR YOURSELF?!

AND *THEM*, CONDEMNED TO SLAVE *FOREVER* IN THE NETHERANIUM MINES! THAT, *TOO*, COULD BE YOUR FATE!

BUT I HOPE YOU WILL BE *INTELLIGENT*--TRULY YOUR FATHER'S *SON*, AND CHOSE TO *SIDE* WITH ME!

AS YOUR FATHER, I OFFER YOU *LIFE ETERNAL*--AND *POWER INCARNATE!* THINK ABOUT IT, AND DECIDE *WISELY*, FOR WHEN NEXT WE MEET, I WILL EXPECT AN *ANSWER!*

AN INSTANT *LATER*, I FOUND MYSELF ON THE FLOOR BACK IN MY *MANSION!* IT WAS AS IF I'D BEEN TRANSPORTED A *MILLION MILES* IN A MATTER OF *SECONDS* --SO RAPIDLY I BEGAN TO WONDER IF I'D FALLEN ASLEEP AND *DREAMED* MY VISIT TO *HELL!*

NO! NOT EVEN MY *SUBCONSCIOUS* COULD CONJURE UP SUCH *HORRORS* AS I HAVE WITNESSED!

IT IS ALL *TRUE!* I AM SATAN'S SON-- AND I'VE CROSSED THE THRESHOLD TO *HELL!* BUT NOW--WHAT DO I *DO* ABOUT IT.?!

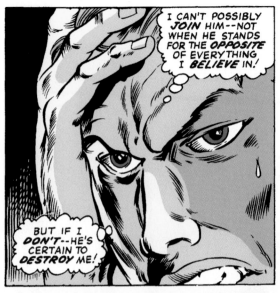

I CAN'T POSSIBLY *JOIN* HIM--NOT WHEN HE STANDS FOR THE *OPPOSITE* OF EVERYTHING I *BELIEVE* IN!

BUT IF I *DON'T*--HE'S CERTAIN TO *DESTROY* ME!

"FOR *HOURS* I WRACKED MY BRAIN, HOPING TO FIND A SENSIBLE *SOLUTION* TO MY DEADLY DILEMMA! THEN, AT LAST, I REALIZED WHAT I SHOULD HAVE KNOWN ALL ALONG--MY ONLY CHOICE WAS TO *FIGHT* HIM!

"SO, DETERMINED AND WELL-RESTED, I BEGAN MY *ASSAULT*--

I ASSUMED THE DOOR WOULD BE *SEALED*--BUT IT'S *OPENING* UNDER ONLY THE SLIGHTEST AMOUNT OF *PRESSURE!*

"ONCE THROUGH THE MYSTIC ENTRANCE IN THE *CELLAR*, I SLOWLY MADE MY WAY *DOWNWARD*--CAUTIOUSLY WINDING MY WAY THROUGH STEAMING CAVERNS TOWARD THE *EARTH'S CORE!*

"TO THIS DAY, I HAVE NO IDEA HOW LONG IT TOOK ME TO *REACH* MY DESTINATION, BUT SHEER *HATRED* KEPT ME GOING UNTIL I REACHED THE *NETHERANIUM MINES*--

MY MOTHER TOLD ME SATAN IS *WEAKENED* BY NETHERANIUM! BUT IF THAT IS *TRUE*--WHY WOULD HE LEAVE THE MINE *UNGUARDED?!*

WHY DON'T THE WRETCHED SOULS WHO TOIL IN THEM *REVOLT*--USE THE ORE *AGAINST* HIM?!

OF *COURSE*--THEY DON'T *KNOW* OF HIS WEAKNESS! BUT *I* DO--AND WITH THEIR *HELP*--PERHAPS BOTH HELL *AND* SATAN CAN BE *DESTROYED!!*

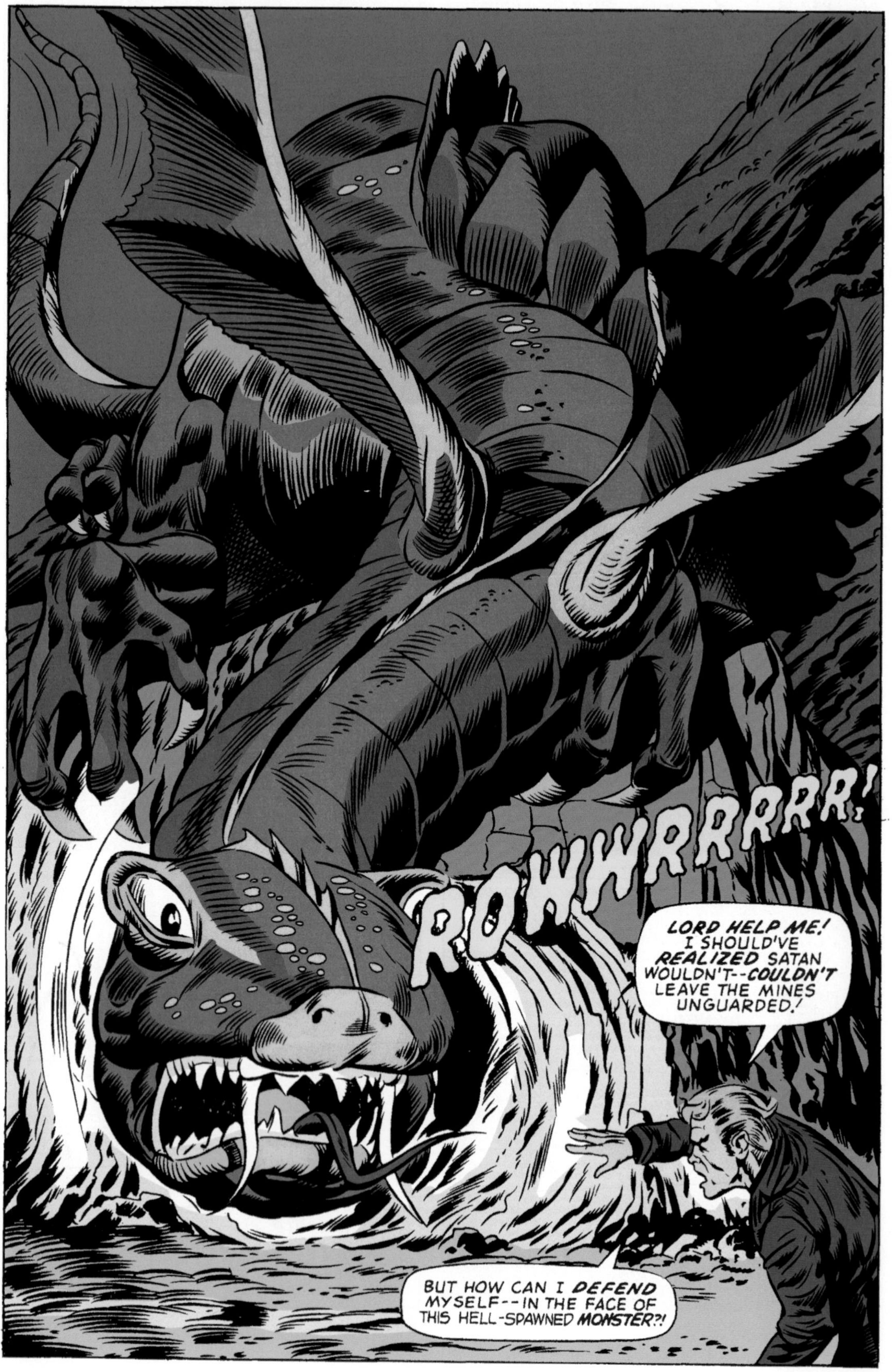
ROWWRRRRRR!
LORD HELP ME! I SHOULD'VE REALIZED SATAN WOULDN'T--COULDN'T LEAVE THE MINES UNGUARDED!
BUT HOW CAN I DEFEND MYSELF--IN THE FACE OF THIS HELL-SPAWNED MONSTER?!

THAT *CAVE*-- PERHAPS I CAN TAKE *SHELTER* THERE--

--AND GAIN PRECIOUS *TIME*-- TIME IN WHICH TO FORMULATE A WAY TO BATTLE THIS DEMON!

"*B*UT I WAS TO BE *GIVEN NO TIME!* NO SOONER DID I *ENTER* THE CAVE THAN THE DRAGON FILLED IT WITH SKIN-SCORCHING *FLAMES*--

"--FORCING ME TO SEEK REFUGE BEHIND A LARGE *BOULDER*--A BOULDER I NOW REALIZE CONTAINED A LARGE AMOUNT OF *NETHERANIUM,* WHICH NOT ONLY *SHIELDED* ME FROM THE DRAGON'S DESTRUCTIVE BREATH--

"*B*UT *DEFLECTED* THE FLAMES DIRECTLY BACK AT THEIR GHASTLY *SOURCE*--

"--*DESTROYING* THAT HORRID APPARITION OF *SATAN* WITH ITS OWN *WEAPON!*

ZAK!

"AND AS THE DEMON **BURNED**, THE SLAVES OF HADES BEGAN TO COME OUT FROM THEIR **HIDING PLACES**--

"--STARING AT ME IN **AWE!** THEN I KNEW WHAT HAD TO BE **DONE**, AND I RAISED MY ARMS AND **SPOKE** TO THEM!

LISTEN TO ME! I CAN **HELP** YOU-- **SAVE** YOU!

WE HAVE AT HAND THE MEANS TO **DESTROY** SATAN--IF ONLY YOU WILL GIVE ME YOUR **AID!**

STOP THEM! THE MASTER **DEMANDS** IT!

"BUT BEFORE I COULD **EXPLAIN**, THE HORDES OF HELL DESCENDED UPON US!

"TO MY **SURPRISE**, THOUGH, THE POOR SOULS WHO'D SLAVED IN THE MINES SEEMED TO **ACCEPT** MY WORD **WITHOUT** FURTHER EXPLANATION--

"--AND THEY **BATTLED** MY FATHER'S MINIONS TO A **STAND-STILL**, RISKING AN EVEN **WORSE** ETERNAL FATE ON THE SLIM CHANCE THAT THEIR TORTURED SOULS MIGHT AT LAST BE **FREED!**

CEASE THIS WORTHLESS FOLLY! I, **SATAN,** COMMAND IT!

THIS BATTLE IS BETWEEN **MYSELF--** AND MY CURSED **OFFSPRING!** THERE IS NO NEED FOR ANYONE ELSE TO BE **INVOLVED!**

"AT THE SOUND OF MY FATHER'S HATE-FILLED **VOICE**, ALL VIOLENCE CAME TO A **HALT!** AND IN THAT MOMENT, I KNEW I WAS LEFT **ALONE**--TO FACE THE FURY OF SATAN!!

I OFFERED YOU *EVERYTHING*-- BUT THE *HUMAN SIDE* OF YOU HAS FORCED YOU TO *SPURN* IT!

THERE-FORE, I HAVE NO *CHOICE!*

BY HIS OWN CHOOSING, THE SON OF SATAN MUST *DIE!*

ZZAAKKKK!

I MUST HAVE BEEN INSANE TO *COME* HERE-- TO *CHALLENGE* HIM!

ZZAAFT!

HE'S FAR TOO *POWERFUL* FOR ME--FOR *ANY* MORTAL!

YET, SINCE I AM HIS *SON*, SURELY *I* POSSESS SOME OF *HIS* POWER!

AND IF I *DO*-- NOW IS THE TIME TO *LEARN* OF THEM--AND UTILIZE THEM *AGAINST* HIM!

BLOTS OF *FIRE*-- SHOOTING FROM MY *HANDS!* ALL I HAD TO DO WAS *WILL* IT!

NOW I *KNOW*, FATHER-- YOUR POWERS ARE *MINE!* AND I WILL USE THEM AGAINST YOU TO THE *DEATH!*

SO I *SEE*--BUT *AGAIN* YOUR MORTAL WAYS AND LOGIC *BETRAY* YOU!

FOR WHILE OUR POWERS ARE NEAR *EQUAL*--I HAVE NO *EMOTIONS*, WHILE *YOURS* WILL PROVE YOUR *UNDOING!!*

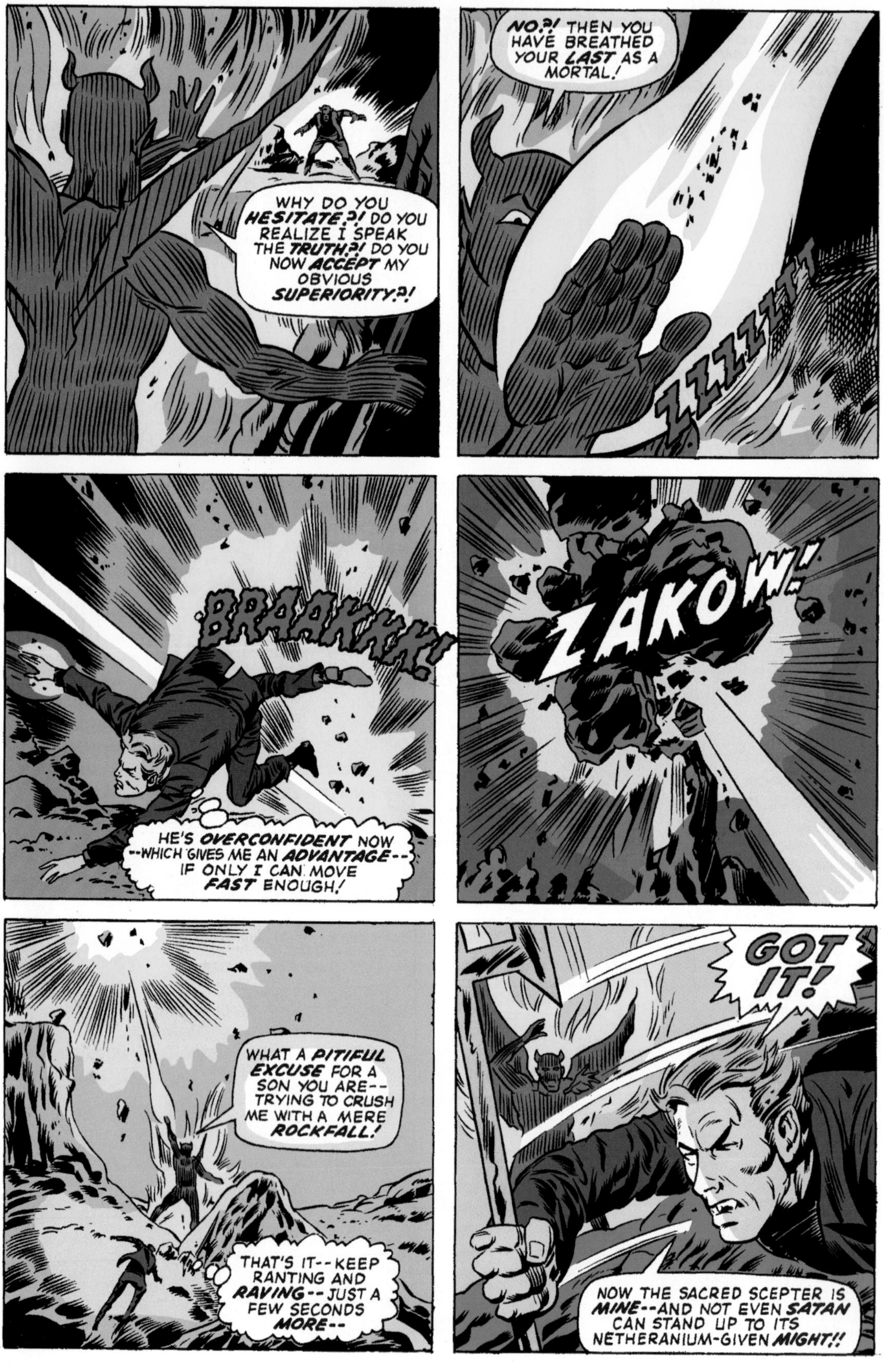
WHY DO YOU HESITATE?! DO YOU REALIZE I SPEAK THE TRUTH?! DO YOU NOW ACCEPT MY OBVIOUS SUPERIORITY?!
NO?! THEN YOU HAVE BREATHED YOUR LAST AS A MORTAL!
ZZZZZZTT
BRAAKKKK!
HE'S OVERCONFIDENT NOW --WHICH GIVES ME AN ADVANTAGE-- IF ONLY I CAN MOVE FAST ENOUGH!
ZAKOW!
WHAT A PITIFUL EXCUSE FOR A SON YOU ARE-- TRYING TO CRUSH ME WITH A MERE ROCKFALL!
THAT'S IT--KEEP RANTING AND RAVING--JUST A FEW SECONDS MORE--
GOT IT!
NOW THE SACRED SCEPTER IS MINE--AND NOT EVEN SATAN CAN STAND UP TO ITS NETHERANIUM-GIVEN MIGHT!!

HE SEES I *HAVE* THE SCEPTER-- AND HE'S *HESITATING!*

NOW IF ONLY IT HAS THE POWER I *SUSPECT*--

--I SHOULD BE ABLE TO BRING FORTH HIS OWN DEMON-DRAWN *CHARIOT* MERELY BY *GESTURING* WITH IT!

YES! THE LAVA PIT IS BEGINNING TO BUBBLE *WILDLY*--THE *SATANIC CHARIOT* COMES FORTH! THE SCEPTER *COMMANDS* IT!

"*A*LL HELL STOOD *STILL* AS THE MOLTEN PIT STEAMED AND HEAVED VIOLENTLY! THEN, A SHATTERING EXPLOSION WRACKED THE NETHERWORLD AS THE EERIE VEHICLE EMERGED FROM THE PIT AND I, THE SON OF SATAN, TOOK CONTROL OF IT!

FAREWELL, MY FATHER! FOR THE FIRST TIME, I HAVE *BESTED* YOU! AND THOUGH I KNOW IT IS ONLY THE *BEGINNING*, I NOW HAVE THE INSTRUMENTS I NEED TO BRING ABOUT YOUR *FINAL DESTRUCTION!!*

"*I* RETURNED TO THE MANSION WITHOUT FURTHER *INCIDENT*, AND SEALED THE ENTRANCE TO HELL WITH MELTED *NETHER-ANIUM*, HOPING THAT WOULD HOLD SATAN AT BAY UNTIL I WAS READY FOR OUR *FINAL DEATH-DUEL*--

BUT NOW THE SEAL HAS BEEN *BROKEN*, AND I CAN SENSE HIS *DEADLY AWESOME PRESENCE*-- WAITING-- WAITING--TO *STRIKE!*

AND THE NEXT BATTLE MAY WELL BE... *THE LAST!*

NEXT ISSUE: **ICE AND HELL-FIRE!**

83

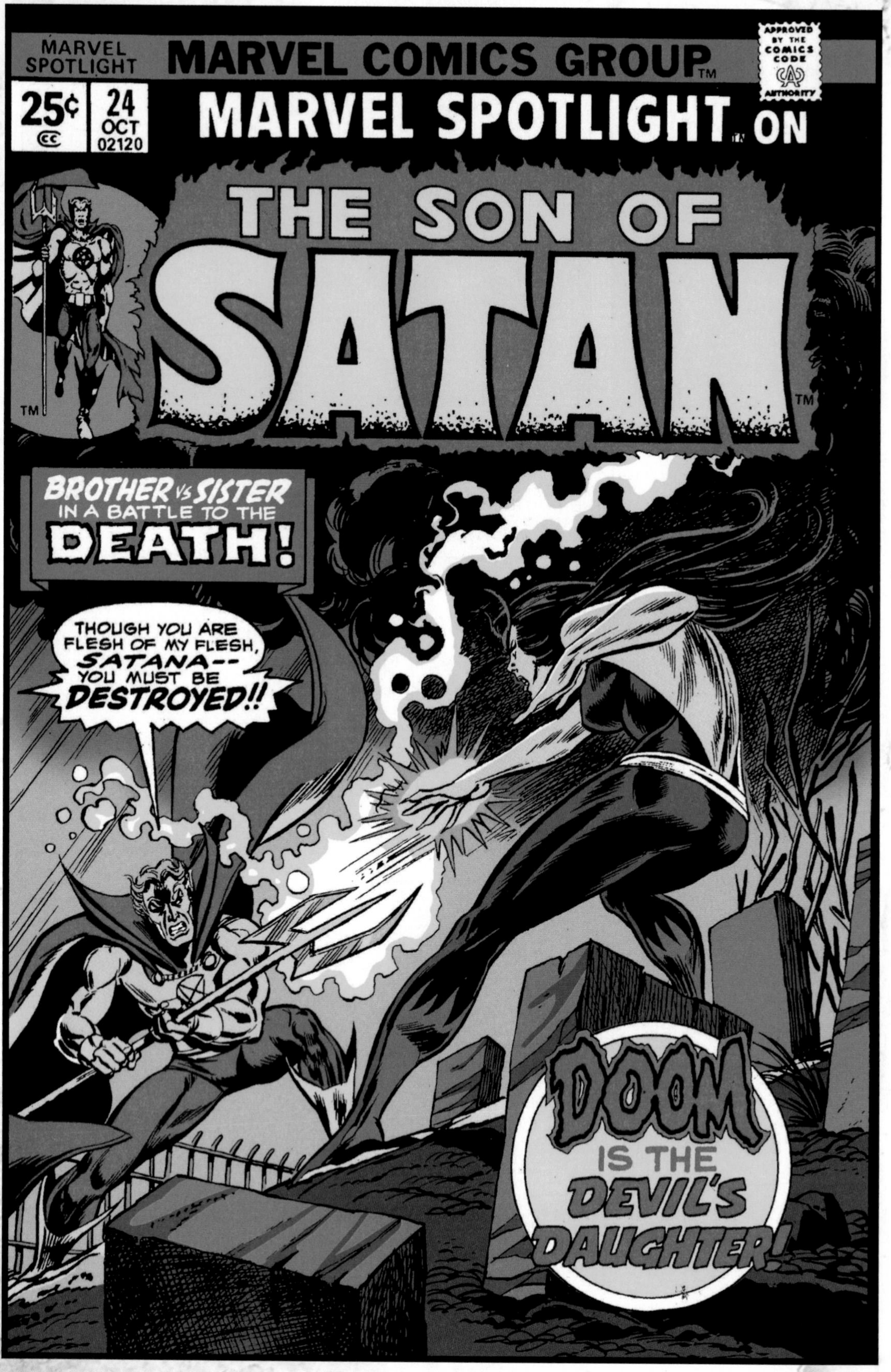
MARVEL SPOTLIGHT
MARVEL COMICS GROUP
APPROVED BY THE COMICS CODE AUTHORITY
25¢
24 OCT 02120
MARVEL SPOTLIGHT ON
THE SON OF SATAN
BROTHER VS SISTER IN A BATTLE TO THE DEATH!
THOUGH YOU ARE FLESH OF MY FLESH, SATANA-- YOU MUST BE DESTROYED!!
DOOM IS THE DEVIL'S DAUGHTER!

He is *Daimon Hellstrom*—spawn of the *devil*, born of *woman*—man of *God*, heir to *hell*—and his two natures are ever at *war!* For though he carries Satan's mark on his chest, he is sworn to drive his Father's minions from the world of men. Exorcist, psychic, demonologist, wielder of the *soulfire*—he is all of these, but within him lurks a *second self*, a savage, satanic side he must constantly fight to control...lest he lose his human heritage *forever!*

STAN LEE PRESENTS: SON OF SATAN ™

| CHRIS CLAREMONT AUTHOR | SAL BUSCEMA ARTIST | BOB McLEOD INKER | JOHN COSTANZA LETTERER | DIANE BUSCEMA COLORIST | LEN WEIN EDITOR |

WALK the DARKLING ROAD!

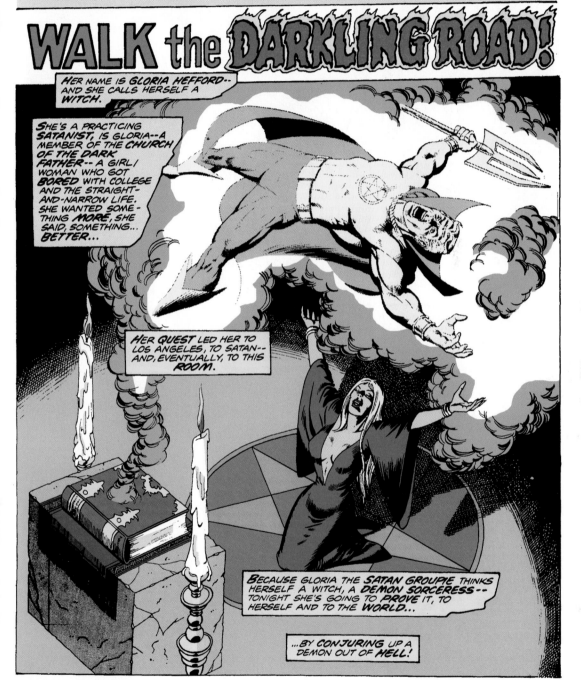

HER NAME IS *GLORIA HEFFORD*-- AND SHE CALLS HERSELF A *WITCH.*

SHE'S A PRACTICING *SATANIST,* IS GLORIA--A MEMBER OF THE *CHURCH OF THE DARK FATHER*-- A GIRL/ WOMAN WHO GOT *BORED* WITH COLLEGE AND THE STRAIGHT- AND-NARROW LIFE. SHE WANTED SOME- THING *MORE,* SHE SAID, SOMETHING... *BETTER...*

HER *QUEST* LED HER TO LOS ANGELES, TO SATAN-- AND, EVENTUALLY, TO THIS *ROOM.*

BECAUSE GLORIA THE *SATAN GROUPIE* THINKS HERSELF A *WITCH,* A *DEMON SORCERESS*-- TONIGHT SHE'S GOING TO *PROVE* IT, TO HERSELF AND TO THE *WORLD...*

...BY *CONJURING* UP A DEMON OUT OF *HELL!*

BUT, FOR ALL HER *TALK*, GLORIA IS STILL AN *AMATEUR*...

BY *Y'GARON*, *Y'GRIANTH* AND *Y'BSALLOTH*-- BY *TRIAD* NAMED AND TRIAD *DAMNED*...

...I *CHARGE* THEE, SPIRIT, COME FORTH AND *SERVE MY WILL!*

...A *CHILD* PLAYING WITH *FIRE*...

WAIT A MINUTE... *WHAT'S* GOING ON...?

THE SPELL'S GONE *WRONG!* THE DEMON'S *HURTING* ME! BUT IT'S *NOT SUPPOSED* TO HURT...

...A CHILD ABOUT TO GET *BURNED*...

...UNTO *DEATH!*

STAY BACK! *STAY BACK!* YOU CAN'T COME INSIDE THE *PENTAGRAM*-- YOU *CAN'T!!*

I'M SUPPOSED TO BE *SAFE* HERE!

SAFE?

HELP ME, SOMEBODY-- *ANYBODY!*

IN GOD'S NAME-- HELP *MEEE!* PLEASE!!

SAFE FROM A *MINOR* SPELL, SAFE FROM A *LESSER* DEMON-- SAFE FROM *THOSE.*

BUT GLORIA HAD WANTED A *TRUE* DEMON-- A *LORD* OF THE *SATANIC* HOST-- SOMEONE *WORTH* HER TIME AND *TROUBLE.*

WELL, SHE GOT WHAT SHE *WANTED.*

MORE FOOL *HER.*

FREE.

AFTER *TEN THOUSAND THOUSAND YEARS*...

...*KTHARA* IS *FREE!*

DO YOU *HEAR*, LORD SATAN-- *DO YOU HEAR!?!*

KTHARA, THE MOTHER OF DEMONS IS FREE--

--AND THE EARTH IS *MINE* TO *RAVAGE* ONCE MORE!!

GLORIA, WHAT'S *GOIN' ON* IN HERE-- WHAT D'YOU THINK YOU'RE *DOIN'?!?*

DIDN'T THE *ELDERS* WARN YOU ABOUT CASTING *SUMMONING SPELLS* ON YOUR *OWN*...?

AYE, THEY *WARNED* THE SOW, HUMAN...

...WARNED HER *TOO LATE.*

TOO LATE FOR HER-- AND TOO LATE FOR *YOU!*

AND AS I TOOK HER *SOUL*, O MAN-- SO DO I TAKE *YOURS.*

NO... PLEASE, NO... I BEG YOU...

WHY SO *FRIGHTENED*, HUMAN? YOU SERVE *SATAN*, DO YOU NOT?

YOU SHOULD *THANK* ME, THEN-- FOR IT IS *KTHARA'S* HAND THAT *SENDS* YOU TO HIM.

ENJOY *HELL*, YOU LITTLE, MORTAL...

...*FOOL!*

HA HA HA HA HA HA

CUT EAST NOW, *FOURTEEN DAYS* AND *FIFTEEN HUNDRED MILES*, TO *ST. LOUIS INTERNATIONAL AIRPORT* ON A RARE, BALMY, *MIDSUMMER'S DAY...*

...TO TWO *FRIENDS* SAYING... *GOODBYE.*

DAIMON HELLSTROM, PROFESSIONAL EXORCIST -- AND *FIRST-BORN* OF THE HOUSE OF HELL -- *THE SON OF SATAN* -- AND *DR. KATHERINE REYNOLDS,* PROFESSOR OF PARAPSYCHOLOGY AT *ST. LOUIS' GATEWAY UNIVERSITY.*

THEY'D FIRST MET OVER A *YEAR* AGO, AND SINCE THEN, KATHY HAS SEEN *DEMONS* AND *NIHILISTS, ANCIENT ATLANTIS* AND A *TAROT DECK* COME TO *LIFE.**...*

...SHE HAS *DIED* AND BEEN *RE-BORN.***

THANK YOU FOR DRIVING ME TO THE *AIRPORT,* KATHERINE.

MY PLEASURE.

D'YOU THINK YOU'LL BE *COMING BACK* TO ST. LOUIS, DAIMON?

* S.O.S. #'S 14-22--LEN. ** LAST ISH--GUESS WHO?

...AND, PERHAPS, FALLEN IN *LOVE.*

WHO CAN SAY, KATHERINE. IF THE *FATES* WILL IT SO, I SHALL RETURN, IF *NOT...*

...THEN *FAREWELL.* MAY THE *LORD* PROTECT YOU AND KEEP YOU.

YOU, TOO...

ONLY TO REALIZE IT *TOO LATE.*

DAIMON?!?

YES, KATHERINE. IS SOMETHING THE *MATTER?*

UH...NO... IT'S *NOTHING,* DAIMON...

...HAVE A *GOOD* FLIGHT.

HE TURNS, AND IN A MOMENT, HE IS *GONE.* WITHOUT A BACKWARD GLANCE, WITHOUT A *WORD...*

...ALMOST AS IF HE'D *NEVER BEEN,* AS IF HE'D NEVER *CARED,* NEVER *LOVED.*

AND, IN TRUTH, MAYBE... HE *HADN'T.*

GOODBYE, DAIMON... GOODBYE, *MY LOVE...*

...GOD KEEP YOU WELL.

BY THE TIME THE PLANE IS *AIRBORNE*, KATHY REYNOLDS IS A *FADING* MEMORY... DAIMON'S MIND OCCUPIED WITH MORE *IMPERATIVE* THOUGHTS...

...SUCH AS A PLEA FOR *HELP* FROM AN *OLD FRIEND.*

"...SINCE HER MOTHER DIED, GLORIA IS ALL I HAVE, DAIMON. AND SOMETHING IS *HAPPENING* TO HER-- I DON'T KNOW WHAT, ONLY THAT IT IS...*EVIL*. HELP ME, DAIMON...HELP *HER*..."

"*SINCERELY, LEWIS HEFFORD*..."

SO, IT BEGINS *AGAIN*...

...A *NEW* CITY, A NEW *BATTLE*, A NEW SOUL HANGING IN THE *BALANCE*.

ONLY *THIS* TIME, THE SOUL *ISN'T* NEW TO YOU...

...AND YOUR *DREAMING* MIND DRIFTS BACK ACROSS THE *YEARS*-- TO THE DAY YOU AND YOUR SISTER WERE *SEPARATED*--AND YOU WERE SENT TO AN *ORPHANAGE*.

YOU HAD *ONE* TRUE FRIEND THERE, THE ORPHANAGE DOCTOR, *LEWIS HEFFORD*-- THE DOCTOR...AND HIS *FAMILY*. HIS WIFE, JUNE, HIS DAUGHTER, *GLORIA*...

BECAUSE OF HEFFORD YOU *STUDIED*...BECAUSE OF *HIM*, YOU FOUND YOUR VOCATION AND ENTERED THE *PRIESTHOOD*...

YOU *LOVED* HIM AS YOU'D *NEVER* LOVED YOUR TRUE FATHER...

A 'MAN' YOU SOON CAME TO KNOW BY HIS *TRUE* NAME...

...*LUCIFER*, PRINCE OF DARKNESS, LORD OF HELL...

...*SATAN!*

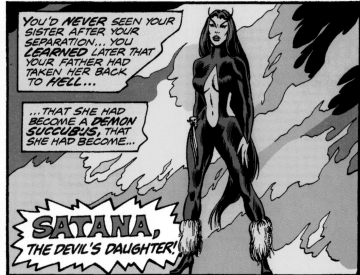

YOU'D *NEVER* SEEN YOUR SISTER AFTER YOUR SEPARATION... YOU *LEARNED* LATER THAT YOUR FATHER HAD TAKEN HER BACK TO *HELL*...

...THAT SHE HAD BECOME A *DEMON SUCCUBUS*, THAT SHE HAD BECOME...

SATANA, THE DEVIL'S DAUGHTER!

HE TRIES TO BREAK *FREE* NOW -- HE HAS DREAMED *ENOUGH*, REMEMBERED *ENOUGH* -- IT'S TIME TO *WAKE UP...*

...BUT HE *CAN'T.* TRY AS HE MIGHT, DAIMON REMAINS *TRAPPED* IN HIS NIGHT- MARE, A PUPPET DANCING TO *SOMEONE ELSE'S* TUNE...

...AND HE SEES HIS *SISTER* FOLLOW HIS FATHER'S PATH TO *EARTH,* WATCHES *HELP- LESSLY* AS SATANA STALKS FIRST *NEW YORK...*

...AND THEN *LOS ANGELES...**

* IN VAMPIRE TALES #'S 2 & 3. --LEN.

...WATCHES AS THE *SUCCUBUS...*

...*KILLS.*

HEY--! WHAT D'YOU THINK YOU'RE *DOING?!*

DOING? I AM *KISSING* YOU, O MAN...

...SATANA IS TAKING YOUR *SOUL!*

WHY SO *FRIGHTENED,* HUMAN? YOU SERVE *SATAN,* DO YOU NOT?

YOU SHOULD *THANK* ME, THEN -- FOR IT IS...*SATANA'S* HAND THAT SENDS YOU TO HIM.

AND SUCH A *TINY* SOUL, TOO. IT HARDLY SEEMS WORTH THE *EFFORT...*

BUT I'M A *POOR HOSTESS,* NOT EVEN GREETING MY *GUEST...*

HELLO, DAIMON, HOW *NICE* TO SEE YOU AGAIN.

WELCOME TO YOUR *DREAM,* BROTHER.

WHAT'S *WRONG?* AREN'T YOU *PLEASED* TO SEE ME? I MEAN YOU *NO HARM.* ALL I WANT TO DO...

...IS *KISS* YOU.

DO NOT *RESIST* ME, BROTHER-- YOU *CANNOT--*

--IN A *MOMENT,* IT WILL BE *ALL OVER...*

NO!!

YOU *DARE,* SUCCUBUS!? YOU DARE THINK MY SOUL IS *YOURS* FOR THE *TAKING--?!*

WRONG *TENSE,* BROTHER...

...YOUR *SOUL* IS *ALREADY* TAKEN.

YOU HAVE LOST, DAIMON--*TRULY LOST*-- THE ONLY THING LEFT FOR YOU TO DO... IS *FALL...*

...FALL, MY *ANGELIC* BROTHER --FALL AS OUR *FATHER* FELL SO MANY *AEONS* AGO--

FALL INTO *HELL,* MY SON--

--AND BE *DAMNED!!*

NOOO

NNOOO!!

MR. *HELLSTROM??* YOU WERE HAVING A *NIGHTMARE,* SIR-- ARE YOU *ALL RIGHT?*

I AM... WELL...

I SEE... PLEASE FASTEN YOUR *SEATBELT*-- WE'RE ABOUT TO LAND IN *LOS ANGELES.*

DREAMS: THE WINDOWS TO A MAN'S *SOUL*, HIS *TRUE SELF*-- OCCASIONALLY, HIS *FATE*...

...DAIMON'S... AND GLORIA HEFFORD'S, THAT MUCH SEEMS *CERTAIN*. AND SATANA SEEMS TO BE THE *CATALYST*...

...OR THE *EXECUTIONER*.

DAIMON! DAIMON HELLSTROM!!

GLORIA-- HELLO.

I HAVEN'T SEEN YOU IN *AGES*, YOU BUM-- DAD PHONED FROM BERKELEY AND ASKED ME TO *MEET YOU*...

...AND I'M *GLAD* I DID. *YOU*, SIR, ARE ONE *SCRUMPTIOUS* HUNK OF MAN.

UHM--YOU... LOOK *WELL*, GLORIA.

I'LL *BET*. I'M GLAD YOU'RE HERE FOR... *OTHER* REASONS, DAIMON. I THINK YOU *KNOW* THAT.

TELL ME ABOUT THEM.

YOU KNOW I'M A MEMBER OF THE *CHURCH OF THE DARK FATHER*-- A *SATANIST* CHURCH...

I KNOW.

FOR *MOST* OF US, IT'S JUST A *GIGGLE*-- WE DON'T TAKE IT VERY *SERIOUSLY*... AT LEAST, WE *DIDN'T*...

...UNTIL ABOUT *SIX* MONTHS AGO, WHEN THIS *NEW WOMAN* JOINED THE CHURCH...

* HAUNT OF HORROR #3. --L.

...AND *RUTH CUMMINS* GOT *MURDERED*.*

THIS WOMAN, DAIMON... SHE TAKES THE CHURCH *SERIOUSLY*. SHE *BELIEVES*.

WE'VE GOTTEN INTO *DARKHOLD* RITES, *BLOOD* RITES... *SACRIFICES*. NO ONE'S *STRONG* ENOUGH TO STOP HER-- SHE HAS THIS WEIRD POWER OVER *MEN*, LIKE THEY WERE HER *SLAVES* OR SOMETHING.

DAIMON, I'M *SCARED*. OF HER, OF WHAT'S *HAPPENING*. IT'S NOT *FUN* ANYMORE-- IT'S?... *EVIL*.

THIS WOMAN--WHAT'S HER *NAME*?

SHE CALLS HERSELF...

...SATANA.

ST. PAUL'S CEMETARY, JUST NORTH OF *L.A.* IT'S A SMALL PLACE, A *PRIVATE* PLACE, GREEN AND *ALIVE* WITH GROWING THINGS, WOODED AND SERENE...

...A *SPECIAL* PLACE, IN IT'S WAY-- A BURIAL GROUND FOR *ROMAN CATHOLIC* PRIESTS.

NOT THE SORT OF PLACE YOU'D EXPECT TO FIND A *SCION* OF THE HOUSE OF HELL.

NOT THE SORT OF PLACE YOU'D EXPECT TO FIND...

...*SATANA.*

BUT SHE'S *HERE* ALL THE SAME.

HERE TO SAY *GOOD-BYE* TO A...*FRIEND.*

A MAN WHO'D *SAVED* HER LIFE-- WHO'D *SHOWN* HER THE HALF OF HER THAT WAS *HUMAN*--

--THE *GLORY* OF IT... AND THE *AGONY*...

FATHER
MICHAEL HERON
1949 —
1947 EN PACE

...A MAN SATANA... *MOURNS.*

A *TOUCHING* SCENE, SATANA, BUT A TRIFLE OUT OF *CHARACTER,* I THINK.

YOU!

HELLO, SATANA. IT'S BEEN A *LONG* TIME.

NOT LONG *ENOUGH,* I THINK, BROTHER.

WHAT BRINGS YOU TO *LOS ANGELES?*

YOU *DO.*

I'M *FLATTERED,* DAIMON.

DON'T BE-- YOU'VE *LITTLE* TO BE FLAT-TERED ABOUT.

I'VE COME ABOUT *GLORIA HEFFORD*...

93

THAT... *CHILD?* YOU'RE *WASTING* YOUR TIME, BROTHER...

...THE CHILD IS *NOTHING* TO ME.

OH?

WHAT ABOUT *RUTH CUMMINS?* OR THIS *DEAD PRIEST* YOU MOURN?

THAT'S *NONE* OF YOUR *BUSI-NESS!*

POSSESSION IS MY BUSINESS, SISTER. POSSESSION AND *EXORCISM*...

...AND *MURDER.*

I DON'T KNOW WHAT YOU'RE *TALKING* ABOUT.

DON'T YOU?! YOU *KILLED* A MAN, SATANA--A FRIEND OF *GLORIA HEFFORD'S*--

YOU'RE *INSANE.*

-- YOU KILLED THE MAN AND YOU TOOK HIS *SOUL*--

--AND NOW YOU'RE GOING TO *PAY!*

YOUR CHEAP *THEATRICS* DON'T IMPRESS ME, BROTHER--OR *FRIGHTEN* ME--I NEVER EVEN MET THIS MAN YOU MENTIONED...

...MUCH LESS TOOK HIS *SOUL.*

LIAR!!

YOU'VE TAKEN A *DOZEN* SOULS THIS PAST FORTNIGHT *ALONE*...

YOU'RE AN *ANIMAL.* STALKING MANKIND AS A *WOLF* STALKS DEER, *SLAYING* WHEN IT PLEASES YOU, WITHOUT *PITY,* WITHOUT MERCY, WITHOUT *REMORSE*--!

BUT *TONIGHT,* YOUR HUNT *ENDS,* SATANA--

--IT *ENDS!!*

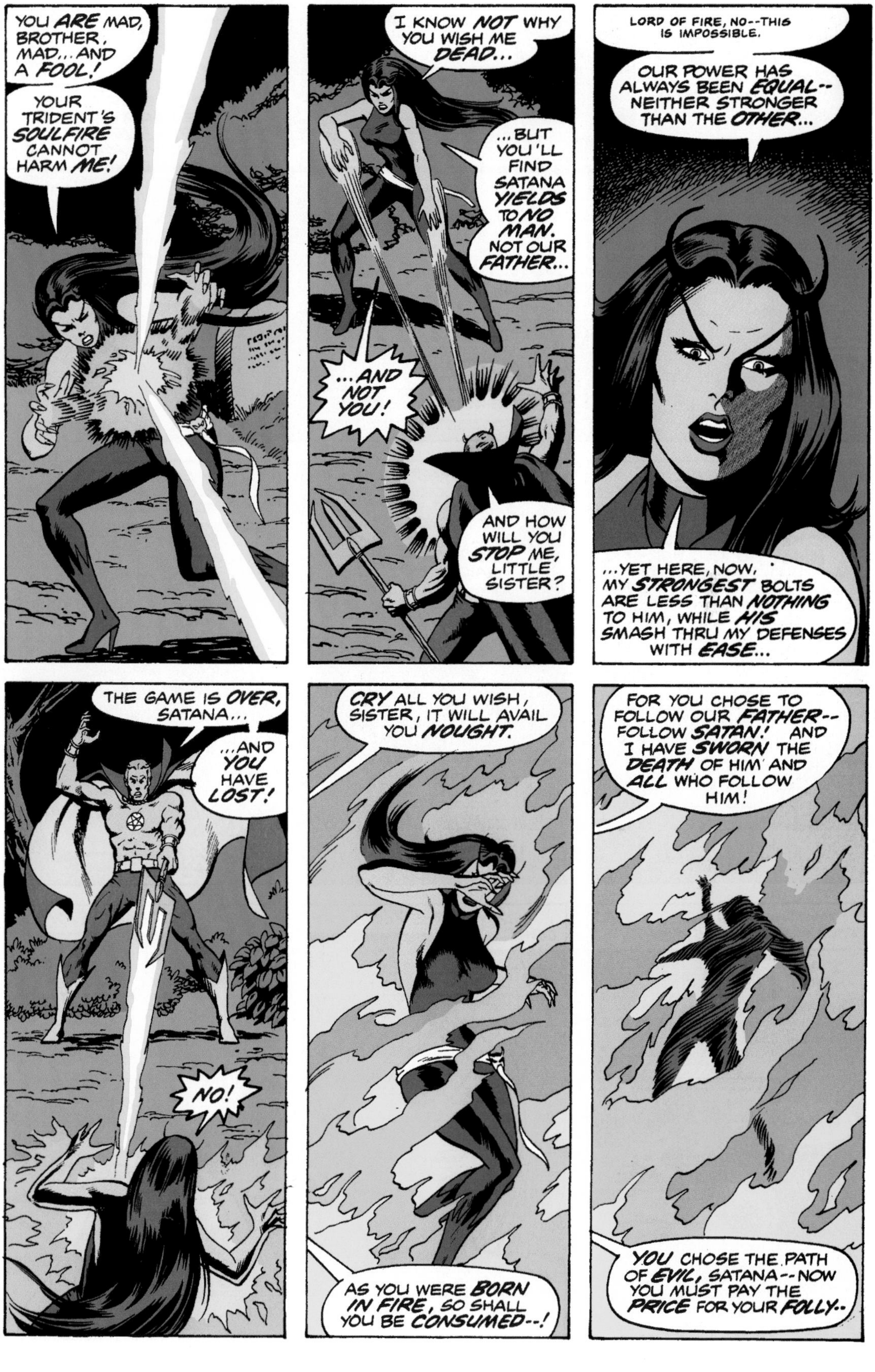
YOU ARE MAD, BROTHER, MAD,... AND A FOOL!
YOUR TRIDENT'S SOULFIRE CANNOT HARM ME!
I KNOW NOT WHY YOU WISH ME DEAD...
...BUT YOU'LL FIND SATANA YIELDS TO NO MAN. NOT OUR FATHER...
...AND NOT YOU!
AND HOW WILL YOU STOP ME, LITTLE SISTER?
LORD OF FIRE, NO--THIS IS IMPOSSIBLE.
OUR POWER HAS ALWAYS BEEN EQUAL-- NEITHER STRONGER THAN THE OTHER...
...YET HERE, NOW, MY STRONGEST BOLTS ARE LESS THAN NOTHING TO HIM, WHILE HIS SMASH THRU MY DEFENSES WITH EASE...
THE GAME IS OVER, SATANA...
...AND YOU HAVE LOST!
NO!
CRY ALL YOU WISH, SISTER, IT WILL AVAIL YOU NOUGHT.
AS YOU WERE BORN IN FIRE, SO SHALL YOU BE CONSUMED--!
FOR YOU CHOSE TO FOLLOW OUR FATHER-- FOLLOW SATAN! AND I HAVE SWORN THE DEATH OF HIM AND ALL WHO FOLLOW HIM!
YOU CHOSE THE PATH OF EVIL, SATANA--NOW YOU MUST PAY THE PRICE FOR YOUR FOLLY..

"--NOW YOU MUST DIE!"

SZRA!!

SEE THE MAN, THE *PROUD,* DETERMINED MAN, THE *EXORCIST SUPREME...*

...THE *MAN* WHO ONCE WISHED TO SERVE *GOD...*

...THE MAN WHO *KILLS!*

GOD FORGIVE ME, WHAT HAVE I DONE?

MY OWN *SISTER--* AND I NEVER EVEN GAVE HER A *CHANCE.* I JUST...*BURNED* HER DOWN. *KILLED* HER.

WHO KILLS, YET STILL IS *HUMAN* ENOUGH TO WONDER *WHY?*

I DIDN'T *MEAN* TO KILL HER-- I DIDN'T *WANT* TO KILL HER-- BUT... I HAD...*NO CHOICE.*

IT WAS AS IF... SOMEONE--SOME-*THING*--MADE ME DO IT.

BUT *WHO?* AND *WHY?* GLORIA SAID *SATANA* WAS THE ONLY *THREAT...*

...*GLORIA* SAID...

HUMAN ENOUGH TO BE *TIRED...* TO BE *CARELESS...* TO REALIZE TOO LATE...

GLORIA? ARE YOU *HERE?*

...THAT HE HAS BEEN PLAYED FOR A *FOOL* THIS NIGHT...

I AM HERE.

WHA--!

...AND NOW THE *TIME* HAS COME...

ALL HAIL TO YOU, DAIMON HELLSTROM, ON *THIS,* THE NIGHT OF YOUR *TRIUMPH...*

...FOR *HIM* TO PAY THE *PIPER.*

...ON *THIS,* THE NIGHT OF YOUR *DEATH!*

He wakes *SHACKLED*, his mind numb, his body twisted with pain, *SEALED* within a *DAEMONIC PENTAGRAM* that saps both strength and *WILL*...

...LEAVING HIM *HUMAN*...

...LEAVING HIM *HELPLESS*.

YOU ARE *AWAKE*, LORD DAIMON-- *GOOD*. THE SPELL WORKS *BEST* WHEN THE SACRIFICE IS *CONSCIOUS* UNDER THE *KNIFE*.

WHO... *ARE* YOU, DEMON?

STILL, YOU KNOW ME *NOT*!

BUT THEN, YOU KNOW SO *FEW* OF YOUR *FATHER'S COURT*.

I AM *KTHARA*, LORD DAIMON, *MOTHER OF DEMONS*, ONE WHO STANDS *HIGH* IN SATAN'S FAVOR...

...ONE WHO SITS ON THE *COUNCIL OF HELL*!

I AM *SHE* WHO RULES THE *OUTER DARK*, AND THIS NIGHT, WHEN *BLOOD* IS SHED AND WORDS OF *POWER* SPOKE...

...MY *RAVAGERS* WILL BE FREE TO *CLAIM* THIS EARTH ONCE MORE. CLAIM -- AND *RULE*!

TWELVE MEN HAVE I *SLAIN*, LORD DAIMON-- *YOU* ARE THE *LAST*...

WITH YOUR *DEATH*, THE SPELL IS *COMPLETE*...

...AND *NO POWER* ON EARTH CAN *SHATTER* IT!

LEAST OF ALL *YOU*.

NO ONE WILL *SAVE* YOU, MY LORD. NOT THE *SOW* WHOSE SHELL I *POSSESS* --SHE IS *DEAD* NOW, DEAD AND *DAMNED*--

--NOT YOUR *SISTER*. SHE IS MERELY... *DEAD*. YOU YOURSELF SAW TO *THAT*-- AIDED OF COURSE, BY SOME SPELLS OF *MINE*.

BUT ENOUGH OF *TALK*. THE HOUR OF SACRIFICE IS *NIGH--REJOICE*, SATANSON, FOR I SEND YOU TO YOUR *FATHER*.

I STRIKE FOR *SATAN*!

I THINK NOT, DEMONESS!

I THINK IT IS *YOU* WHO WILL DIE *THIS NIGHT*...

SATANA!

BY THE *GREAT PIT*, THIS CANNOT BE...

...YOU SHOULD BE *DEAD* SUCCUBUS.

AND DEAD YOU *SHALL BE* WHEN MY PETS HAVE *CRUSHED* YOUR BONES TO *PASTE!*

SATANA! CUT ME LOOSE!

EASIER *SAID* THEN DONE, DEMON-MOTHER--

BE *SILENT,* BROTHER-- I HAVEN'T *FORGOTTEN* YOU.

STOP HIM, MY PETS--! HE *MUSTN'T* REACH HIS *TRIDENT!*

TOO LATE, KTHARA--

--THE TRIDENT IS *MINE* ONCE MORE-- ITS *SOULFIRE* MINE TO *COMMAND* ONCE MORE...

...AND *NONE* MAY STAND AGAINST ME!

I AM *COMING* FOR YOU, KTHARA, AND NONE OF YOUR 'PETS' ARE GOING TO *STOP-- EH?!!*

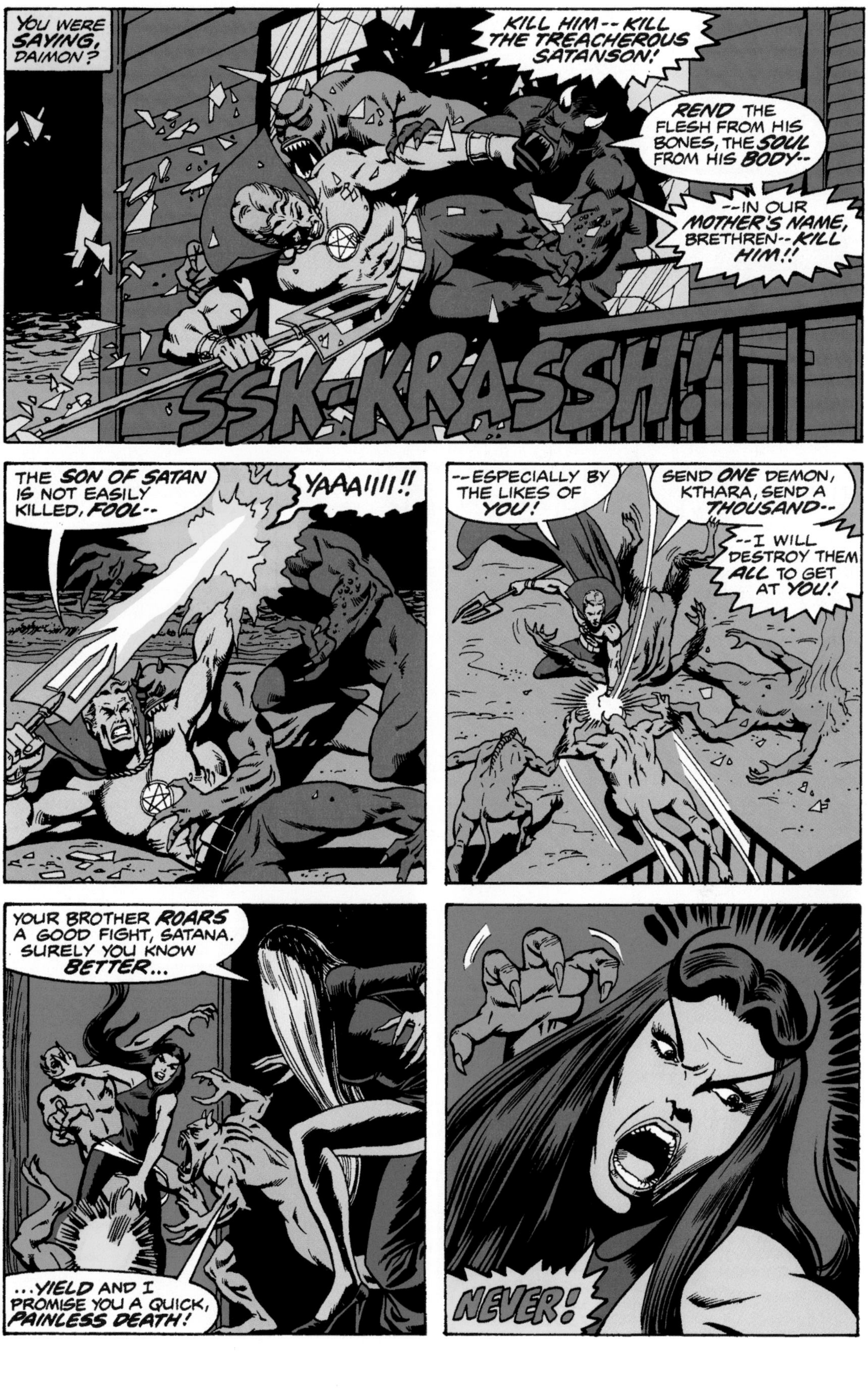
YOU WERE SAYING, DAIMON?
KILL HIM--KILL THE TREACHEROUS SATANSON!
REND THE FLESH FROM HIS BONES, THE SOUL FROM HIS BODY--
--IN OUR MOTHER'S NAME, BRETHREN--KILL HIM!!
SSK-KRASSH!
THE SON OF SATAN IS NOT EASILY KILLED, FOOL--
YAAAIIII!!
--ESPECIALLY BY THE LIKES OF YOU!
SEND ONE DEMON, KTHARA, SEND A THOUSAND--
--I WILL DESTROY THEM ALL TO GET AT YOU!
YOUR BROTHER ROARS A GOOD FIGHT, SATANA. SURELY YOU KNOW BETTER...
...YIELD AND I PROMISE YOU A QUICK, PAINLESS DEATH!
NEVER!

SO BE IT! LET *YOUR* FATE-- THE *FATE* OF THIS EARTH YOU FOOLS CALL *HOME*-- BE ON *YOUR HEAD*--!

HEAR ME, YOU *GODS* WHO WALK THE *DARKLING ROAD*...

...I AM *ONE* OF YOU, *BOUND* TO YOU BY BLOOD AND *SACRIFICE*...

...I AM *KTHARA*-- HEAR ME AND *OBEY!*

AWAY, DEMON-SPAWN--

--I'LL HAVE *NO MORE* OF YOU!

KTHARA-- BY ALL THE *FIRES OF HELL*--

--BY ALL THE *TORMENTS* OF THE *ETERNAL PIT*--

--*BEGONE* FROM THIS *CHILD'S* BODY!

IN THE NAME OF *GOD*, BEGONE.!!

POOR, FOOLISH *HALFBREED*-- I AM NOT SOME *LESSER SPIRIT*, TO BE *AFRIGHTED* BY A BLAST OF FIRE AND THE NAMING OF *GREAT NAMES*...

...TONIGHT I CLAIM MY *BIRTHRIGHT*, LORD DAIMON.

I CLAIM THIS *EARTH*-- AND THERE IS *NOTHING* YOU CAN DO TO *STOP ME!*

NOT SO!

FOR *I* CAN STOP YOU, KTHARA. I CAN...

...AND I *WILL*.

BASILISK, I *SUMMON* THEE...

HEAR SATANA'S CALL, MY *BASILISK*...

...COME THEE FORTH...

...AND **SLAY!**

THERE IS *LIGHT* FIRST, AN *UNHOLY* BRILLIANCE THAT FLARES FROM SATANA'S EYES LIKE THE DAWNING OF SOME *OBSCENE, NEWBORN SUN*...

...AND THEN, THE *BASILISK* IS FREE, *RAVENING* OUT FROM SATANA'S *SOUL* TO STRIKE AT KTHARA AND *SMASH HER DOWN*...

...TO REND HER BODY AND *RAVAGE HER SOUL*...

...AND DRAG HER, *SCREAMING*, BACK TO *HELL*.

THERE WILL BE ONLY... *THE BASILISK*.

AND AS KTHARA DIES, *SATANA* DIES. AND IS *REBORN*. KNOWING THAT THE *BASILISK* IS THAT MUCH *STRONGER* WITHIN HER, WATCHING, *WAITING*; KNOWING THAT THE DAY WILL COME WHEN SATANA WILL BE *NO MORE*.

AND THE *MEN* WHO LIVE TO *SEE* THAT DAY WILL CALL IT...

...ARMAGEDDON.

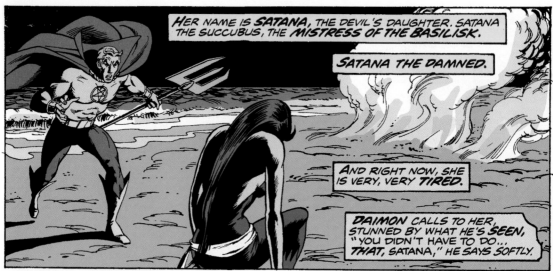

HER NAME IS **SATANA**, THE DEVIL'S DAUGHTER. SATANA THE SUCCUBUS, THE **MISTRESS OF THE BASILISK.**

SATANA THE **DAMNED.**

AND RIGHT NOW, SHE IS VERY, VERY **TIRED.**

DAIMON CALLS TO HER, STUNNED BY WHAT HE'S **SEEN**, "YOU DIDN'T HAVE TO DO... **THAT,** SATANA," HE SAYS SOFTLY.

THE SUCCUBUS ONLY...**SMILES.**

I **KNOW** I DIDN'T, BROTHER.

I...**WANTED** TO.

YOU TRIED TO **KILL** ME TONIGHT, DAIMON, **BURN** ME DOWN WITHOUT A **SECOND THOUGHT...**

...THE **BASILISK** SAVED MY LIFE **THEN,** TOO. AT A **COST.**

SATANA, LET ME **EXPL--**

DON'T **TOUCH** ME, DAIMON-- DON'T YOU **EVER** TOUCH ME!

WE CHOSE OUR **DESTINIES** A LONG TIME AGO, BROTHER...

...**YOU** THE RIGHT-HAND PATH OF **GOOD** AND I THE **LEFT,** AND WE'LL **WALK** THOSE ROADS UNTIL WE **DIE.** STILL, WE MIGHT HAVE BEEN **FRIENDS**...ONCE!

BUT **NO MORE!**

CROSS MY PATH AGAIN, BROTHER, AND I'LL LOOK ON YOU AND SEE A **CRINGING,** SHIVER- ING, PITIFUL LITTLE **MORTAL MAN...**

...I'LL **LOOK** ON YOU...

"...AND I WILL **TAKE** ...YOUR... **SOUL!!**

"AND **LAUGH** AT THE **TAKING** OF IT!"

HIS NAME IS **DAIMON HELLSTROM**-- HE IS THE **SON OF SATAN.** AND THIS NIGHT HE HAS **LEARNED** THAT THE PATH HE **WALKS...**

...HE WALKS **ALONE.**

MAY **GOD** HAVE **MERCY** ON HIS SOUL.

FIN

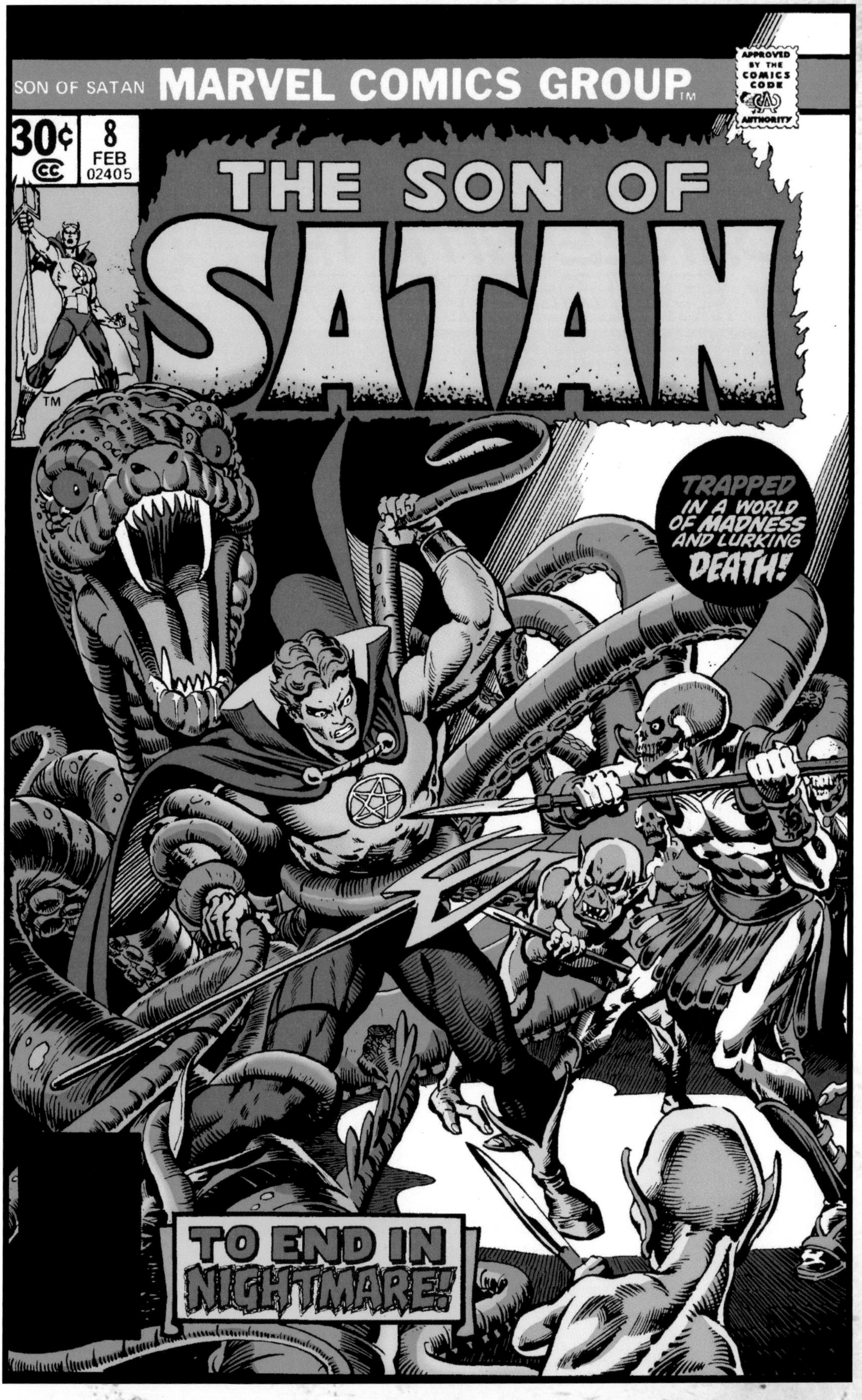
SON OF SATAN
MARVEL COMICS GROUP
TM
APPROVED BY THE COMICS CODE AUTHORITY
30¢
CC
8
FEB
02405
THE SON OF SATAN
TM
TRAPPED IN A WORLD OF MADNESS AND LURKING DEATH!
TO END IN NIGHTMARE!

He is *Daimon Hellstrom*—spawn of the *devil*, born of *woman*—man of *God*, heir to *hell*—and his two natures are ever at *war!* For though he carries Satan's mark on his chest, he is sworn to drive his Father's minions from the world of men. Exorcist, psychic, demonologist, wielder of the *soulfire*—he is all of these, but within him lurks a *second self*, a savage, satanic side he must constantly fight to control...lest he lose his human heritage *forever!*

Stan Lee PRESENTS: SON OF SATAN™

BILL MANTLO	RUSS HEATH	KAREN MANTLO	DON WARFIELD	ARCHIE GOODWIN
WRITER	ARTIST	LETTERER	COLORIST	EDITOR

BRING YOU TO THE REALM OF NIGHTMARE AND BACK IN A BLOOD-CHILLING TERROR TALE CALLED...

"...DANCE WITH THE DEVIL MY RED-EYED SON!"

I HAVE *COME*... IN RESPONSE TO A *PSYCHIC SUMMONS* THAT COULD NOT BE *IGNORED!* WHO ARE YOU? WHY HAVE YOU CALLED ME?

I AM ONE WHO *CARES* FOR YOU, DAIMON. ONE WHO *LOVES* YOU. BUT *HURRY.* THE OTHERS ARE WAITING!

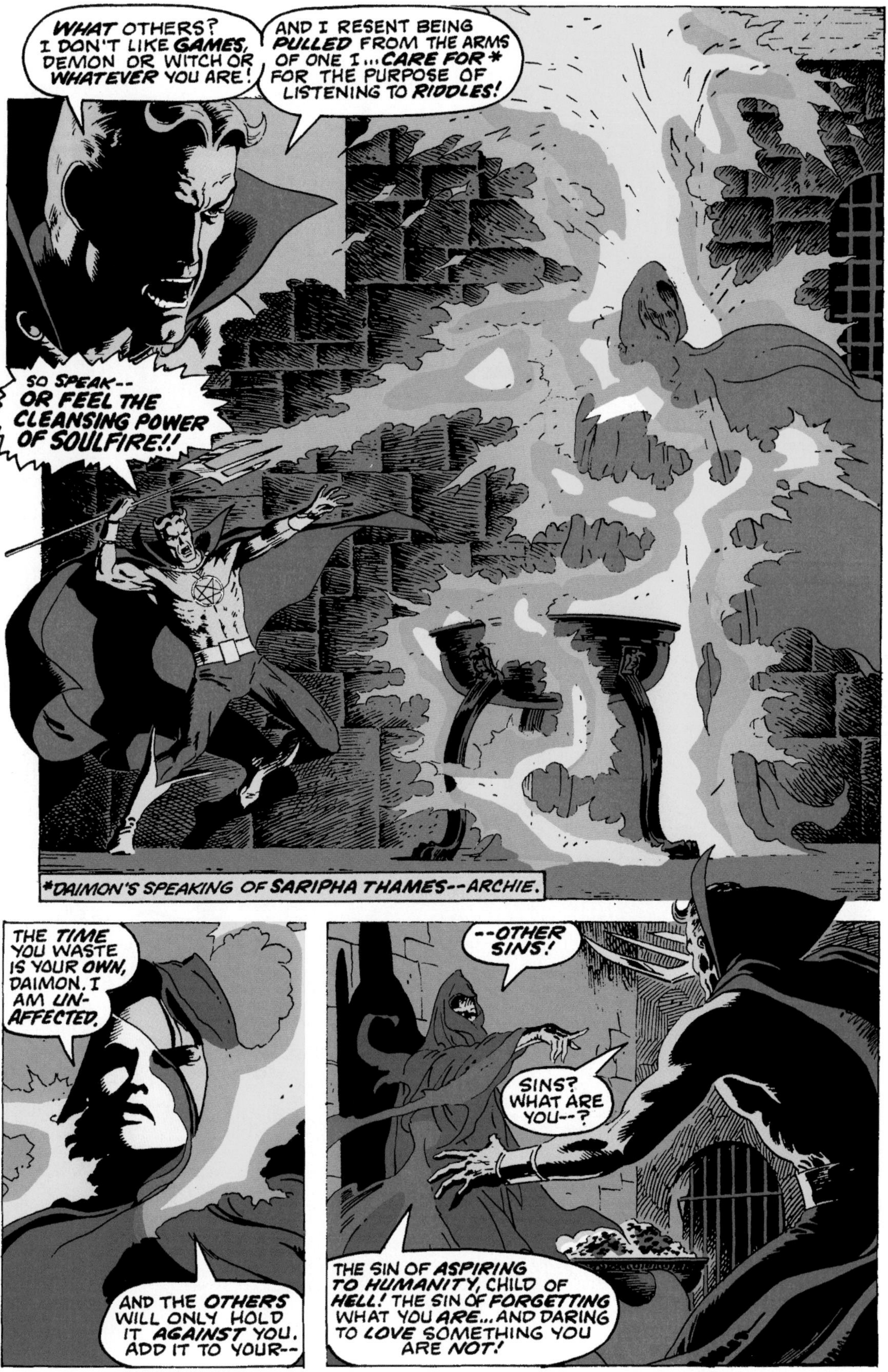
WHAT OTHERS? I DON'T LIKE GAMES, DEMON OR WITCH OR WHATEVER YOU ARE!
AND I RESENT BEING PULLED FROM THE ARMS OF ONE I... CARE FOR* FOR THE PURPOSE OF LISTENING TO RIDDLES!
SO SPEAK-- OR FEEL THE CLEANSING POWER OF SOULFIRE!!
*DAIMON'S SPEAKING OF SARIPHA THAMES--ARCHIE.
THE TIME YOU WASTE IS YOUR OWN, DAIMON. I AM UN-AFFECTED.
AND THE OTHERS WILL ONLY HOLD IT AGAINST YOU. ADD IT TO YOUR--
--OTHER SINS!
SINS? WHAT ARE YOU--?
THE SIN OF ASPIRING TO HUMANITY, CHILD OF HELL! THE SIN OF FORGETTING WHAT YOU ARE... AND DARING TO LOVE SOMETHING YOU ARE NOT!

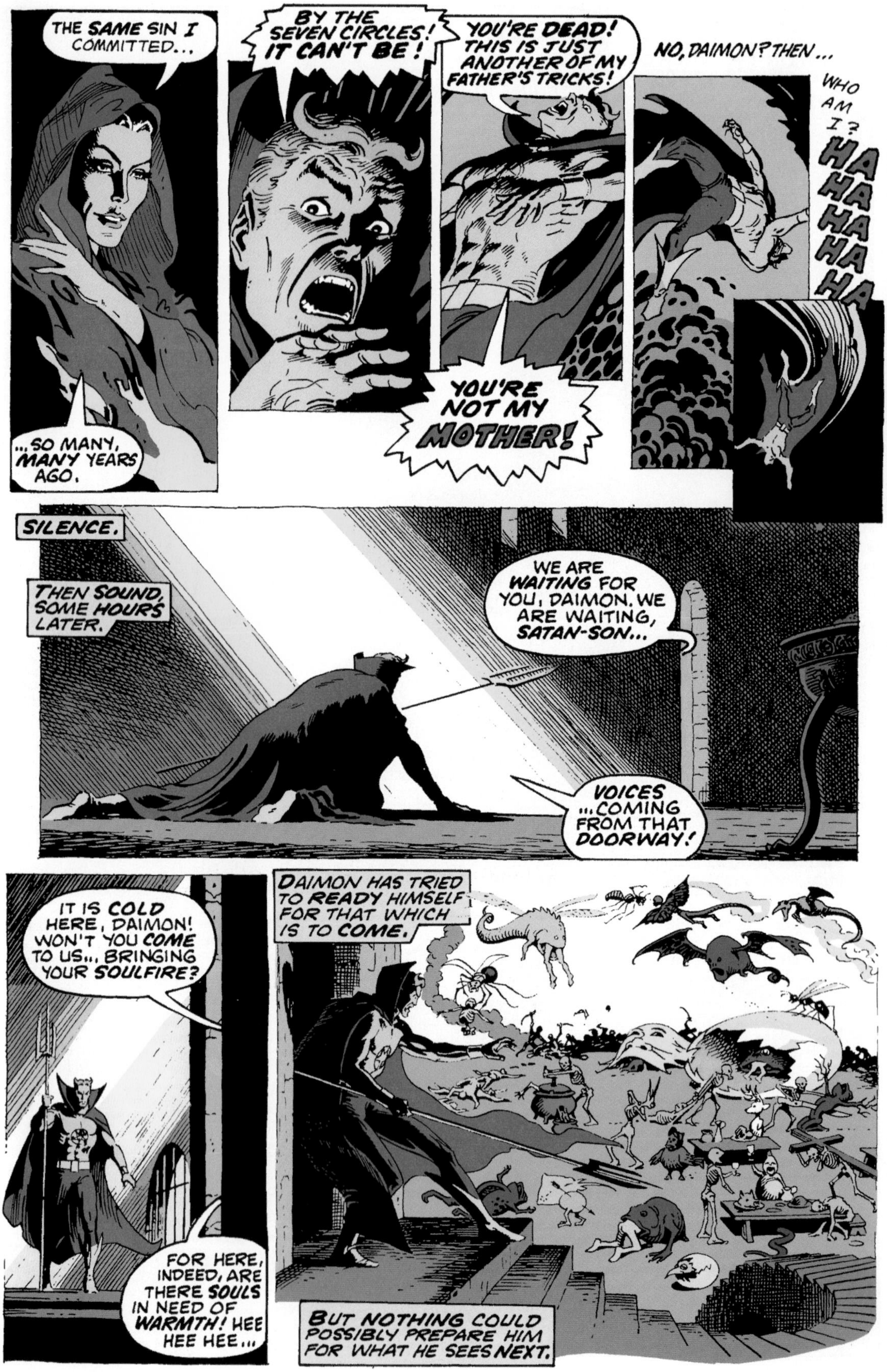
THE SAME SIN I COMMITTED...
...SO MANY, MANY YEARS AGO.
BY THE SEVEN CIRCLES! IT CAN'T BE!
YOU'RE DEAD! THIS IS JUST ANOTHER OF MY FATHER'S TRICKS!
YOU'RE NOT MY MOTHER!
NO, DAIMON? THEN...
WHO AM I?
HA HA HA HA HA HA
SILENCE.
THEN SOUND, SOME HOURS LATER.
WE ARE WAITING FOR YOU, DAIMON. WE ARE WAITING, SATAN-SON...
VOICES ...COMING FROM THAT DOORWAY!
IT IS COLD HERE, DAIMON! WON'T YOU COME TO US... BRINGING YOUR SOULFIRE?
FOR HERE, INDEED, ARE THERE SOULS IN NEED OF WARMTH! HEE HEE HEE...
DAIMON HAS TRIED TO READY HIMSELF FOR THAT WHICH IS TO COME.
BUT NOTHING COULD POSSIBLY PREPARE HIM FOR WHAT HE SEES NEXT.

HORRORS OF HELL!

YES, *MOST OF* THEM *ARE* QUITE HORRIBLE. BUT NOT ALL OF US ENTERED THIS VALE THROUGH *EVIL!* I FOR INSTANCE...

...AM HERE BECAUSE I DARED PURSUE *DELIGHT.* WILL YOU TAKE MY HAND, DAIMON, I AM TO LEAD YOU.

IT'S BAD *ENOUGH* HERE WITHOUT DWELLING ON THE THINGS THAT MAKE IT *WORSE!* WE WERE HOPING *YOU* WOULD HAVE *CHANGED* ALL THAT, DAIMON.

TO MY *FATHER?*

SHH. SPEAK OF *PLEASANTER* THINGS.

I HAVE NO *PART* OF THIS, GIRL. MY PLACE IS--

YOUR PLACE *WAS* TO HAVE BEEN *HERE,* PRINCE. YOUR FATHER WOULD HAVE *GROOMED* YOU FOR *COMMAND*--

--WHILE WE PLACED *OUR* HOPES IN YOUR MOTHER'S INFLUENCE, AND PRAYED FOR A DAY WHEN A MORE...*HUMAN* OVERLORD, ONE WHO UNDERSTOOD *PASSION,* WOULD...

THE WOMAN DOES NOT FINISH. THE EVIDENCE OF HIS EYES CONCLUDES THE SENTENCE FOR HER.

107

WHAT YOU ASK IS *IMPOSSIBLE!* THE DAMNED ARE *TRULY* DAMNED, THROUGH PACTS THEY MADE *LONG* BEFORE MY TIME.

EVEN *WERE* MY FATHER ...*DEPOSED* I COULD NOT CHANGE THE COURSE OF A *SOUL* THAT HAD SEALED ITS *OWN FATE!*

PERHAPS.

BUT WHAT OF THOSE WHOSE PATH HAS NOT BEEN *FINALIZED?* THERE IS GREAT *GOOD* YOU COULD DO, DAIMON--OR DO YOU PREFER TO JUST *READ* OF US IN DRY BOOKS ON *EXORCISM?*

WE ARE NOT FOUND IN *BOOKS,* DOCTOR...

...BUT IN *NIGHTMARES!*

THE *SOUNDS* REACH HIS EARS, WAILS, MOANS, CRIES, PLEAS, ALL AT ONCE, ALL IN A *RUSH* TO COME AND *WRITHE* BEFORE HIM.

"*HELP US, SATAN-SON!* BETRAY US AND YOU BETRAY YOURSELF!"

"WHAT WAS *OUR* SIN? THAT WE LIVED *TOO LONG* TO *CARE* OR TOO SHORT TO LEARN TO LOVE?"

"WHAT OF ME, DAIMON? WAS *MY* CRIME SO GREAT THAT I DESERVE PERDITION...WHILE OTHERS, WHOSE LISTS WERE *LONGER,* RECEIVED ABSOLUTION FOR A *DONATION* TO THE RIGHT *PLACE* AT THE RIGHT TIME?"

OH, MY GOD.

NOT SO *LOUD,* DAIMON. YOU MIGHT ...*WAKE HIM!*

"WAKE...? YOU MEAN TO SAY THE DEVIL SLEEPS?!"

"ON THIS DAY, SATAN-SON... ALWAYS! WE POOR CREATURES ARE LEFT TO OUR-SELVES AND OUR TORMENTS--"

"--WHILE HE WITHDRAWS FROM A CERTAIN ... EVENT WHICH IS TO TRANSPIRE THIS NIGHT ON THE HUMAN PLANE.

WHAT IS THERE TO CONCERN MY FATHER IN THE DOINGS OF MAN?

AT MOST TIMES VERY LITTLE, SATAN-SON.

--BUT TONIGHT... TONIGHT IS DIFFERENT, AND ITS DIFFERENCE IS FELT EVEN IN HELL.

FOR THE LESSER BEINGS, IT IS A MOMENT OF REST FROM THE TORTURES OF DAMNATION. FOR THE UNDERLINGS OF THE MASTER IT IS A TIME OF FEAR.

BUT FOR THE MASTER HIMSELF... IT IS A TIME TO WITH-DRAW UNTIL THE MADNESS ABOVE IS SPENT. UNTIL HUMANKIND IS RETURNED TO ITS NORMAL POSTURE OF PETTY EVILS AND GREED.

IT IS CHRISTMAS EVE, DAIMON--THE NIGHT LORD SATAN SLEEPS!

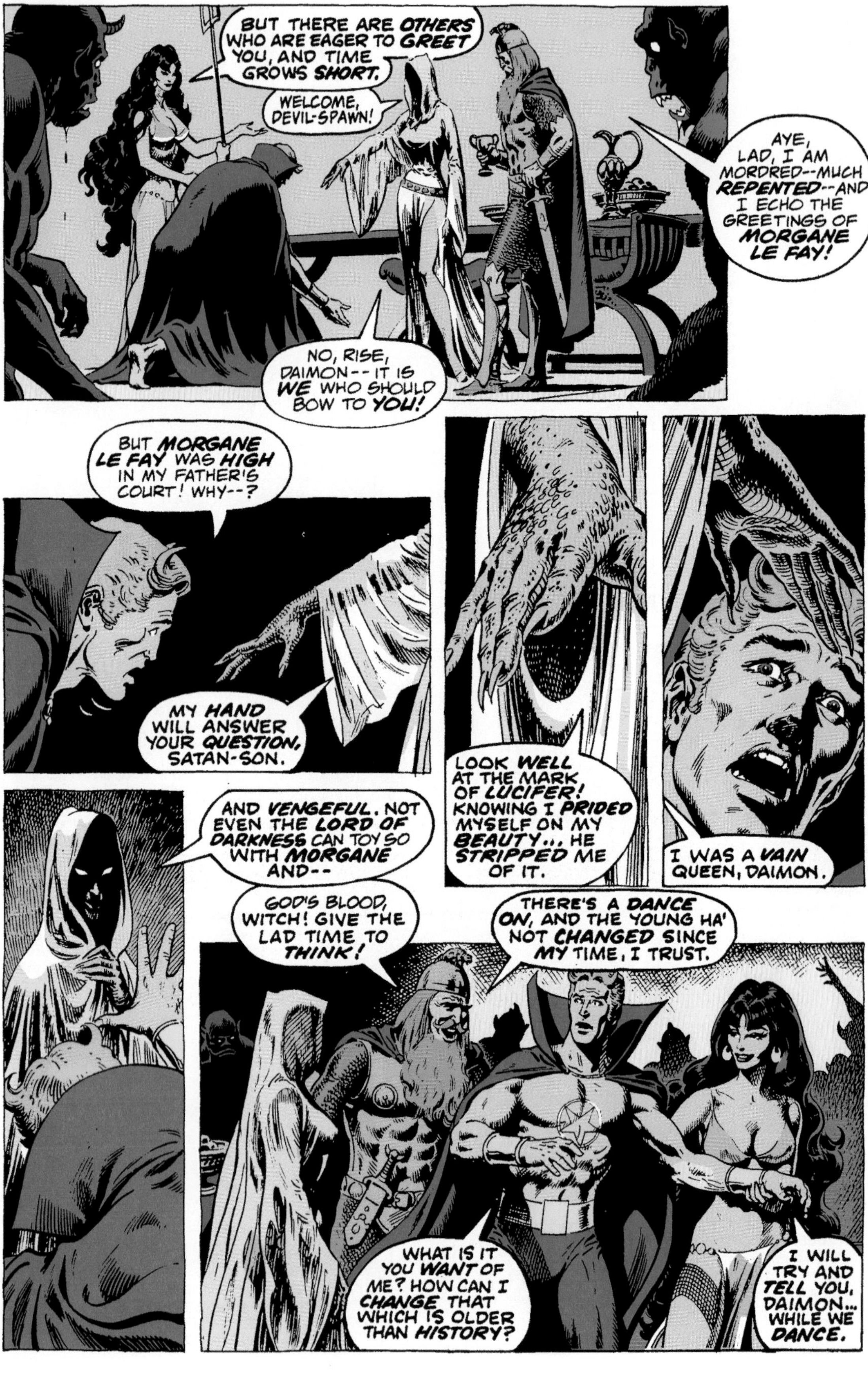

BUT THERE ARE OTHERS WHO ARE EAGER TO GREET YOU, AND TIME GROWS SHORT.
WELCOME, DEVIL-SPAWN!
AYE, LAD, I AM MORDRED--MUCH REPENTED--AND I ECHO THE GREETINGS OF MORGANE LE FAY!
NO, RISE, DAIMON--IT IS WE WHO SHOULD BOW TO YOU!
BUT MORGANE LE FAY WAS HIGH IN MY FATHER'S COURT! WHY--?
MY HAND WILL ANSWER YOUR QUESTION, SATAN-SON.
LOOK WELL AT THE MARK OF LUCIFER! KNOWING I PRIDED MYSELF ON MY BEAUTY... HE STRIPPED ME OF IT.
I WAS A VAIN QUEEN, DAIMON.
AND VENGEFUL. NOT EVEN THE LORD OF DARKNESS CAN TOY SO WITH MORGANE AND--
GOD'S BLOOD, WITCH! GIVE THE LAD TIME TO THINK!
THERE'S A DANCE ON, AND THE YOUNG HA' NOT CHANGED SINCE MY TIME, I TRUST.
WHAT IS IT YOU WANT OF ME? HOW CAN I CHANGE THAT WHICH IS OLDER THAN HISTORY?
I WILL TRY AND TELL YOU, DAIMON... WHILE WE DANCE.

HISTORY BRINGS *CHANGE*, DAIMON, EVEN *HERE*. YOUR FATHER SCHEMED FOR A DAY WHEN THE *GODS* WOULD BE *FORGOTTEN*---BUT HE DIDN'T FORSEE THAT, WHEN THAT DAY *COMES*--

--MAN WOULD FIND A WAY TO SET ASIDE *SATAN* AS WELL.

HE IS *FRIGHTENED*, DAIMON! *TIRED*! HIS HOLD IS *WEAKENING* EVEN HERE--

--AND WITH EACH NEW *DEFEAT* WE TASTE OF A *FREEDOM* WHICH HE CAN NO LONGER *DENY*!

I WOULDN'T HAVE THOUGHT IT *POSSIBLE*! WHILE I WAS WORKING TOWARDS PREPARING *MANKIND* TO BATTLE HIS *INFLUENCE*--

--THERE WAS A *REVOLUTION* BREWING IN HIS OWN *KINGDOM*! I-- THE *MUSIC*!

WHY HAVE THEY STOPPED *PLAYING*?

HUSH, DAIMON, IT'S NOT *IMPORTANT*!

WHAT *IS* IS THAT YOU *UNDERSTAND*! WE CAN *TRUST* YOU!

YOU *ARE* WITH US, DAIMON, *AREN'T* YOU?

I...

YOU *ARE*! I *KNOW* YOU ARE! *SAY* IT, DAIMON!

SAY: "I AM WITH YOU!"

"I AM *ONE* OF YOU!" SAY IT!

NO! DON'T *OPEN YOUR EYES*! YOU'LL *RUIN* EVERYTHING!

BUT THE SON OF THE PRINCE OF DARKNESS DOES OPEN HIS EYES--

--JUST IN TIME TO REALIZE HOW DEVIOUS HIS FATHER CAN REALLY BE.

GET AWAY FROM ME, TEMPTRESS! BY ALL THAT'S HOLY--

-- GET AWAY!!

PIG OF EVIL! I ALMOST HAD YOU, DEVIL'S SUCKLING!

BUT A SECOND MORE AND YOUR PRECIOUS DARKSOUL WOULD HAVE JOINED US IN THE FIRE!

BUT YOU'RE NOT OUT YET, HUMAN-CHILD! NOT YET!

NOT WHILE THE HORDES OF HELL HUNGER TO PLEASE THE MASTER--

-- BY SERVING UP HIS DISOBEDIENT WHELP!!

"AND YOU, FOR ALL YOUR BOOK-LEARNING, DAIMON--

NO!!

"--WERE SUCKED IN AS EASILY AS THE REST!"

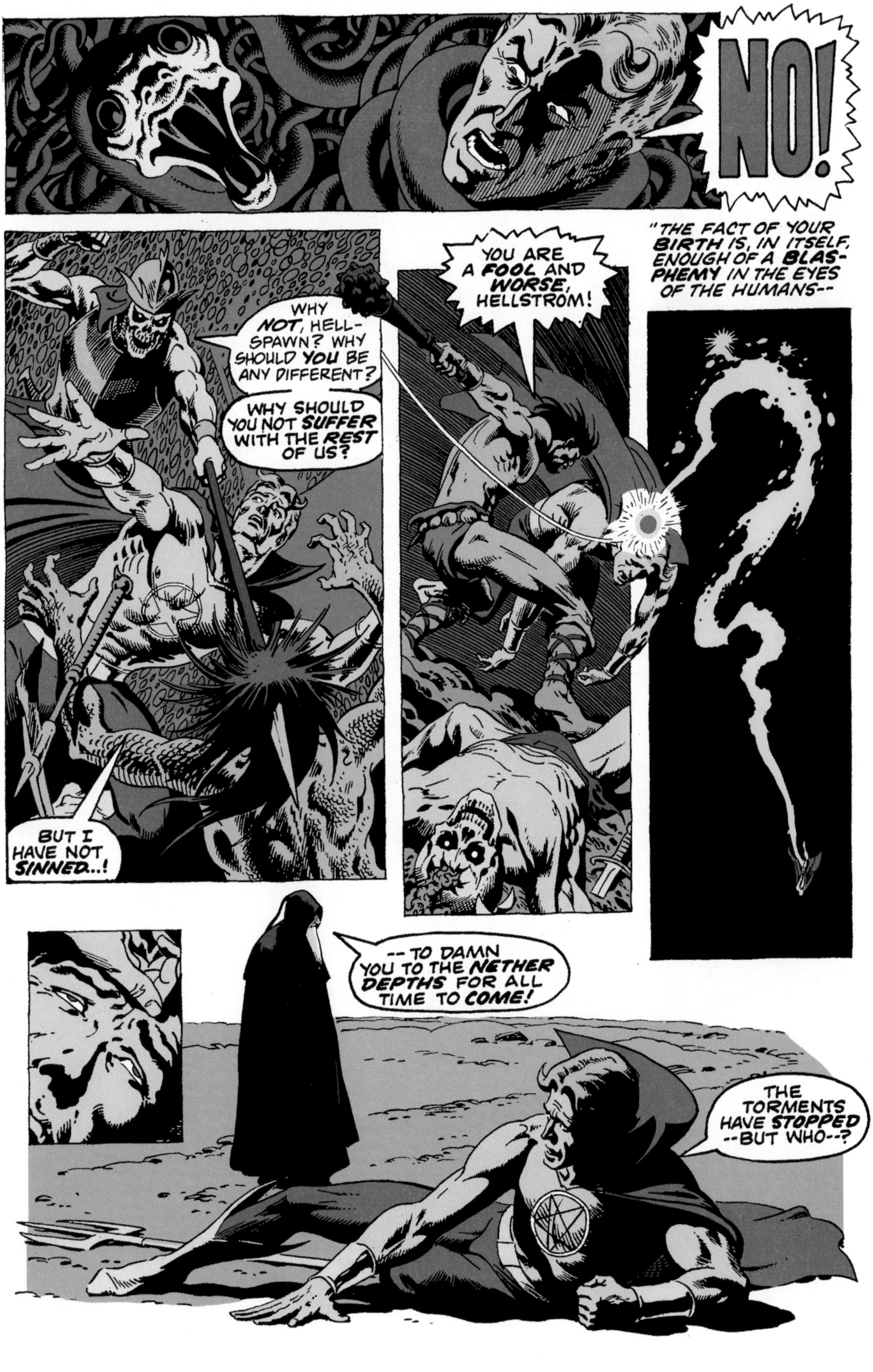
NO!
WHY NOT, HELL-SPAWN? WHY SHOULD YOU BE ANY DIFFERENT?
WHY SHOULD YOU NOT SUFFER WITH THE REST OF US?
BUT I HAVE NOT SINNED...!
YOU ARE A FOOL AND WORSE, HELLSTROM!
"THE FACT OF YOUR BIRTH IS, IN ITSELF, ENOUGH OF A BLASPHEMY IN THE EYES OF THE HUMANS--
-- TO DAMN YOU TO THE NETHER DEPTHS FOR ALL TIME TO COME!
THE TORMENTS HAVE STOPPED --BUT WHO--?

COME, DAIMON. I AM YOUR *GUIDE*. THERE IS SO *LITTLE* TO SEE--

-- AND SO *MUCH* TIME.

COME.

DAIMON *FOLLOWS*, HIS MIND A WHIRLING MAELSTROM OF *BABBLE*, HIS THOUGHTS REFUSING TO *COALESCE*.

AND THE INCREDIBLE MELEE OF *SOUNDS* FROM THE TOWER ON THE PLAINS BEFORE HIM SEEMS TO *FEED* ON HIS CON-FUSION, *TAUNTING* HIM--

--UNTIL HE *SURRENDERS* TO IT, EXHAUSTED, CAPABLE ONLY OF *JOINING* WITH THE THRONG THAT HAS MADE ITS PILGRIMAGE ACROSS THIS DUSTY LANDSCAPE TO...

THE *CITY*, DAIMON. IT *HAS* BORNE OTHER NAMES.

BUT IT IS *ONLY* THE CITY, NOW. A PLACE WHERE *EVENTS* ARE ENACTED IN ENDLESS *REPEAT*, AND TIME *PASSES*, ECHOING ITSELF. COME.

BUT WHAT WILL I *SEE* HERE? WHY--

BY THE *SEVEN CIRCLES!* THAT MAN ON THE BALCONY--!

HE IS *ME!*

114

FROM A SUDDENLY DARKLING SKY, UNNATURAL *THUNDER* PEALS. *LIGHTNING* SLASHES THE SCENE, DESTROYING ALL *COLOR* WITH ITS TERRIBLE BRILLIANCE, AS THOUGH *MEANT* TO REDUCE WHAT DAIMON HELLSTROM BEHOLDS TO THE RIGID BLACK AND WHITE OF STARK, UNYIELDING *TRUTH!*

NO! THE FIGURE WHICH SEEMED TO BE *ME* ALTERS, CHANGES... BECOMES...

BECOMES THAT WHICH YOU HAVE *ALWAYS* TRULY BEEN!

THESE *FOOLS* GUESSED IT AND TRIED TO *CONTAIN* ME WITH THEIR BONDS OF MYSTIC *YEW THORNS.*

NOW I SUMMON FORTH ALL THE POWERS OF THE PIT TO *PUNISH* THEM FOR THAT ACT!

W-WAIT! YOU WRONG US! WE DID NOT *ACTUALLY* KNOW OR MEAN TO--

TAKE THEM! DESTROY THEM! THEY KNOW EXACTLY WHAT THEY DO!

HA-HA-HA HA HA-HA HA HA

IT IS A PERVERSION, A COSMIC, SOUL-SEARING WARPAGE OF THAT MOST FRAGILE OF HUMANITY'S MYTHS ...FAITH IN A BELIEF OF INHERENT GOOD--

-- IN THE FACE OF UNDENIABLE ...ABSOLUTE... EVIL!

AND FOR THE SON OF SATAN, IT HAS A SPECIAL TWIST.

THE PERVERSION MIGHT HAVE EASILY BECOME THE REALITY--

-- FOR WAS HE NOT INTENDED TO HAVE BEEN...

DEAR LORD, HOW COULD I HAVE BEEN SO BLIND?

ALL THE RITUAL! ALL THE LORE! IT SHOULD HAVE PREPARED ME... WARNED ME!

BUT NO! I CLUNG TO REASON! TO FAITH THAT EVIL COULD ALWAYS BE EXORCISED! THAT THERE HAD TO BE GOOD, BURIED SOMEWHERE BENEATH!

EVEN MY FATHER, BEFORE HE FELL! EVEN LORD SATAN HIMSELF HAD TO HAVE POSSESSED THAT SEED OF GLORY!

BUT WHAT IF A BEING EXISTED WHO WAS NOTHING MORE THAN A LIVING INCARNATION OF EVIL?

SO OVERWHELMINGLY EVIL THAT THE SHEER ENORMITY OF IT MIGHT DRIVE HIM... WAIT--THAT FIGURE ON THE TAPESTRY--

POSTULATE:

YOU, DAIMON HELLSTROM, HAVE ALWAYS CONSIDERED YOURSELF A BEING DIVIDED. WHAT IF THAT DIVISION WERE ...ILLUSORY?

POSTULATE:

WHAT GOOD WOULD EXIST IN YOU WERE IT PROVED THAT BOTH YOUR PARENTS--

-- WERE TOTALLY AND ABSOLUTELY...EVIL?

THE UNICORN.

PURITY, DAIMON, MAY EXIST BOTH IN ITS LIGHT...AND DARK FORMS.

MOTHER!

NO! IT'S NOT TRUE!!

I WILL NOT LET IT BE TRUE!

SHH-FWOOSH!

LET IT? DON'T BE ABSURD, BOY. NO ONE "LETS" TRUTH! IT JUST IS!

ISN'T THAT RIGHT, DEAR?

OF COURSE, MY LORD.

MOTHER, PLEASE...

YOU SEE, DAIMON, IF OUR POSTULATION WERE TO FORMULATE ITSELF INTO TRUTH, THEN THE FORMULATION WOULD BE QUITE INESCAPABLE. AND YOU MY DEAR EXORCIST, FOR ALL YOUR DELUSIONS TO THE CONTRARY (THOUGH WE WILL NOT DISCOUNT THE POSSIBILITY THAT THE TRUTH MAY HAVE DRIVEN YOU MAD, FORCING YOU TO THE POINT WHERE YOU HAD TO HIDE THE TRUTH, EVEN FROM YOURSELF) ARE, AND WERE CREATED TO BE--

--EVIL?! ONLY IF I ACCEPT ALL YOU SAY AS TRUTH!

BUT THIS IS *YOUR* REALM AND THE ONLY TRUTHS ARE *YOURS*--

I *REJECT* YOUR "TRUTHS," FATHER... AS LONG AGO, I *REJECTED* YOU!

AND THE *SOULFIRE'S* SEARING FLAMES PROVE ME *RIGHT!*

NO! YOU WERE *WEAKENING!* IT CANNOT END LIKE *THIS*...!

IT MUST NOT BE *OVER,* UNTIL...

BUT *ALL NIGHTMARES* END WHEN THE *SLEEPER* WAKES...

... EVEN WHEN THE DREAMER IS *SATAN* HIMSELF.

IT IS *OVER,* MASTER... CHRISTMAS EVE IS *PAST!*

YOU ARE *FREE* TO *WAKE!*

YOUR SLEEP, SIRE... I HOPE IT WAS NOT--

TROUBLED, BELIAL...?

A *VICTORY* WAS IN MY GRASP... IT PROVED TO BE A *DREAM.*

BUT THE *BATTLE* IS *REAL,* MY SERVANT. AND WHATEVER THE OUTCOME, IT MUST AS ALWAYS...

...GO ON.

END

50¢
CC
92
FEB
02152
MARVEL® COMICS GROUP
APPROVED BY THE COMICS CODE CA AUTHORITY
©1980 MARVEL COMICS GROUP
TM
THE DEFENDERS®
A PIECE OF ETERNITY IS MISSING!
AT LONG LAST...THE RETURN OF SON OF SATAN!
EH/AM

Stan Lee PRESENTS: THE DYNAMIC DEFENDERS!

ETERNITY...HUMANITY...OBLIVION!

| J. M. DeMATTEIS WRITER | DON PERLIN & PABLO MARCOS ARTISTS | DIANA ALBERS LETTERER | GEORGE ROUSSOS COLORIST | AL MILGROM EDITOR | JIM SHOOTER EDITOR-IN-CHIEF |

FRIENDSHIP HAS BEEN A MOST PRECIOUS-- AND RARE--COMMODITY TO *THE INCREDIBLE HULK.* FEW HAVE DARED TO OFFER THAT FRIENDSHIP, AND FEWER STILL HAVE REMAINED BY HIS SIDE FOR LONG, AFTER THE OFFER HAS BEEN MADE.

NO WONDER THEN THAT--WHEN THE LONELINESS IN HIS TOR- TURED HEART BECOMES TOO MUCH TO BEAR--THE MASSIVE MAN-BRUTE SEEKS THE COM- PANY OF A CERTAIN MAGICIAN WHO HAS BEEN A COMFORTING CONSTANT IN A LIFE OF EPHEMERA.

LOOK AT HIM, STEPHEN-- SO ENGROSSED IN HIS PLAY...MORE LIKE A CHILD THAN THE HATEFUL MONSTER THE WORLD BELIEVES HIM TO BE.

INDEED. BUT LET US NOT FORGET, CLEA, HOW *DANGEROUS* THAT CHILD CAN BE WHEN PROVOKED.

THEN BIG WIZARD SAY TO FIRE-HEAD "HELLO--WANT TO COME TO MY HOUSE AND SING SONGS?"

BEFORE THE MASTER OF THE MYSTIC ARTS CAN FURTHER EXPOUND ON HIS THOUGHTS, HE SUDDENLY WHIRLS, FACE TIGHT WITH CONCENTRATION. HE SNAKES HIS FINGERS IN A MYSTIC GESTURE...

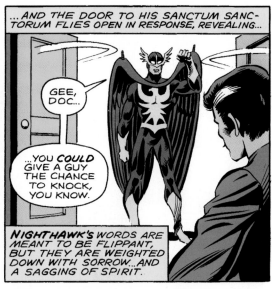

...AND THE DOOR TO HIS SANCTUM SANCTORUM FLIES OPEN IN RESPONSE, REVEALING...

GEE, DOC...

...YOU **COULD** GIVE A GUY THE CHANCE TO KNOCK, YOU KNOW.

NIGHTHAWK'S WORDS ARE MEANT TO BE FLIPPANT, BUT THEY ARE WEIGHTED DOWN WITH SORROW...AND A SAGGING OF SPIRIT.

BIRD-NOSE IS HERE! HELLO, BIRD-NOSE--WANT TO HAVE FUN WITH HULK?

BIRD-NO UH... **KYLE** LOOKS A BIT UNDER-THE-WEATHER, HULK-- BUT I'D LOVE TO BE BIG WIZARD!

I GUESS I'M NOT DOING A SPECTACULAR JOB OF HIDING MY EMOTIONS, HUH?

MAYBE I SHOULDN'T HAVE COME OVER.

NONSENSE-- YOU ARE ALWAYS WELCOME HERE.

BUT TELL ME, KYLE--WHAT IS WRONG?

I COULD SENSE YOUR DESPAIR ROILING THE ETHERS A BLOCK AWAY.

SOMETHING...HAPPENED TO ME LAST NIGHT, DOC, OR SHOULD I SAY **SOME** ONE. A GIRL FROM MY PAST. A VERY CONFUSED GIRL NAMED MINDY. *

SEE MARVEL TEAM-UP #101--AL.

SHE GAVE ME A GLIMPSE OF THE REAL KYLE RICHMOND--THE SPOILED, RICH BRAT BENEATH THE ADVENTURER'S MASK, WHO'S SPENT HIS ENTIRE LIFE SIDESTEPPING RESPONSIBILITY...

...THE BUNGLER WHO'S NEARLY WRECKED HIS FATHER'S BUSINESS--AND LET DOWN EVERY WOMAN HE'S LAUGHINGLY ATTEMPTED TO LOVE.

2

NOT ONLY IS YOUR SELF-PITY DISTASTEFUL, KYLE--BUT IT HAS DISTORTED YOUR PERCEPTIONS BEYOND BELIEF! NEED I REMIND YOU OF THE COUNTLESS TIMES YOU HAVE RISKED DEATH TO LITERALLY SAVE THE WORLD? IF THAT IS NOT TAKING RESPON-SIBILITY-- THEN WHAT...

...IS...?!

DORMAMMU'S DEMONS!

DID YOU FEEL THAT?!

STEPHEN--IT SEEMED AS IF--FOR A MOMENT-- ALL OF REALITY SIMPLY...

...CEASED TO EXIST...

THIS IS ONE OF DUMB MAGICIAN'S STUPID TRICKS?

3

I CAN ASSURE YOU, HULK, THAT THIS IS NO TRI--

MY LOVE-- WHAT IS IT?

--YAKKK!

I DON'T THINK HE CAN HEAR YOU, CLEA. IT'S LIKE HE'S BEEN...SHUT DOWN--LIKE SOME POWER HAS REACHED OUT AN--OH LORD! HIS EYES, CLEA...

...LOOK AT HIS EYES!

AND, IF HUMAN SIGHT WERE CAPABLE OF PEERING DEEPER INTO THOSE TWIN POOLS OF SHIMMERING LIGHT, SHAPE, AND COLOR, IT WOULD NO DOUBT REVEAL WINDING CORRIDORS OF SOUL...

...CORRIDORS THAT LEAD TO AN ELDRITCH DIMENSION FARTHER AWAY THAN THE MOST DISTANT STAR-- YET NEARER THAN A SINGLE THOUGHT.

FLAMES OF THE FALTINE! MY ASTRAL BODY HAS BEEN FORCIBLY RIPPED FROM MY CORPOREAL SHELL--PLUCKED LIKE SOME RIPENED FRUIT AND HURLED HERE! BUT...WHERE AM I?

WAIT! THIS ARCH OF SERAPHIC ENERGY IS FAMILIAR--I KNOW THIS PLACE! OF COURSE--I FIRST TRAVELED HERE YEARS AGO--WHEN SEEKING TO SAVE MY DEPARTED MENTOR, THE ANCIENT ONE, FROM THE CLUTCHES OF THE VILE BARON MORDO!*

THIS IS THE DOMAIN OF THE MINDSTAGGERING ENTITY WHOSE VERY BEING ENCOMPASSES ALL OF CREATION...

*STRANGE TALES #138--AL.

YES, MAGICIAN--IT IS ETERNITY WHO DREW YOU HERE!

FORGIVE THE ABRUPT MANNER IN WHICH YOU WERE SUMMONED, BUT AS THE DISPLACEMENT OF REALITY YOU EXPERIENCED SO ELOQUENTLY TESTIFIED--THERE IS A DIRE CRISIS AT HAND... AND I NEED YOUR AID.

OMNIPOTENT ETERNITY-- ASKING FOR THE HELP OF AN EARTHBORN SORCERER? THIS IS EITHER UTTER MADNESS... OR DOOMSDAY! (4)

I READ YOUR THOUGHTS, STRANGE--AND THEY ARE CHILLINGLY ACCURATE. DARK OBLIVION MAY AWAIT US AND--IN PART--THE BLAME IS MINE.

BUT--TO FULLY UNDERSTAND--YOU MUST FIRST CONSIDER WHAT IT MEANS TO BE WHAT I AM--TO COMPRISE TOTALITY ITSELF! HAS IT NEVER OCCURRED TO YOU THAT TO BE ALL IS ALSO TO BE...UNUTTERABLY *ALONE*?

THERE CAME A POINT WHEN I WAS TORN BY THIS COSMIC SOLITUDE THAT BEGGARS DESCRIPTION--WHEN I DESPERATELY CRAVED EXPERIENCE OF DUALITY... OTHERNESS.

TO ASSUAGE THIS SENSATION, I CREATED *FORMS* FOR MYSELF--MORTAL BODIES THAT I INFUSED WITH A PORTION OF MY INFINITE CONSCIOUSNESS...AND SCATTERED ACROSS THE MULTIVERSE.

"I BESTOWED UPON THESE FORMS FALSE IDENTITIES-- FUNCTIONAL EGOS THAT VEILED FROM THEM THEIR TRUE NATURES. AND SO, UNKNOWING, THEY WALKED THE WORLDS OF MEN...

"...LEARNING THE *MEANING* OF OTHERNESS..."

"...LEARNING OF SUFFERING..."

"...OF STRUGGLE..."

"...OF LOVE AND REJOICING."

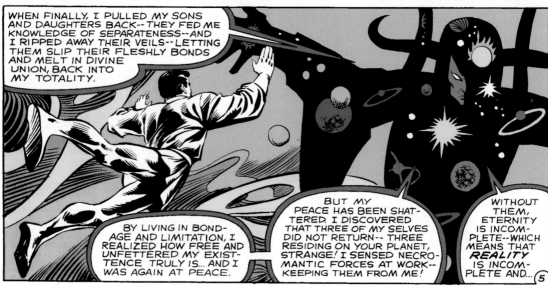

WHEN FINALLY, I PULLED MY SONS AND DAUGHTERS BACK--THEY FED ME KNOWLEDGE OF SEPARATENESS--AND I RIPPED AWAY THEIR VEILS--LETTING THEM SLIP THEIR FLESHLY BONDS AND MELT IN DIVINE UNION, BACK INTO MY TOTALITY.

BY LIVING IN BONDAGE AND LIMITATION, I REALIZED HOW FREE AND UNFETTERED MY EXISTENCE TRULY IS... AND I WAS AGAIN AT PEACE.

BUT MY PEACE HAS BEEN SHATTERED. I DISCOVERED THAT THREE OF MY SELVES DID NOT RETURN-- THREE RESIDING ON YOUR PLANET, STRANGE! I SENSED NECROMANTIC FORCES AT WORK-- KEEPING THEM FROM ME!

WITHOUT THEM, ETERNITY IS INCOMPLETE--WHICH MEANS THAT *REALITY* IS INCOMPLETE AND... 5

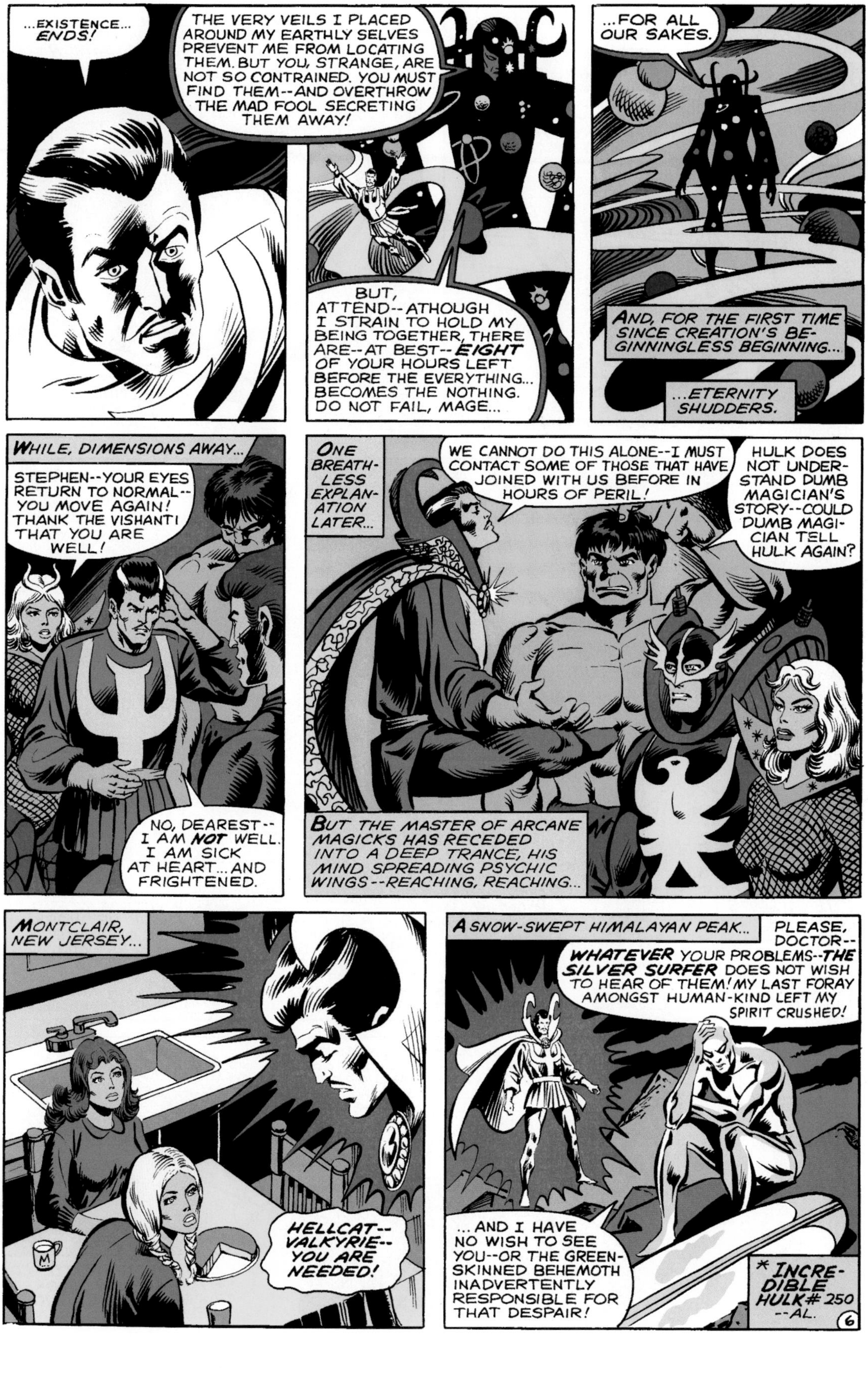
...EXISTENCE... ENDS!
THE VERY VEILS I PLACED AROUND MY EARTHLY SELVES PREVENT ME FROM LOCATING THEM. BUT YOU, STRANGE, ARE NOT SO CONTRAINED. YOU MUST FIND THEM--AND OVERTHROW THE MAD FOOL SECRETING THEM AWAY!
BUT, ATTEND--ATHOUGH I STRAIN TO HOLD MY BEING TOGETHER, THERE ARE--AT BEST--EIGHT OF YOUR HOURS LEFT BEFORE THE EVERYTHING... BECOMES THE NOTHING. DO NOT FAIL, MAGE...
...FOR ALL OUR SAKES.
AND, FOR THE FIRST TIME SINCE CREATION'S BEGINNINGLESS BEGINNING...
...ETERNITY SHUDDERS.
WHILE, DIMENSIONS AWAY...
STEPHEN--YOUR EYES RETURN TO NORMAL--YOU MOVE AGAIN! THANK THE VISHANTI THAT YOU ARE WELL!
NO, DEAREST--I AM NOT WELL. I AM SICK AT HEART...AND FRIGHTENED.
ONE BREATHLESS EXPLANATION LATER...
WE CANNOT DO THIS ALONE--I MUST CONTACT SOME OF THOSE THAT HAVE JOINED WITH US BEFORE IN HOURS OF PERIL!
HULK DOES NOT UNDERSTAND DUMB MAGICIAN'S STORY--COULD DUMB MAGICIAN TELL HULK AGAIN?
BUT THE MASTER OF ARCANE MAGICKS HAS RECEDED INTO A DEEP TRANCE, HIS MIND SPREADING PSYCHIC WINGS--REACHING, REACHING...
MONTCLAIR, NEW JERSEY...
HELLCAT--VALKYRIE--YOU ARE NEEDED!
M
A SNOW-SWEPT HIMALAYAN PEAK...
PLEASE, DOCTOR--WHATEVER YOUR PROBLEMS--THE SILVER SURFER DOES NOT WISH TO HEAR OF THEM! MY LAST FORAY AMONGST HUMAN-KIND LEFT MY SPIRIT CRUSHED!
...AND I HAVE NO WISH TO SEE YOU--OR THE GREEN-SKINNED BEHEMOTH INADVERTENTLY RESPONSIBLE FOR THAT DESPAIR!
*INCREDIBLE HULK #250 --AL.
6

UNDAUNTED, STEPHEN STRANGE TURNS HIS ATTENTION TO THE SUNKEN KINGDOM OF ATLANTIS...

...AND THAT FABLED REALM'S HAUGHTY MONARCH, THE SAVAGE SUB-MARINER!

FOR THE SAKE OF HIS PEOPLE--AND HIS WORLD--NAMOR WILL COME!

FINALLY, THE EN-CHANTER APPEARS IN GEORGETOWN, DIS-TRICT OF COLUMBIA...

...BEFORE A SOMBRE DAIMON HELLSTROM--NOTED DEMON-OLOGIST, EXORCIST... AND FIRST-BORN SON OF SATAN!

I HAVE BEEN EXPECTING YOU, DOCTOR STRANGE-- AND I AM READY.

AFTER AN ADROITLY-WOVEN SPELL OF TELE-PORTATION SWEEPS THE MOTLEY GROUP TOGETHER...

THE CAULDRON OF THE COSMOS HAS REVEALED TO ME THE LAST LOCATIONS OF ETERNITY'S VANISHED CHILDREN! THUS, IN TEAMS OF TWO, I SHALL DISPATCH YOU TO...

...A SECLUDED INDIAN TEMPLE DEDICATED TO THE HINDU GOD, RAMA-- A SMALL ISLAND OFF THE COAST OF PATRAS, GREECE-- AND A BACKWARD VILLAGE IN NORTHERNMOST RUSSIA!

MEAN-WHILE, CLEA AND I --ALONG WITH A WORLD-WIDE NETWORK OF DEDICATED SEERS--WILL ATTEMPT TO MYSTIC-ALLY BOLSTER ETERNITY'S WANING LIFE-FORCE!

IF I SEEM BRUSQUE, MY FRIENDS--IT IS ONLY THE URGENCY OF OUR SITUATION WEIGHING HEAVILY UPON ME. GO--AND MAY THE VISHANTI SMILE UPON YOU!

THERE IS A HASTILY-MUTTERED INCANTATION AND SIX COLOR-FUL FIGURES DISSOLVE LIKE TRAILS OF RIMEY BREATH...

7

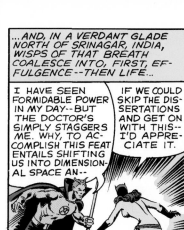

...AND, IN A VERDANT GLADE NORTH OF SRINAGAR, INDIA, WISPS OF THAT BREATH COALESCE INTO, FIRST, EFFULGENCE--THEN LIFE...

I HAVE SEEN FORMIDABLE POWER IN MY DAY--BUT THE DOCTOR'S SIMPLY STAGGERS ME. WHY, TO ACCOMPLISH THIS FEAT ENTAILS SHIFTING US INTO DIMENSIONAL SPACE AN--

IF WE COULD SKIP THE DISSERTATIONS AND GET ON WITH THIS--I'D APPRECIATE IT.

OH... HEY--I'M SORRY. THIS WHOLE SITUATION'S GOT ME NERVOUS. EVERYTHING WE KNOW COULD GO BLOOEY AND TH--

NO. THAT IS NOT IT. I SENSE A DISTURBANCE IN YOUR SOUL--A BLACKNESS HOVERING AROUND YOU.

THE ONLY BLACKNESS HOVERING AROUND ME, MR. HELLSTROM, IS MY MOTHER'S DEATH*--AND I'D RATHER NOT TALK ABOUT IT... OR HER. SO LET'S CHECK OUT THE TEMPLE.

OF COURSE. BUT--IF IT HELPS--KNOW THAT I, TOO, HAVE BEEN TORN BY CONFLICTING FEELINGS TOWARD A PARENT.

*SEE DEFENDERS #89--AL.

AS STRANGE MAY HAVE TOLD YOU--MY FATHER IS THE...

DEVIL! DEVIL!

FROM THE TORCH-LIT SHADOWS, A DOZEN ROBED FIGURES SWARM OVER THE STARTLED DEFENDERS LIKE ANTS OVER A HALF--ROTTED CORPSE.

WHILE, AROUND THEM, THE GLITTERING, JEWELED STATUES OF LORD RAMA, HIS WIFE SITA, AND THE GOD'S PERFECT SERVANT--HANUMAN, THE MONKEY--STAND IN IMPASSIVE JUDGEMENT.

YOU ARE TOO LATE, DEVIL! HE IS SAFE... AND YOU...

...ARE DOOMED!

EITHER DOC'S PROVIDED US WITH A SPELL OF UNDERSTANDING...OR I'VE PICKED UP HINDI IN LESS THAN A MINUTE!

AMUSING. BUT THIS GIFT OF TRANSLATION WILL DO US NO GOOD.

8

...WITH THESE LUNATICS UPON OUR BACKS!

THERE IS AN EXPLOSION OF UNHOLY SOULFIRE...

...AND ALL IS SILENCE, IN THE TEMPLE OF RAMA.

WOW. THAT'S IMPRESSIVE.

WORDLESSLY, EYES FLAMING, THE SATAN-SPAWN REACHES FOR ONE OF THE STUNNED ACOLYTES...

...AND... HEAR ME, WOMAN-- I WILL BROOK NO SUBTERFUGE! WHY WERE WE ATTACKED?

ANSWER ME, WITCH-- OR I WILL TEAR YOUR HEART OUT AND FEED IT TO THE DOGS!

ANSWER ME!

WHOA--TAKE IT EASY, HELLSTROM! YOU'RE FRIGHTENING THIS POOR GAL HALF OUT OF HER WITS!

LISTEN. WE DON'T WANT TO HURT YOU. WE JUST WANT TO KNOW IF SOMETHING ODD HAS BEEN GOING ON HERE--PERHAPS SOMEONE HAS BEEN KIDNAPPED OR--

Y- YES! THAT IS WHY WE ATTACKED! W-WE THOUGHT YOU WERE THE DEMONS SENT TO CAPTURE OUR BELOVED MASTER, SAI ANAND. BUT YOUR EYES--ARE PURE.

"YOU SEE, DAYS AGO, HANUMAN HIMSELF APPEARED BEFORE OUR TEMPLE-- BRINGING A WARNING FROM RAMA.

"EVIL ONES, HANUMAN SAID, WERE COMING FOR THE GURU-- FOR HE WHO HAS TAUGHT US THE MEANING OF LOVE AND DEVOTION.

"BUT THE SACRED MONKEY HAD COME TO PROTECT SAI ANAND-- TO TAKE HIM TO THE BLESSED ABODE OF RAMA--WHERE HE WOULD BE SAFE."

INDEED! MY TRIDENT BURNS--ITS PSYCHO-SENSITIVE METAL IS ALIGHT!

CLEARLY, SAI ANAND IS A PART OF ETERNITY-- THIS BOGUS HANUMAN IS AN AGENT OF THE ONE HOLDING HIM. WE MUST FOLLOW THE VIBRATIONS--IMMEDIATELY!

OKAY--BUT COOL OUT, WILL YOU? I DON'T MIND TELLING YOU THAT YOU'RE SCARING ME!

SO BEGINS AN HOURS-LONG HUNT IN THE MANY-HUED MOUNTAINS BEYOND THE TEMPLE...

9

...AND STRANGELY--FOR HE HAS NEVER BEEN ONE TO ALLOW INTIMACY--DAIMON HELLSTROM FINDS HIMSELF OPENING UP...

--YOU MEAN THIS *DARKSOUL*--THIS OTHER PART OF YOU JUST TAKES CONTROL?

NOT COMPLETE-LY--BUT MY INFERNAL HERITAGE OFTEN URGES ME TO ACTIONS WHICH LATER LEAVE ME QUITE...

...ASHAMED...

UH--DAIMON? I HAVE A FUNNY FEELING THAT WE'VE JUST FOUND HANUMAN...

GRROWR....!

...AND HE LOOKS LIKE ONE *APE* APE!

WOMP!

OH-OH! THE DARK SOUL MAY FEED DAIMON SOME- AMAZING ABILI- TIES BUT FELINE AGILITY, LIKE MINE, SURE ISN'T ONE OF THEM!

...TO *WRAP* THIS THING UP WITH MY CLAW-LINE GRAPPLE!

WHICH MEANS THAT IT'S ON ME...

NOT BAD-- IF I SAY SO MYSELF!

FZZAKT!

THANK YOU PATSY--FOR GRANTING ME THE MOMENTS I NEEDED TO REGAIN MY EQUILIBRIUM.

"HANUMAN" WILL SOON LOSE SUBSTANCE. AS I SUSPECTED, HE IS NOTHING MORE THAN A PSYCHO-KINETIC CONSTRUCT--A PAWN OF OUR UNNAMED FOE.

AND-- UNLESS I AM MISTAKEN--WE WILL *FIND* THAT FOE...

--THERE!

THE PAIR RACES FORWARD, DAIMON HELLSTROM NOTING THAT THERE IS NO AURA OF EVIL EMANATING FROM THE SEPULCHRAL STRUCTURE BEFORE THEM--JUST LAYERS OF DESPERATION... AND GRAY CONFUSION.

A CONFUSION NOT UNLIKE THAT EXPERIENCED BY NIGHTHAWK AND THE HULK, SOME TIME EARLIER, WHEN THEY BURST INTO BEING...

... BACK IN THE U.S.S.R.! TALK ABOUT YOUR BASIC SPEEDY SERVICE!

HULK CONFUSED WHEN DUMB MAGICIAN TALK ABOUT E-TERN-TY AND TINY E-TERN-TYS-- BUT HULK NOT CON-FUSED NOW!

SNOW MEN SMASH PEOPLE-- MAKE THEM SCARED...

SO HULK WILL SMASH THEM RIGHT BACK!

SKAK!

YOU KNOW, HULK-- SOMETIMES YOUR LOGIC IS SIMPLY IN-CONTROVERTIBLE!

I'D BET MY LAST SHRED OF SELF-RESPECT THAT THESE CREATURES ARE HERE TO KEEP US FROM OUR GOAL!

WAK!

Z-WASH!

THAT MEAN HULK IS DOING GOOD, BIRD-NOSE?

11

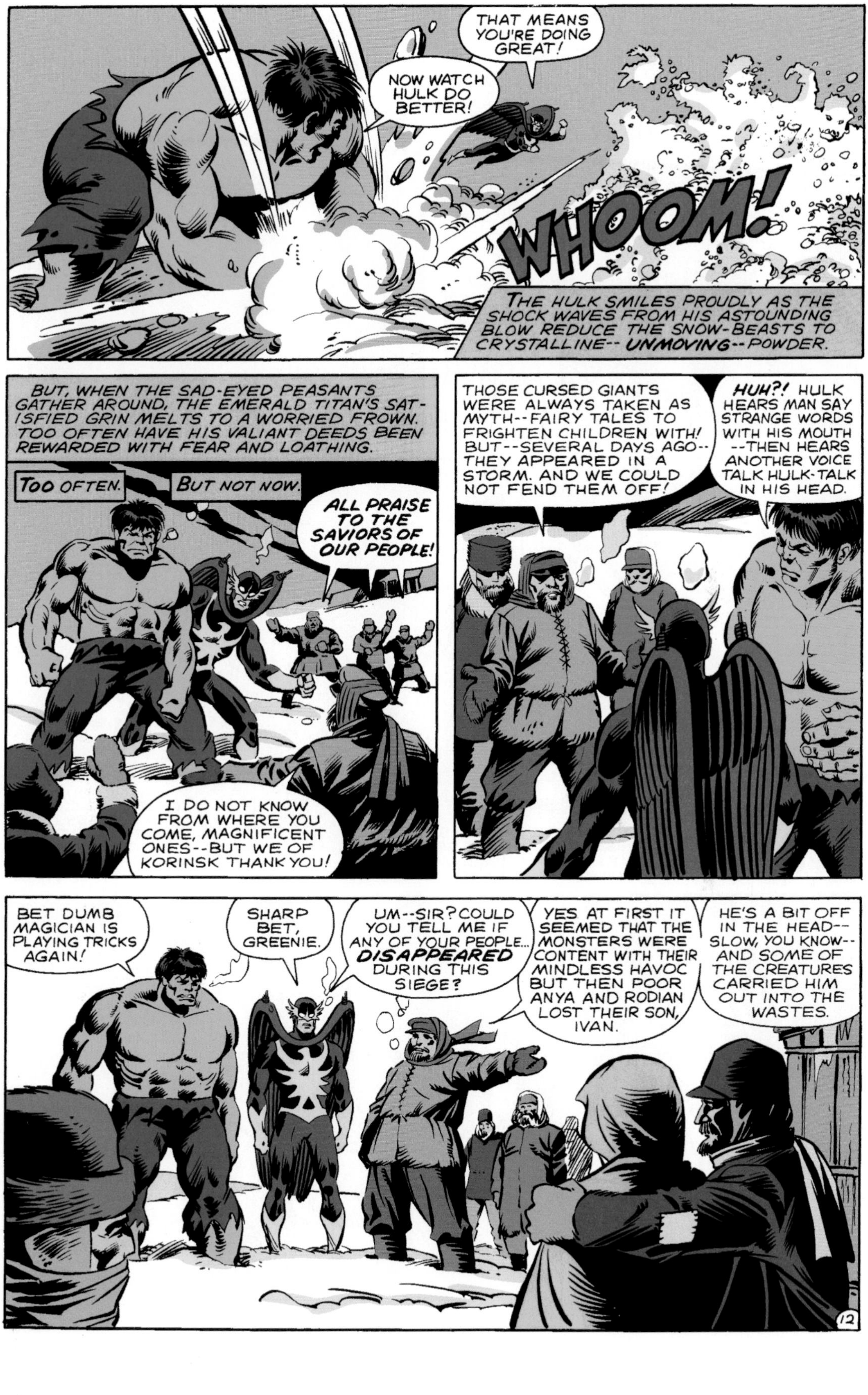
NOW WATCH HULK DO BETTER!
THAT MEANS YOU'RE DOING GREAT!
WHOOM!
THE HULK SMILES PROUDLY AS THE SHOCK WAVES FROM HIS ASTOUNDING BLOW REDUCE THE SNOW-BEASTS TO CRYSTALLINE-- UNMOVING-- POWDER.
BUT, WHEN THE SAD-EYED PEASANTS GATHER AROUND, THE EMERALD TITAN'S SATISFIED GRIN MELTS TO A WORRIED FROWN. TOO OFTEN HAVE HIS VALIANT DEEDS BEEN REWARDED WITH FEAR AND LOATHING.
TOO OFTEN.
BUT NOT NOW.
ALL PRAISE TO THE SAVIORS OF OUR PEOPLE!
I DO NOT KNOW FROM WHERE YOU COME, MAGNIFICENT ONES--BUT WE OF KORINSK THANK YOU!
THOSE CURSED GIANTS WERE ALWAYS TAKEN AS MYTH--FAIRY TALES TO FRIGHTEN CHILDREN WITH! BUT--SEVERAL DAYS AGO--THEY APPEARED IN A STORM. AND WE COULD NOT FEND THEM OFF!
HUH?! HULK HEARS MAN SAY STRANGE WORDS WITH HIS MOUTH --THEN HEARS ANOTHER VOICE TALK HULK-TALK IN HIS HEAD.
BET DUMB MAGICIAN IS PLAYING TRICKS AGAIN!
SHARP BET, GREENIE.
UM--SIR? COULD YOU TELL ME IF ANY OF YOUR PEOPLE... DISAPPEARED DURING THIS SIEGE?
YES AT FIRST IT SEEMED THAT THE MONSTERS WERE CONTENT WITH THEIR MINDLESS HAVOC BUT THEN POOR ANYA AND RODIAN LOST THEIR SON, IVAN.
HE'S A BIT OFF IN THE HEAD--SLOW, YOU KNOW--AND SOME OF THE CREATURES CARRIED HIM OUT INTO THE WASTES.
12

OUR IVAN WANDERED INTO KORINSK WHEN BUT A CHILD--SO TERRIFIED. ALL THESE YEARS WE HAVE LOVED HIM--TENDED HIM... AND HE HAS GIVEN US SO MUCH IN RETURN.

THE LAD CANNOT CARE FOR HIMSELF. EVEN IF THOSE HORRORS SET HIM FREE--HE WILL DIE! *PLEASE* BRING US BACK OUR SON!

GOD! HOW DO I EXPLAIN THE TRUTH OF THIS TO THEM. WHAT DO I SAY...?

"UH--PARDON ME, BUT THE BOY YOU ADORE SO ISN'T REALLY *HUMAN*-- HE'S JUST AN EXTENSION OF AN ALL-POWERFUL BEING NAMED ETERNITY--AND THE FATE OF THE UNIVERSE DEPENDS ON HIS *NEVER* COMING BACK?"

WILL YOU HELP US?

YEAH. RIGHT. I'LL... DO MY BEST.

SCARLET WINGS AND MIGHTY THEWS PROPEL THEM SKYWARD...

...AND THE SEARCH BEGINS.

THEN--AFTER HOURS OF SCOUTING THE TRACKLESS BARRENS...

WHAT GOING ON?! HULK FEELS SO COLD-- ICE GROWING ALL OVER HIM--!

W-W-WE MUST BE G-GETTING CLOSE... AND I GUESS OUR HIDDEN NEMESIS W-WANTS TO MAKE SURE TH-THAT WE GO...

...DOWN...

WHUPP!

...BUT NOT...

...OUT!

KR-AK!

13

NEM-E-SIS MUST BE STUPID TO THINK ICE CAN HOLD HULK FOR LONG! HULK IS STRONGER THAN ICE-- STRONGER THAN ANYTHING!

BUT BIRD-NOSE IS NOT STRONG LIKE HULK! BIRD-NOSE IS HURT! HULK MUST GET BIRD-NOSE OUT OF--

BRIGHT LIGHT LEADS HULK TO FUNNY ICE-HOUSE! COULD BE PLACE TO HELP BIRD-NOSE-- OR COULD BE WHERE NEM-E-SIS IS! BUT...

--HEY!

...HULK MUST HELP FRIEND.

HOW LONG WILL THIS GO ON? SINCE THE DAY WE MET, THAT MAN OF MAGIC HAS BEEN COAXING ME INTO BATTLING OCCULT MENACES AND AIDING A HUMANKIND THAT ABHORS ME!

AND SINCE THAT DAY YOU'VE DONE NOTHING BUT *COMPLAIN* ABOUT IT, NAMOR! I THINK-- BENEATH IT ALL-- YOU LIKE IT THAT WAY. WHY ELSE IS IT THAT YOU'VE RARELY IGNORED STEPHEN'S...

P-SHANG! P-SHOKK!

...PLEAS...?

OVER THERE, NAMOR--THOSE GUARDS!

RUT-DUT-DUT-DUT-DUT

FIVE WORDS SPOKEN-- AND THEY ARE ENOUGH-- THIS PAIR HAS NO NEED OF IDLE BANTER TO BOLSTER COURAGE.

HE IS A KING--LORD OF THE OCEANS-- AND SHE IS AN IMMORTAL OF MANY-SPIRED ASGARD-- LORD ODIN'S HAND-PICKED CHOOSER OF THE SLAIN! TOGETHER...

...THEY ARE UN-STOPPABLE...

SK-

YANG!

WHA-BOOM!

(14)

133

...TO SAY THE LEAST!

GUARDS-- STOP! STOP THIS INSTANT!

THE MAN IS KNOWN TO ME-- HE IS A HERO FROM THE GREAT WAR!

DURING MY CHILDHOOD IN LONDON, I SAW HIM FIGHT VALIANTLY-- SIDE BY SIDE WITH CAPTAIN AMERICA AND THE HUMAN TORCH!

YOU'RE ...BRI-TISH.

QUITE. THE FORMER LIZZIE LANGWOOD--NOW MRS. ELIZABETH CARVOPOLIS-- WIFE OF SOCRATES CARVOPOLIS, THE SHIPPING MAGNATE. BUT--YOU MUST KNOW THAT, IF YOU'RE HERE.

CARVOPOLIS INTERNATIONAL *DID* HIRE YOU TO INVESTIGATE MY HUSBAND'S DISAPPEARANCE, DIDN'T THEY?

ER...IN A WAY.

"THEN YOU'VE HEARD ABOUT THE *HARPY*-- THE IMPOSSIBLE BEAST FROM GREEK MYTH...

"...THAT SWOOPED DOWN UPON OUR ISLAND HOME AND CARRIED SOCRATES SCREAMING INTO THE NIGHT."

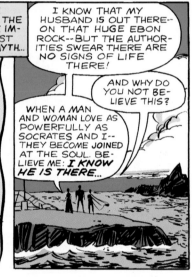

I KNOW THAT MY HUSBAND IS OUT THERE-- ON THAT HUGE EBON ROCK--BUT THE AUTHORITIES SWEAR THERE ARE NO SIGNS OF LIFE THERE!

AND WHY DO YOU NOT BELIEVE THIS?

WHEN A MAN AND WOMAN LOVE AS POWERFULLY AS SOCRATES AND I-- THEY BECOME JOINED AT THE SOUL. BELIEVE ME; *I KNOW HE IS THERE...*

...JUST AS I KNOW THAT YOU WILL FIND HIM.

MRS. CARVOPOLIS--I AM SORRY...

WE *HAVE* INVESTIGATED THOROUGHLY-- AND THE SITUATION IS HOPELESS...

YOUR HUSBAND IS DEAD.

15

NAMOR--WHY DID YOU TELL HER THAT--?

LET HER GRIEVE NOW-- INSTEAD OF WASTING YEARS IN VAIN WAITING FOR ONE WHO CAN NEVER RETURN. I--

BECAUSE THE MAN THAT SHE LOVES IS A FICTION-- A GOD'S IMAGINING THAT MUST WALK THE WORLD NO MORE IF THE COSMOS IS TO SURVIVE.

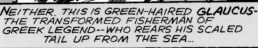

--NEPTUNE!

DEMONS OF THE NORN!

SMAKK!

NEITHER. THIS IS GREEN-HAIRED GLAUCUS-- THE TRANSFORMED FISHERMAN OF GREEK LEGEND--WHO REARS HIS SCALED TAIL UP FROM THE SEA...

...AND HE IS NOT ALONE!

RAWWWK!

THERE IS A MOMENT OF SUDDEN SHOCK, AND DISBELIEF...

...FOLLOWED BY AN EXPLOSION OF REGAL RAGE...

...AND THE BLOOD-SOAKED FURY OF ONE OF HELA'S OWN!

THEN, A FLURRY OF THRASHING LIMBS AND FRANTICALLY-BEATING WINGS--

16

--FOLLOWED BY SILENCE... THEN...

...VICTORY!

PRESENTLY...

SOMEHOW I THINK THE AUTHORITIES WERE SPARED THOSE... OBSTACLES WHEN THEY MADE THEIR AMBIT OF THIS ISLE.

THAT CAN ONLY MEAN THAT MRS. CARVOPOLIS' INTUITION WAS CORRECT. IF WE WERE NOT NEAR OUR GOAL--THEN WHOEVER HAS ETERNITY'S CHILDREN WOULD NOT HAVE ATTACKED.

STILL, THAT DOES NOT CHANGE THE FACT THAT THIS ROCK *IS* INDEED "LIFELESS." WHERE DO WE BEGIN TO LOO--

HOLD!

DO YOU HEAR IT, VALKYRIE--THAT OMINOUS CHANTING... FROM WITHIN THE CAVE?

SHE HEARS...

...THEY ENTER...

...AND--FOR WHAT SEEM LIKE HOURS--THEY DESCEND THROUGH STINKING LABYRINTHS, ALWAYS FOLLOWING THE BONE CHILLING DRONE...

...UNTIL...

THE CHANTING--IT'S COMING FROM DIRECTLY BEHIND THIS DOOR. FIRST WE ARE WAYLAID--*THEN* WE ARE DELIBERATELY LED *HERE?* WHY, NAMOR--WHY?

THAT IS SOMETHING ONLY OUR FOEMAN CAN TELL US, VALKYRIE...

...AND I SEE NO REASON TO KEEP HIM WAITING!

ONE MUSCLE-RIPPLING HEAVE...

17

...AND SANITY COLLAPSES LIKE A HOUSE OF CARDS!

WELCOME, FRIENDS--WE TRUST THE SHOCK OF THE DIMENSION-SPANNING JOURNEY WAS NOT TOO MUCH FOR YOU. AH--BUT YOU APPEAR SO BAFFLED-- SO CONFUSED.

DID NONE OF YOU SUSPECT THAT *NO* OUTSIDE FORCE TOOK US AWAY FROM ETERNITY-- THAT WE CHOSE TO HIDE *OURSELVES?*

BUT WHY? DON'T YOU REALIZE THAT YOU ARE MINUTES AWAY FROM WRITING AN ENDING TO ALL THAT EXISTS?!

OF COURSE! IT WAS SO OBVIOUS THAT WE NEVER CONSIDERED IT!

OUR LIVES HERE ON EARTH HAVE RUN THE GAMUT OF EXPERIENCE-- WE HAVE TASTED THE BEAUTY OF BEING HUMAN--THE INTENSITY OF EMOTION...

...HOW CAN WE GO BACK TO THE INFINITE SOLITUDE THAT IS ETERNITY, AFTER SUCH LIVES? IT IS BETTER TO DIE HUMAN--THAN TO LIVE FOREVER AS *THAT!*

WE HAVE BEEN FOOLS! YOU WANTED US TO TRACE YOU-- TO DALLY IN THE SEARCH--IN BATTLE WITH YOUR PSYCHO-KINETIC CONSTRUCTS...

...BECAUSE THE MORE TIME WE SPENT IN THESE PURSUITS--THE CLOSER THE MULTIVERSE WOULD COME TO DESTRUCTION!

18

CLEARLY-- YOU LEAVE US NO CHOICE! YOU MUST BE RETURNED TO ETERNITY-- YOU MUST BE DRIVEN FROM THOSE BODIES!

IT MAY TAKE ALL MY HELL-BORN POWERS--BUT YOU MUST ALL *DIE!*

FWOOSH!

OOOF!

ZAKT!

B-BECAUSE WE R-R-RE- SPECT Y-YOUR BRAVERY--WE WERE GOING TO L-LET YOU S-STAY ALIVE U-UNTIL THE F-FINAL MOMENT. B-BUT--I... GUESS WE CAN'T.

THEY MAY YET WITNESS THE FINALE, MY SON. EVEN NOW REALITY BEGINS TO LOSE SUB- STANCE--WHILE THE GOOD DOCTOR STRANGE AND HIS FELLOW MYSTICS STRIVE VAINLY TO HOLD IT IN PLACE.

HULK IS NOT SURE WHAT YOU ARE DOING...

...BUT HULK THINKS YOU ARE DOING BAD THING-- AND HULK WILL STO-- *HUH?!*

FEEL FUNNY--HEAD BANGING--CAN'T SEE! WHERE DID NEM-E-SIS MEN GO?

THERE YOU ARE, NEM-E-SIS MEN! HULK WILL STOP YOU NOW! HULK WILL DO GOOD AGAIN!

BUNNT!

THE BRUTE HAS BEEN ENSORCELED-- HE MISTAKES THE VALKYRIE FOR ONE OF OUR ENEMIES!

WHY DOES FISH-MAN SAY THAT NEM-E-SIS IS SWORD-GIRL? HULK KNOW NEM-E-SIS WHEN HULK...

...SEES...

19

AND AS A BEWITCHED **BRUCE BANNER** JOINS VALKYRIE IN THE DEPTHS OF UNCONSCIOUSNESS...

...A SHIVERING NIGHTHAWK STRUGGLES PAINFULLY TO RISE UP FROM THOSE DEPTHS.

...WHILE THE TWO REMAINING DEFENDERS MAKE A LAST, DESPERATE STAND.

BUT--AS WITH MANY LAST STANDS THIS ONE SEEMS DESTINED TO END...

...IN FAILURE!

ARGH! HEAT-- SO MUCH DAMNABLE HEAT-- DRAINING THE LIFE-SUSTAINING WATERS FROM ME!

OOOPS! LOOKS LIKE SUBBY'S HAD IT! I HOPE THAT I CA--

NO IT CAN'T BE--!

MOTHER!!

IN TRUTH, IT IS MERELY *ANOTHER* PSYCHO-KINETIC CONSTRUCT...

...BUT THE EFFECT IS THE SAME.

NOOOOO

SLAM!

HELLCAT DROPS...

...AND HER FADING MOANS COULD BE CREATION'S EPITAPH.

20

AND, ELSEWHERE...

DO YOU UNDERSTAND, KYLE?

THE EIGHT HOURS HAVE *PASSED!* WITH EACH SECOND, OUR EFFORTS TO STAVE OFF OBLIVION GROW WEAKER! BUT THEY HAVE FORGOTTEN ABOUT YOU--*YOU MUST GET UP!*

GET UP-- AND DO WHAT?

THE STRAIN OF PROJECTING THIS ASTRAL IMAGE IS TOO MUCH TO BEAR...

...ALL I CAN SAY IS...

...LOOK TO YOUR HEART...

HE STANDS FACING THEM, ACROSS THIS INSANE EXPANSE OF SURREALITY, FEELING HIMSELF PHASE IN AND OUT OF EXISTENCE ALONG WITH THE TERRAIN AROUND HIM.

WHAT CAN HE DO, HE WONDERS, WHEN THE LIKES OF NAMOR AND THE HULK HAVE FAILED? AND THEN HE PONDERS DOCTOR STRANGE'S WORDS: "LOOK TO YOUR HEART."

HE DOES.

AND HE SPEAKS.

YOU SAY YOU'VE LEARNED WHAT IT MEANS TO BE HUMAN--AND YET YOU'D SEE US ALL WIPED OUT RATHER THAN ENDURE A FATE YOU FIND... UNPLEASANT. THAT'S NOT HUMANITY--THAT'S THE DARKNESS THAT EATS *AWAY* AT HUMANITY!

REAL HUMANITY MEANS SACRIFICE IN THE NAME OF LOVE-- THE SAME KIND OF SELFLESS LOVE OTHERS HAVE SHOWN *YOU!* UNTIL YOU'VE LEARNED *THAT*--YOU'LL *NEVER* BE HUMAN!

"THINK OF YOUR FAMILIES...

"... OF THOSE THAT EVEN NOW, ARE CRYING FOR THE THE LOSS OF YOU!

"WILL YOU SEE THEM PERISH BECAUSE OF YOUR OWN FEARS...

"... OR WILL YOU BE *TRULY* HUMAN?!"

21

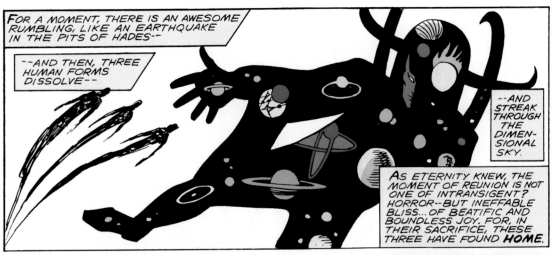

FOR A MOMENT, THERE IS AN AWESOME RUMBLING, LIKE AN EARTHQUAKE IN THE PITS OF HADES--

--AND THEN, THREE HUMAN FORMS DISSOLVE--

--AND STREAK THROUGH THE DIMENSIONAL SKY.

AS ETERNITY KNEW, THE MOMENT OF REUNION IS NOT ONE OF INTRANSIGENT? HORROR--BUT INEFFABLE BLISS...OF BEATIFIC AND BOUNDLESS JOY. FOR, IN THEIR SACRIFICE, THESE THREE HAVE FOUND **HOME.**

INSTANTANEOUSLY, IN GREENWICH VILLAGE, EIGHT EXHAUSTED HEROES...**COME DOWN**...

I AM PROUD OF YOU, KYLE. VERY PROUD. I KNEW THAT ONE OF YOUR SPIRIT COULD BE COUNTED ON TO FIND THE KEY.

YOU HAVE SHOWN THAT THE REAL KYLE RICHMOND IS NOT THE INEPT BUNGLER YOU BELIEVE HIM TO BE...

...BUT A MAN OF GREAT WORTH-- AND GREAT UNDERSTANDING.

HUH? WHAT'D YOU SAY, DOC. I WASN'T LISTENING.

I WAS JUST THINKING ABOUT TWO SWEET OLD PEOPLE IN RUSSIA...

...WHO ARE GOING TO FEEL VERY ALONE TONIGHT.

NEXT: "THE WOMAN BEHIND THE MAN!"

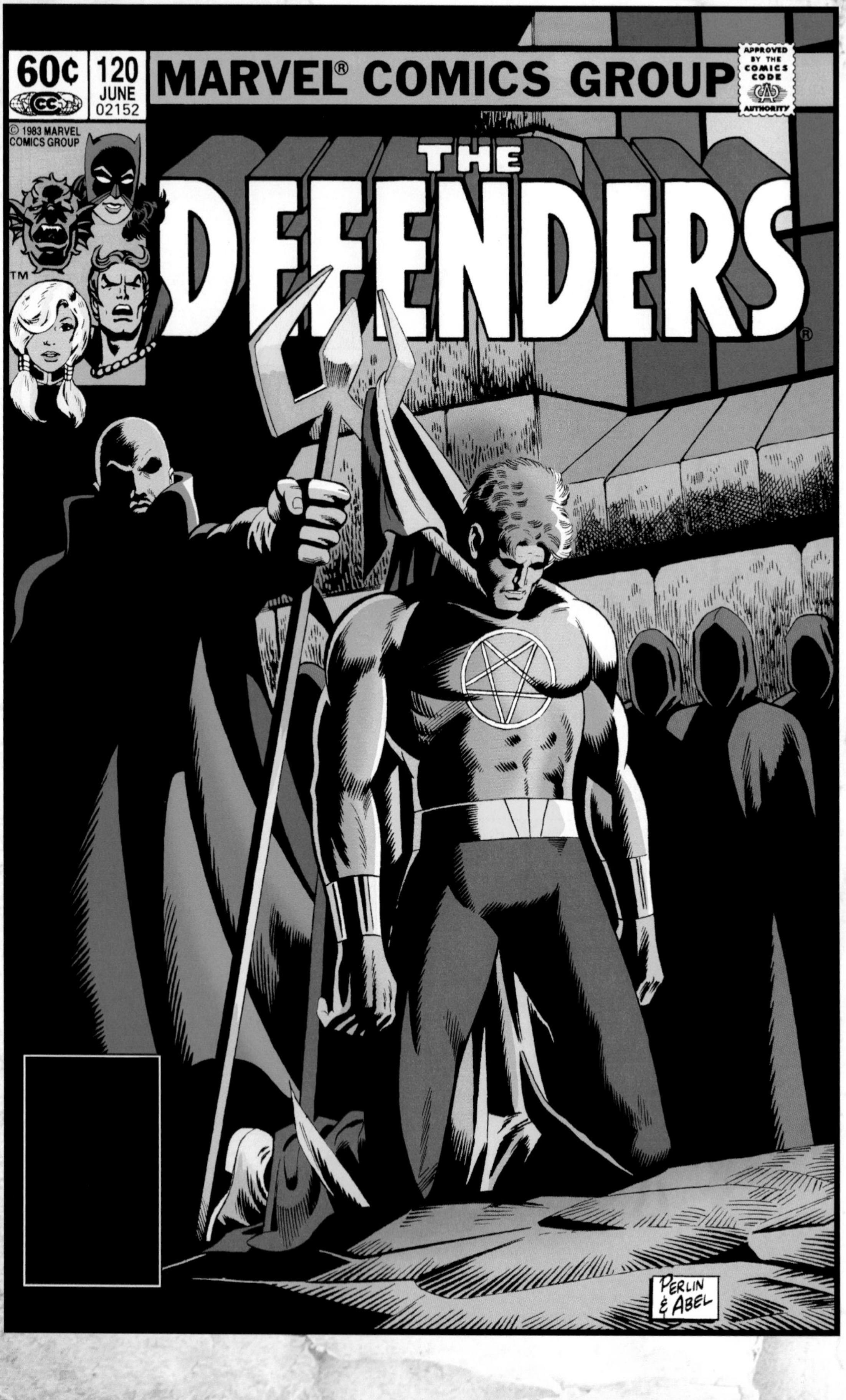

60¢
120
JUNE
02152
MARVEL® COMICS GROUP
APPROVED BY THE COMICS CODE AUTHORITY
© 1983 MARVEL COMICS GROUP
TM
THE
DEFENDERS®
PERLIN & ABEL

STAN LEE PRESENTS: THE DYNAMIC DEFENDERS!™

Sanctuary!

J.M. DeMATTEIS
scripter

DON PERLIN
penciler
ABEL, DeMULDER
& MUSHYNSKY
inkers

SHELLY LEFERMAN
letterer

GEORGE ROUSSOS
colorist

ALLEN MILGROM
editor

JIM SHOOTER
chief

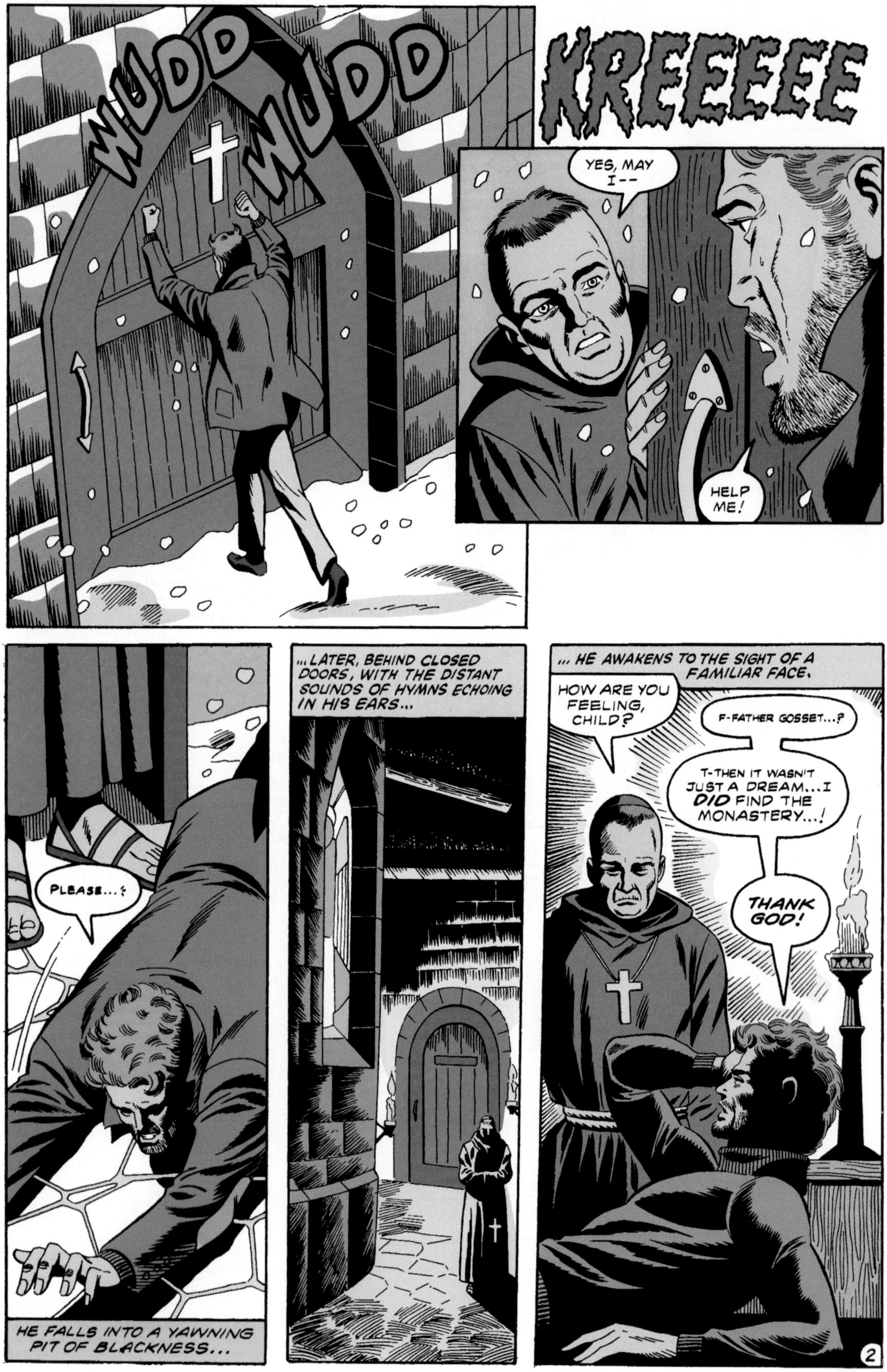
WUDD WUDD
KREEEEEE
YES, MAY I--
HELP ME!
PLEASE...!
HE FALLS INTO A YAWNING PIT OF BLACKNESS...
...LATER, BEHIND CLOSED DOORS, WITH THE DISTANT SOUNDS OF HYMNS ECHOING IN HIS EARS...
... HE AWAKENS TO THE SIGHT OF A FAMILIAR FACE.
HOW ARE YOU FEELING, CHILD?
F-FATHER GOSSET...?
T-THEN IT WASN'T JUST A DREAM...I DID FIND THE MONASTERY...!
THANK GOD!
2

PLEASE, DAIMON... LIE BACK. YOU MUST REST.

N-NO. I'VE COME SO FAR...TO TALK TO YOU. I... DON'T KNOW HOW MANY DAYS IT'S BEEN...SINCE I LEFT WASHINGTON *...HOW LONG I'VE BEEN WANDERING...LIKE A MAN IN A DREAM. BUT A VOICE *WITHIN* THAT DREAM SAID... "FIND FATHER GOSSET ...IF ANY MAN CAN HELP YOU...*HE* CAN...

*ISSUE #118 - AL.

I'M NOT THE SAME RAYMOND GOSSET WHO TAUGHT YOU AT THE SEMINARY THOSE LONG YEARS AGO, DAIMON. LIFE AS ABBOT OF THIS MONASTERY HAS CHANGED ME -- EVEN AS LIFE IN THE WORLD OUTSIDE HAS CHANGED *YOU*. BUT YOU KNOW THAT I *WILL* HELP... IN WHATEVER WAY I CAN.

O-OF COURSE I KNOW. WHEN THOSE HORRIBLE VISIONS AND SEIZURES HAUNTED MY NIGHTS AT THE SEMINARY... I TURNED TO YOU -- AND YOU EASED MY TROUBLED HEART.

AND WHEN I *LEFT* THAT CLOISTERED LIFE BEHIND, DISCOVERING THAT THOSE SEIZURES HAD BEEN THE FIRST SIGNS OF MY SATANIC HERITAGE RISING TO THE FORE...YOU WERE THE ONLY ONE I *DARED* SHARE THAT TRUTH WITH.

ALL THESE YEARS WE'VE CORRESPONDED, FATHER. ALL THESE YEARS YOU'VE BEEN THERE FOR ME. BUT I NEED MORE THAN YOUR LETTERS NOW--

--I NEED *YOU!*

DAIMON, THE LAST I HEARD YOU HAD FINALLY BROKEN *AWAY* FROM YOUR ACCURSED FATHER'S INFLUENCE. * "AT LAST THERE IS HOPE," YOU WROTE.

AND THERE *WAS!* MY DARKSOUL'S HOLD ON ME HAD DIMINISHED, CONTROLLED AND WEAKENED BY A NEW-FOUND INNER RESOLVE... AN EVER-GROWING FAITH!

*DEFENDERS #105.

BUT BATTLING THE DARKSOUL WAS THE ONLY LIFE I'D KNOWN! WITHOUT THAT BATTLE TO GIVE ME PURPOSE AND MEANING, I WAS LEFT TO CONFRONT *NOT* THE FIRST-BORN *SON OF SATAN* ...BUT A *MAN* NAMED DAIMON HELLSTROM!

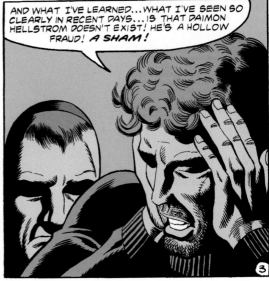

AND WHAT I'VE LEARNED...WHAT I'VE SEEN SO CLEARLY IN RECENT DAYS...IS THAT DAIMON HELLSTROM DOESN'T EXIST! HE'S A HOLLOW FRAUD! *A SHAM!*

3

145

THERE'S A WOMAN I'VE FALLEN IN LOVE WITH, FATHER... A WOMAN NAMED PATSY WALKER--WHO'S TOUCHED ME AS NO OTHER SOUL HAS BEFORE. BUT--HOW CAN I OFFER MYSELF TO HER--*IF I DON'T KNOW WHO I AM!*

DAIMON... *CHILD--*

--TWO SIDES OF YOUR NATURE HAVE WAGED A LONG AND SAVAGE WAR, NEARLY DESTROYING EACH OTHER IN THE PROCESS. IT WILL TAKE *TIME* FOR YOUR SOUL TO HEAL ITSELF...TO *FIND* ITSELF.

BUT-- WHAT IF THERE'S *NOTHING* TO FIND?!

WHAT IF MY ONLY DESTINY--

--IS TO BE--

--*THIS?!*

DEAR GOD--!

④

146

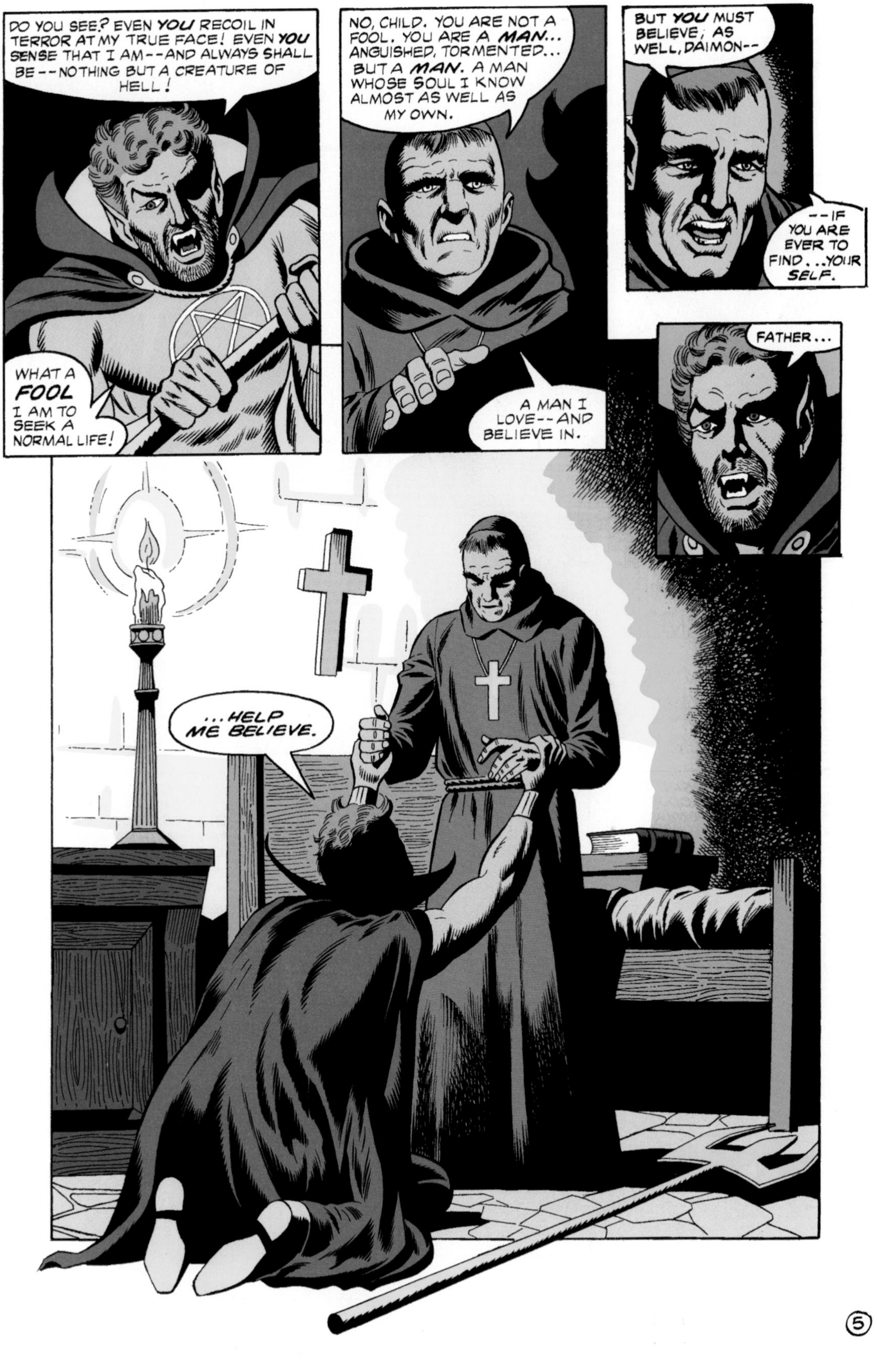
DO YOU SEE? EVEN YOU RECOIL IN TERROR AT MY TRUE FACE! EVEN YOU SENSE THAT I AM--AND ALWAYS SHALL BE--NOTHING BUT A CREATURE OF HELL!
WHAT A FOOL I AM TO SEEK A NORMAL LIFE!
NO, CHILD. YOU ARE NOT A FOOL. YOU ARE A MAN... ANGUISHED, TORMENTED... BUT A MAN. A MAN WHOSE SOUL I KNOW ALMOST AS WELL AS MY OWN.
A MAN I LOVE--AND BELIEVE IN.
BUT YOU MUST BELIEVE, AS WELL, DAIMON--
--IF YOU ARE EVER TO FIND...YOUR SELF.
FATHER...
...HELP ME BELIEVE.
5

A NEW DAWN.

EXCUSE ME, MY FRIEND--

--ARE YOU DAIMON...THE ABBOT'S OLD STUDENT-- WHO'S COME TO STAY WITH US FOR A WHILE?

I AM.

I'M--*BROTHER JOSHUA.* I JUST WANTED TO INTRODUCE MYSELF...AND OFFER WHATEVER HELP I CAN TO MAKE YOUR STAY WITH US A FRUITFUL ONE.

BUT I MUST BE DISTURBING YOU. WE CAN TALK LATER, WHEN--

NO, BROTHER--YOU WEREN'T DISTURBING ME. I WAS ONLY WATCHING THE MONKS IN MEDITATION...DRINKING IN THE SILENCE--AND THE PEACE.

WELL, THEN-- WOULD YOU CARE TO JOIN ME FOR A WALK? SOME PLACE WHERE OUR CHATTER WON'T BOTHER THE OTHERS?

I'D LIKE THAT VERY MUCH.

HAVE YOU BEEN HERE LONG, JOSHUA?

I CAME TO THE MONASTERY SOME MONTHS AGO--A PITIABLE, CONFUSED WRECK OF A MAN--WITH NO MEMORY OF WHO I WAS...WHERE I HAD COME *FROM.*

THE BROTHERS TOOK ME IN...NURTURED ME BACK TO HEALTH...BROUGHT ME ALIVE --PHYSICALLY, MENTALLY, AND SPIRITUALLY.

AND YOU STAYED?

INDEED I DID. IN FOUR DAYS I'LL BE TAKING MY FORMAL VOWS.

6

148

YET YOU AREN'T INSIDE-- MEDITATING WITH THE OTHERS.

I'M SLIGHTLY UNCOMFORTABLE WITH ALL THE POMP AND TRADITION. IT'S THE SIMPLICITY AND HONESTY OF THIS LIFE THAT APPEALS TO ME MOST.

AND *THAT* YOU CAN SEE...FEEL... ALL AROUND US.

I PRAY I CAN TAKE SOME OF THAT FEELING *WITH* ME AFTER I'VE LEFT.

AT THE VERY LEAST, I HOPE I CAN COME TO BETTER UNDERSTAND... MYSELF.

ALL THE ANSWERS ARE INSIDE US, DAIMON.

WHY, SOMETIMES I THINK THAT-- IN MY HEART-- IS THE GREATEST POWER MAN COULD EVER KNOW. AND I FEEL AS IF I'LL BE ABLE TO *FIND* THAT POWER-- AND THE SELF-KNOWLEDGE THAT MUST COME WITH IT-- RIGHT...

...HERE--?

STRANGE. I WONDER WHAT FRIGHTENED HER SO.

WHO KNOWS? MAYBE OUR HEADY CONVERSATION WAS TOO MUCH TO BEAR.

I *DO* HAVE A TENDENCY TO DIVE INTO THE GREAT MYSTERIES AT THE DROP OF A HAT. I...HOPE I HAVEN'T BORED YOU, DAIMON.

BORED ME? NO. I SENSE THAT WE ARE...MUCH ALIKE, YOU AND I.

BUT YOU'LL HAVE TO EXCUSE ME, BROTHER JOSHUA. I PROMISED TO LET THE ABBOT TAKE ME ON A TOUR OF THE MONASTERY-- AND I DON'T WANT TO KEEP HIM WAITING. YOU KNOW HOW HE IS ABOUT PUNCTUALITY.

THEN I WON'T HOLD YOU ANY LONGER. TAKE CARE--

--BROTHER.

⑦

NEW YORK CITY: THE UPPER WEST SIDE BROWNSTONE THAT IS HOME AND HEADQUARTERS TO FOUR OF THE DYNAMIC DEFENDERS...

OH, MY--!

WUZZAT?

THAT CAME FROM PATSY'S ROOM!

LOOK ALIVE, GROUP--THIS COULD BE TROUBLE!

WORRY NOT, BEAST, THE VALKYRIE STANDS READY!

EASE OFF, FOLKS... THERE'S NO SUPER-VILLAIN AT WORK HERE--

--JUST A NASTY OLD NIGHTMARE.

IT'S OKAY, PATSY. IT WAS ONLY A DREAM.

I WISH IT WERE ONLY A DREAM, ISAAC...

WHAT DO YOU MEAN, PAT?

IT'S DAIMON, HANK. HE'S IN TROUBLE. HE NEEDS US. I... SAW HIM.

YOU WERE SLEEPING, PATSY. YOU SAW WHAT YOUR MIND WANTED YOU TO SEE.

YOU CAN DOUBT ME IF YOU WANT-- BUT I KNOW WHAT I FELT.

I-I'VE BEEN SLOWLY COMING TO GRIPS WITH MY RETURNING MENTAL POWERS ...TRYING TO SORT THEM OUT ...UNDERSTAND THEM--AND THEIR LIMITS.

ONE THING I'M SURE OF IS THAT I'VE BECOME... IN TUNE WITH THE PEOPLE I CARE ABOUT... SENSITIVE TO THEIR MOODS, THEIR WANTS, THEIR FEARS.

AND I FEEL IN TUNE WITH DAIMON-- MOST OF ALL.

BELIEVE ME, HANK-- THIS ISN'T A HUNCH.

HE'S IN TROUBLE.

8

THE MONASTERY... THREE DAYS LATER.

WELL, DAIMON--

--YOU'RE CERTAINLY THROWING YOURSELF INTO YOUR WORK WITH GREAT ENTHUSIASM.

THAT TRACTOR'S BEEN NEEDING ADJUSTMENTS FOR WEEKS.

I FEEL...WONDERFUL, FATHER! THIS WORK, THIS LIFE--IS SO SIMPLE... YET SO FULFILLING!

MORE AND MORE I WANT TO REMAIN HERE WITH YOU, AND WITH GOD.

DON'T LET A MOMENT'S PEACE FOOL YOU, CHILD. YOU CAN RETREAT HERE--BUT YOU CAN'T *HIDE.* YOU HAVE TO LIVE, SIDE-BY-SIDE WITH YOUR BROTHER MONKS-- DEALING WITH EACH OTHER'S COMPLEX PERSONALITIES AND ALL-TOO-HUMAN FOIBLES!

ALL IN ALL, IT'S A MICROCOSM OF THE WORLD OUTSIDE. THE PRESSURES CAN BE EVERY BIT AS POWERFUL HERE.

BUT YOU'VE GOT SO MUCH *LOVE* TO SUSTAIN YOU. WHY, WHEN I WAS TALKING TO BROTHER JOSHUA...

WHAT IS IT, FATHER? YOU LOOK... DISTURBED.

I DON'T KNOW. THERE IS SOMETHING *ABOUT* BROTHER JOSHUA THAT-- I WISH I COULD PUT MY FINGER ON IT. HE REMINDS ME OF...

YES?

OH...IT'S PROBABLY NOTHING MORE THAN AN OLD MAN'S MIND, PLAYING TRICKS ON HIM. PLEASE-- FORGET THAT I MENTIONED ANYTHING.

WELL, DON'T JUST STAND THERE DAY- DREAMING, MY BOY-- THERE'S WORK TO BE DONE!

9

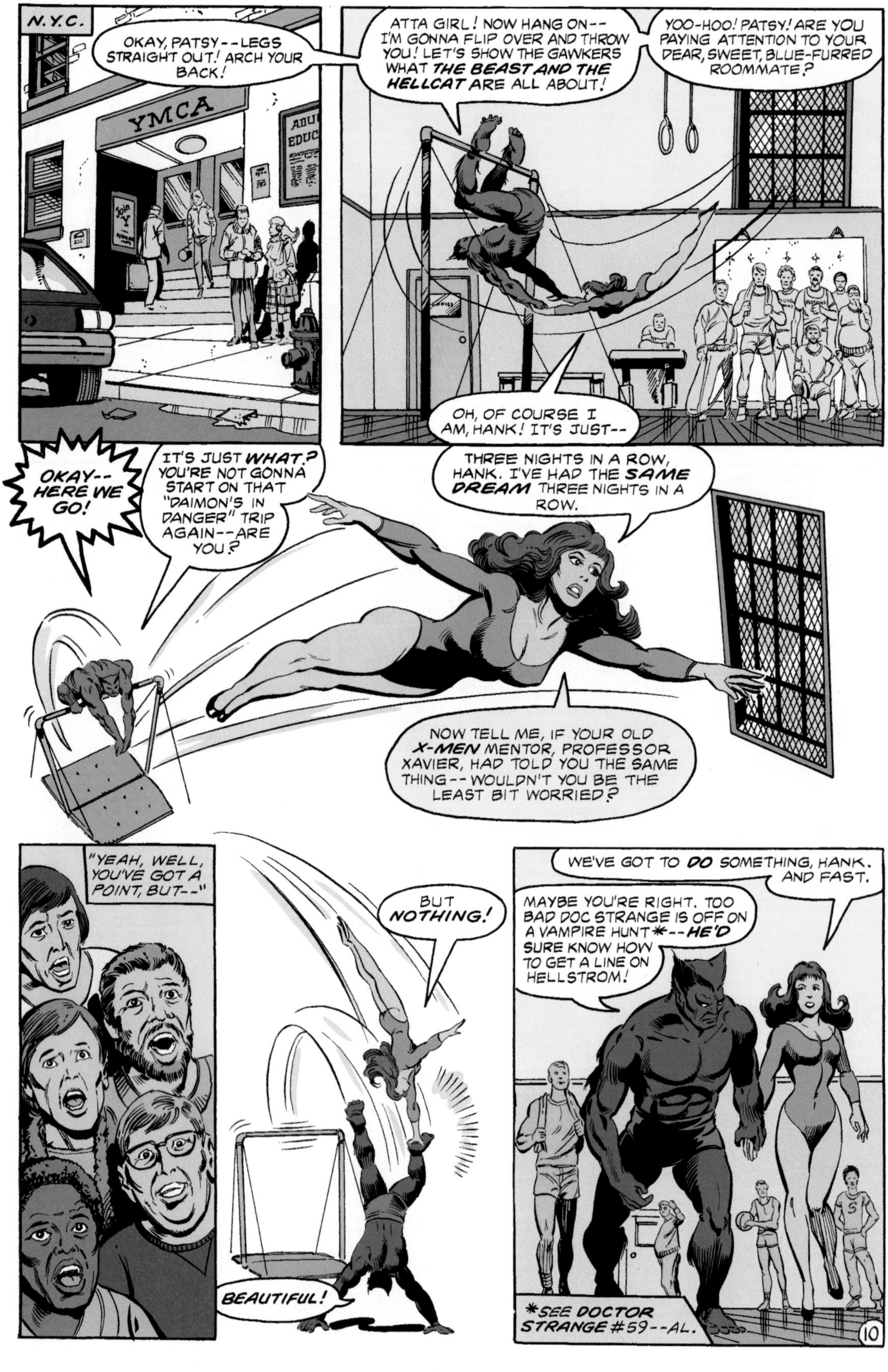
N.Y.C.
OKAY, PATSY--LEGS STRAIGHT OUT! ARCH YOUR BACK!
YMCA
ATTA GIRL! NOW HANG ON-- I'M GONNA FLIP OVER AND THROW YOU! LET'S SHOW THE GAWKERS WHAT THE BEAST AND THE HELLCAT ARE ALL ABOUT!
YOO-HOO! PATSY! ARE YOU PAYING ATTENTION TO YOUR DEAR, SWEET, BLUE-FURRED ROOMMATE?
OH, OF COURSE I AM, HANK! IT'S JUST--
OKAY-- HERE WE GO!
IT'S JUST WHAT? YOU'RE NOT GONNA START ON THAT "DAIMON'S IN DANGER" TRIP AGAIN--ARE YOU?
THREE NIGHTS IN A ROW, HANK. I'VE HAD THE SAME DREAM THREE NIGHTS IN A ROW.
NOW TELL ME, IF YOUR OLD X-MEN MENTOR, PROFESSOR XAVIER, HAD TOLD YOU THE SAME THING-- WOULDN'T YOU BE THE LEAST BIT WORRIED?
"YEAH, WELL, YOU'VE GOT A POINT, BUT--"
BUT NOTHING!
BEAUTIFUL!
WE'VE GOT TO DO SOMETHING, HANK. AND FAST.
MAYBE YOU'RE RIGHT. TOO BAD DOC STRANGE IS OFF ON A VAMPIRE HUNT*--HE'D SURE KNOW HOW TO GET A LINE ON HELLSTROM!
*SEE DOCTOR STRANGE #59--AL.
10

"LET'S GO SEE WHAT VAL'S UP TO...MAYBE *SHE'LL* HAVE SOME SAGE ADVICE!"

CHECK IT OUT, HOWIE! THE CHICK THINKS SHE CAN DEAD LIFT THREE HUNDRED AND FIFTY POUNDS.

NOT ONLY THAT, PAT--BUT SHE THINKS SHE'S GONNA DO IT WITH ONLY--

-- ONE HAND.?.?!!!

THIS HAS GOTTA BE A TRICK! WHAT ARE YOU, LADY--ONE OF THEM RUSSIAN ATHLETES WHO'S REALLY A GUY IN DISGUISE?

I AM *THE VALKYRIE,* GODDESS OF ASGARD! AND YOU WOULD DO WELL TO UNHAND ME, WRETCH!

HEY, WHAT'RE YOU GETTIN' SO UPTIGHT ABOUT! I JUST WANNA--

I SAID--

--UNHAND ME!

OH-OH!

Y'KNOW, LADIES -- I THINK THE NEXT TIME WE WANT TO WORK OUT A LITTLE, WE SHOULD TRY *AVENGERS MANSION!*

THIS PLACE DEFINITELY HAS ITS LIMITATIONS!

NO SMOKING

EXIT

11

MIDNIGHT--AND THE MONASTERY IS WRAPPED IN BLANKETS OF SILENCE AND SLEEP.

BUT THERE IS ONE TO WHOM SLEEP IS A STRANGER THIS NIGHT...

...AND WHO BREAKS THE SILENCE WITH A TORRENT OF WORDS.

WORDS OF ADJURATION.

WORDS OF PRAYER.

FOR THE FIRST TIME IN OVER A DECADE, DAIMON HELLSTROM HAS KNEELED BEFORE HIS GOD, AND ASKED FOR HELP. FOR GUIDANCE.

FOR A SIGN.

SUDDENLY--AS IF IN RESPONSE TO HIS ENTREATY--HELL-STROM'S LUNGS SEEM TO SHRIVEL UP...

...HIS BREATH COMES HARD--IN SHALLOW GASPS...

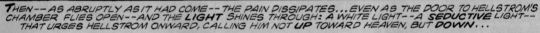

...AND RAZOR-TIPPED FINGERS OF PAIN DIG DEEP INTO HIS HEART, SLAMMING HIM DOWN LIKE SOME WEIGHTLESS DOLL.

THEN--AS ABRUPTLY AS IT HAD COME--THE PAIN DISSIPATES...EVEN AS THE DOOR TO HELLSTROM'S CHAMBER FLIES OPEN--AND THE *LIGHT* SHINES THROUGH: A WHITE LIGHT--A *SEDUCTIVE* LIGHT-- THAT URGES HELLSTROM ONWARD, CALLING HIM NOT *UP* TOWARD HEAVEN, BUT *DOWN*...

12

...TOWARD DESTINY!

A DESTINY THAT WEARS THE ROBES OF BROTHER JOSHUA.

A DESTINY THAT KNEELS WITHIN A NIMBUS OF BLINDING LIGHT.

BUT, AT HELLSTROM'S APPROACH, THE NIMBUS DIMS, DIES...MELTING AWAY INTO THE SHADOWS.

THAT WAS...MOST INTERESTING.

JOSHUA...?

HELLSTROM-- WHAT ARE YOU DOING?

DON'T TOUCH ME!

YARRGH!

OH, LORD...OH, LORD... I DON'T UNDERSTAND! WHAT IS IT? WHAT'S HAPPENING TO ME?

DAIMON...PLEASE...DON'T TELL THEM! DON'T TELL THEM WHAT YOU'VE JUST SEEN! Y-YOU'LL MAKE THEM AFRAID ...AND THEY'LL...THEY'LL DRIVE ME OUT!

PLEASE, DAIMON--I BEG OF YOU!

BE STILL, JOSHUA. BE CALM.

I WILL TELL THEM NOTHING.

THAT THERE IS SOME STRANGE POWER ALIVE WITHIN YOU IS ALL-TOO-CLEAR. BUT I HAVE KNOWN SUCH POWER IN MY DAY--

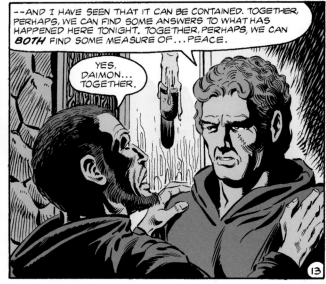

--AND I HAVE SEEN THAT IT CAN BE CONTAINED. TOGETHER, PERHAPS, WE CAN FIND SOME ANSWERS TO WHAT HAS HAPPENED HERE TONIGHT. TOGETHER, PERHAPS, WE CAN BOTH FIND SOME MEASURE OF...PEACE.

YES, DAIMON... TOGETHER.

13

TWO A.M.--THE GREENWICH VILLAGE SANCTUM OF THE SORCERER SUPREME, *DOCTOR STRANGE*.

THE DOCTOR IS *OUT*...

...BUT HIS HIGHLY UNUSUAL HOUSE-GUEST--THE MULTI-MINDED BEING CALLED *THE OVER-MIND*--IS IN...

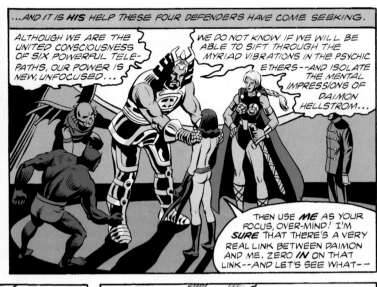

...AND IT IS *HIS* HELP THESE FOUR DEFENDERS HAVE COME SEEKING.

ALTHOUGH WE ARE THE UNITED CONSCIOUSNESS OF SIX POWERFUL TELE-PATHS, OUR POWER IS NEW, UNFOCUSED...

WE DO NOT KNOW IF WE WILL BE ABLE TO SIFT THROUGH THE MYRIAD VIBRATIONS IN THE PSYCHIC ETHERS--AND ISOLATE THE MENTAL IMPRESSIONS OF DAIMON HELLSTROM...

THEN USE *ME* AS YOUR FOCUS, OVER-MIND! I'M *SURE* THAT THERE'S A VERY REAL LINK BETWEEN DAIMON AND ME. ZERO *IN* ON THAT LINK--AND LET'S SEE WHAT--

--HAPPENS...?

WHAT IN SAM HILL--?!

MOST...EXTRA-ORDINARY. YOUR MIND, PATSY WALKER, IS QUITE FORMIDABLE. THE PSIONIC FEEDBACK CAUSED US --MUCH PAIN.

BUT WE *WERE* ABLE TO UNVEIL AN IMAGE ...A LOCATION... A DIRECTION TO FOLLOW...

YEAH, I CAN SEE IT TOO, NOW. WELL, WHAT'RE WE WAITING FOR, TROOPS? DAIMON NEEDS US!

WHEN THE MASTER RETURNS, MISS WALKER --WHERE SHALL I TELL HIM YOU HAVE GONE?

MASSACHUSSETS, WONG! AND I'M AFRAID I CAN'T BE MUCH MORE SPECIFIC--

--YET!

14

MORNING. THE TIME, AT LAST, HAS COME WHEN BROTHER JOSHUA MUST TAKE THE FINAL STEP; DRIVE THE FINAL WEDGE BETWEEN HIMSELF AND THE OUTSIDE WORLD; SPEAK THE VOWS THAT WILL MAKE HIM ONE WITH THE BROTHERS OF THE ORDER.

NEARBY, DAIMON HELLSTROM WATCHES THE CENTURIES-OLD CEREMONY UNFOLD, HIS HEART TORN BETWEEN A STRANGE SENSE OF DREAD-- AND AN EVEN STRANGER... ENVY.

...DEAR BROTHER--

--THROUGH BAPTISM YOU ARE ALREADY DEAD TO SIN AND RISEN IN THE LORD.

WILL YOU LIVE OUT YOUR DAYS IN THIS MONASTERY-- LIVE FOR GOD ALONE-- IN SOLITUDE AND SILENCE-- FAITHFUL UNTO DEATH?

I... WILL.

DO YOU WISH NOW TO UNITE YOURSELF MORE CLOSELY TO HIM-- THROUGH THE BOND OF MONASTIC LIFE?

15

157

RISE THEN, BROTHER JOSHUA-- AS ONE OF US.

RISE, ABBOT? YES... YES! I *HAVE* RISEN. BUT NOT--I FEAR --AS YOU BELIEVE!

I REMEMBER!!

THIS CEREMONY-- HAS STIRRED SOMETHING IN THE DEEPEST CAVERNS OF MY BEING! WASHED THE BLINDNESS FROM MY EYES! I...I...

JOSHUA'S EYES...HIS VOICE...HIS ENTIRE *BEARING* SEEMS --TRANSFORMED! WHAT HAS HA--

YARRRR!

MY CHEST! I BURN! I BURN!

I SEE NOW WHY I WAS DRAWN *HERE* OF ALL PLACES --TO THIS SEAT OF GREAT POWER, WHERE THE BELIEF IN MIRACLES IS STRONG, INVIOLATE!

A BELIEF POWERFUL ENOUGH TO SHATTER MY AMNESIA--AND MAKE ME ONCE AGAIN--

16

--THE MIRACLE MAN!!! *

--I AM YOUR MASTER!

HA-HA-HA! FLY, LITTLE BROTHERS, LIKE THE ANGELS YOU SO WISH TO BE!

THEN PERHAPS I SHALL ALLOW YOU TO KNEEL BEFORE ME!

DO YOU SEE, FOOLS? YOU SOUGHT TO MAKE ME YOUR BROTHER, WHEN IN TRUTH --

*LAST SEEN IN MARVEL TWO-IN-ONE #8

BEFORE THE ONLY MAN ALIVE WHO CAN TRULY--MAKE MIRACLES!

THIS IS...INSANE! G-GOSSET...NEEDS ME... AND I...CAN HARDLY... MOVE!

MY CHEST... MY CHEST!

JOSHUA--WHATEVER THIS POWER IS YOU POSSESS... CAN'T YOU SEE THAT IT'S UNHOLY? A TRANS-GRESSION AGAINST GOD?

I AM MY OWN GOD NOW, OLD MAN--

--AND MINE IS THE WILL THAT CONTROLS YOU ALL!

MINE, THE WHIM THAT CAN RAISE YOU UP--

--OR CAST YOU DOWN!

17

159

PLEASE, JOSHUA -- WHAT YOU ARE DOING IS NOT RIGHT! YOU MOCK GOD'S WILL!

SPARE ME YOUR SERMONS ABOUT GOD'S WILL, OLD MAN!

YOU REMIND ME OF *THE CHEEMUZWA* --THE INDIAN MYSTICS WHO FIRST TAUGHT ME HOW TO UNLEASH THE MIRACULOUS POWERS OF MY SOUL!

THOSE BEAD-BEDECKED, HEAD-DRESSED MORONS THWARTED ME TIME AND AGAIN IN MY EFFORTS TO MASTER MANKIND! AND ALWAYS DID THEY LECTURE ME ABOUT THE CREATOR'S LIFEPLAN!*

*BACK IN FANTASTIC FOUR #138 --AL.

WELL -- I HAVE HAD ENOUGH LECTURES!

YOUR ILK SPEAKS AS IF YOUR EVERY PIOUS UTTERANCE SHOULD BE ENGRAVED IN STONE-- SO STONE YOU SHALL BE... NOW AND FOREVER!

JOSHUA --HEAR ME! I UNDERSTAND YOU! WE ARE, AS I ONCE SAID, TWO OF A KIND!

I, OF ALL MEN, KNOW WHAT IT IS TO BE SEDUCED BY A DARKLING POWER! I, OF ALL MEN, KNOW WHAT IT IS TO BE TEMPTED BY SIN!

AND I, OF ALL MEN--

--HAVE THE MEANS TO STOP YOU!

18

160

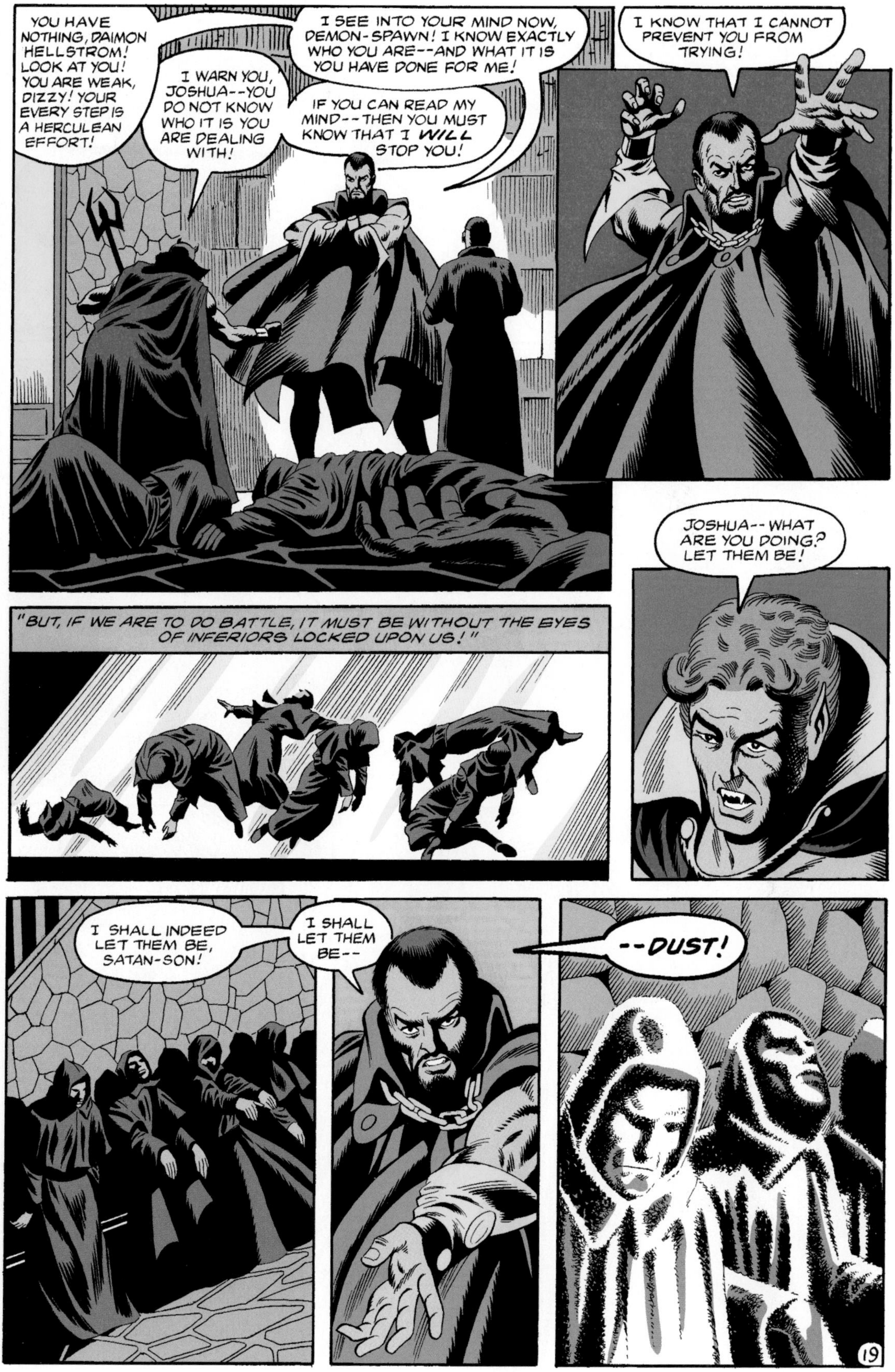
YOU HAVE NOTHING, DAIMON HELLSTROM! LOOK AT YOU! YOU ARE WEAK, DIZZY! YOUR EVERY STEP IS A HERCULEAN EFFORT!
I WARN YOU, JOSHUA--YOU DO NOT KNOW WHO IT IS YOU ARE DEALING WITH!
I SEE INTO YOUR MIND NOW, DEMON-SPAWN! I KNOW EXACTLY WHO YOU ARE--AND WHAT IT IS YOU HAVE DONE FOR ME!
IF YOU CAN READ MY MIND--THEN YOU MUST KNOW THAT I WILL STOP YOU!
I KNOW THAT I CANNOT PREVENT YOU FROM TRYING!
"BUT, IF WE ARE TO DO BATTLE, IT MUST BE WITHOUT THE EYES OF INFERIORS LOCKED UPON US!"
JOSHUA--WHAT ARE YOU DOING? LET THEM BE!
I SHALL INDEED LET THEM BE, SATAN-SON!
I SHALL LET THEM BE--
--DUST!
19

YOU HAVE WORKED YOUR LAST MIRACLE, MONSTER!

TASTE OF MY SOULFIRE --AND FALL!

TASTE IT? DON'T YOU UNDERSTAND YET, HELLSTROM?

I AM FEASTING UPON IT!

FEAST, THEN, UPON MY TRIDENT, TOO! FEAST UPON MY RAGE!

YOUR RAGE IS IMPOTENT, WRETCH-- AS ARE YOU!

BUT I SEE I MUST SPELL IT OUT FOR YOU!

N-NO...WHAT ARE YOU DOING?

I AM ROBBING YOU OF YOUR BIRTHRIGHT DAIMON HELLSTROM!

I AM ABSORBING THAT BLACK FORCE WHICH ACCELERATED MY AWAKENING FROM THE MYSTICALLY-INDUCED AMNESIA WHICH THOSE ACCURSED CHEEMUZWA PLACED UPON ME AS PUNISHMENT FOR MY PAST MISDEEDS!

BY THE SEVEN CIRCLES! I UNDERSTAND!

AT LAST-- I UNDERSTAND!

MY... DARK... SOUL...

OF COURSE, YOU IDIOT! IT WAS YOUR *DARKSOUL* THAT CALLED TO ME--YOUR *DARKSOUL* THAT SENSED THE LATENT POWER STIRRING INSIDE ME AND URGED IT TO LIFE!

FOR TOO LONG HAVE YOU DENIED YOUR SECOND-SELF! FOR TOO LONG HAVE YOU REPRESSED AND DILUTED IT! IT WAS *DYING*, DAIMON! BUT NOW, WITHIN MY BREAST--

--THE DARKSOUL IS UNLEASHED--

AND THE MIRACLE MAN STANDS SUPREME!

21

ELSEWHERE--A HASTILY-BORROWED AVENGERS QUINJET ARCS GRACEFULLY THROUGH THE STARLIT SKY.

IT'S A BEAUTIFUL SIGHT...MOONLIGHT GLINTING OFF THE SHIP'S SURFACE, ITS SLEEK, SILVERY FORM DOING AIR-DANCES OVER THE EAST RIVER.

BUT, INSIDE THE CRAFT, THE AMBIENCE IS SOMEWHAT MORE...GRIM.

THE BEAST, THE VALKYRIE, AND THE GARGOYLE UNDERSTAND, AT LAST, THAT ONE OF THEIR NUMBER IS IN TERRIBLE DANGER, THEY UNDERSTAND, TOO, THAT THEIR FAILURE TO BELIEVE HELLCAT'S *WARNINGS* ABOUT THAT DANGER COULD VERY WELL HAVE COST DAIMON HELLSTROM HIS LIFE.

AND SO THERE IS NO CONVERSATION AS THE SHIP MOVES WESTWARD TOWARD MASSACHUSSETS. THERE IS ONLY THE DISCOMFORTING SOUND OF THE QUINJET'S ENGINES...

...SCREAMING IN THE NIGHT.

NEXT: IT'S THE DEFENDERS VERSUS THE MIRACLE MAN! Plus THE SON OF SATAN'S LAST STAND!

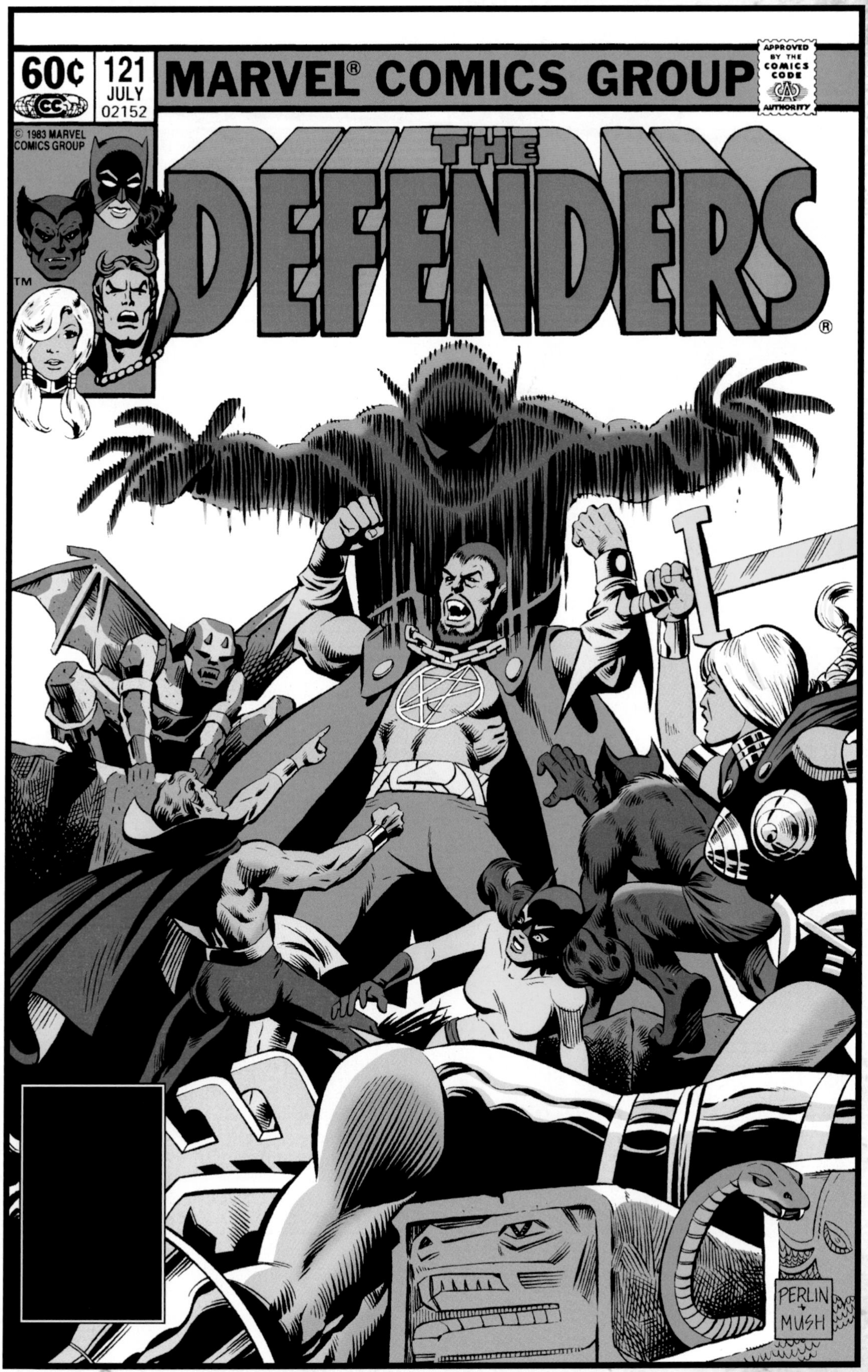

60¢
121
JULY
02152
MARVEL® COMICS GROUP
APPROVED BY THE COMICS CODE AUTHORITY
© 1983 MARVEL COMICS GROUP
TM
THE DEFENDERS®
PERLIN + MUSH

STAN LEE PRESENTS: THE DYNAMIC DEFENDERS!™

Savior!

A BORROWED AVENGERS QUINJET ARCS LOW OVER MASSACHUSSETS WOODS, ITS CHROME GLEAMING AGAINST A GRAY, CLOUD-COVERED SKY.

INSIDE, FIVE GRIM-VISAGED DEFENDERS SIT IN SILENCE, SCANNING THE HORIZON. JUST WHAT THEY'RE SCANNING FOR THEY CANNOT SAY.

BUT IT MOST CERTAINLY IS NOT...

THIS!

OH, MY STARS AND GARTERS!

HANK, WHAT IS IT? WHERE DID IT COME FROM?

WHAT IT IS IS A STATUE, TALL AS A SKYSCRAPER-- AND IT SEEMS TO HAVE SPRUNG UP FROM... NOWHERE!

J.M. DeMATTEIS, scripter and DON PERLIN penciler CO-PLOTTERS
ABEL·MUSHYNSKY KUPPERBERG inkers·SHELLY LEFERMAN letterer
ALLEN MILGROM, Editor · JIM SHOOTER, chief

AND NO SOONER DOES HANK McCOY -- THE BOUNDING BEAST -- EXPERTLY SWERVE THE QUINJET ASIDE, THAN A SECOND GRANITE GARGANTUA APPEARS!

AND THEN A THIRD!

THIS AIRSHIP CAN TURN ON A DIME, CAN SWOOP AND DIVE ALMOST LIKE A LIVING THING.

BUT ALL MACHINES HAVE THEIR LIMITATIONS!

SHRAK

AS DO THE MEN THAT GUIDE THEM!

THOSE THINGS POPPED UP TOO FAST -- THERE WAS NO MANEUVERING ROOM!

HANG TIGHT, GROUP!

KRUNK

WE'RE GOING DOWN!

SHOOP!

THE STATUES ARE...*GONE*-- AS IF THEY HAD NEVER BEEN THERE!

THERE'S SOMETHING *AWFULLY* SCREWY GOING ON AROUND HERE!

YOU CAN SAY THAT AGAIN, ISAAC! WE CAME HERE TRYING TO TRACK DOWN *DAIMON HELLSTROM*--AND WE SEEM TO HAVE LANDED SMACK IN THE MIDDLE OF A--

--*MYSTERY*...?

ODIN'S EYE! THAT RUMBLING!

RUMMMMMM

THE VERY GROUND BENEATH THE DEFENDERS' FEET PULSES, TREMBLES, CRACKS, AND HEAVES-- *UNTIL*--

THAT...*WHATEVER-IT-IS* SEEMED TO JUST GROW UP OUT OF THE SNOW! BUT--*HOW?*

IF WE WANT TO STAY ALIVE TO FIND OUT THE ANSWER TO THE COGENT QUERY, HELLCAT--WE'D BETTER SCATTER...*FAST!*

I SEE IT--

--BUT I DON'T BELIEVE IT!

GARGOYLE! WHILE PATSY AND I EVER-SO-AGILELY DIVERT GODZILLA'S ATTENTION, YOU ZAP HIM WITH YOUR *BIO-MYSTIC* BOLTS!

SEE IF SIPHONING OFF A LITTLE *LIFE-FORCE* WILL SLOW HIM DOWN!

UH...THERE'S ONE MINOR PROBLEM, HANK! IN ORDER TO *HAVE* A LIFE-FORCE, A THING HAS GOT TO BE *ALIVE!*

AND *THIS* BEASTIE--

ISN'T!

THWAK!

3

BY ASGARD'S GLEAMING SPIRES --I HAVE HAD ENOUGH OF THIS!

VAL--*DON'T!* YOU CAN'T GO CHARGING IN LIKE THAT! WE'VE GOT TO WORK AS A *TEAM* OR ELSE--

SAVE THY BREATH, BEAST--

MONSTER-- THE VALKYRIE SHALL BRING THEE DOWN WITH ONE SWIPE OF HER *ENCHANTED* BLADE!

SHIKKK

--FOR DRAGONFANG AND I--

--HAVE ALREADY WON THE DAY!

CHOKKK

OH, NO!

THE CREATURE TOPPLES TOWARD US--

--AND WE ARE TOO SLOW, TOO CLUMSY, TO--

WHOOOM!

GREAT JOB, VAL! YOU STOPPED THE BIG, BAD MONSTER--

--AND KILLED THE OVER-MIND IN THE PROCESS!

EASY, HANK! THE OVER-MIND'S BODY HAS TAKEN WORSE THAN THIS! HE--

SHRREEE

NOW, WHAT?

BOOOM!

FORGIVE US, DEAR FRIENDS--BUT WE HAVE NOT YET LEARNED TO PROPERLY...CONTAIN OUR PSIONIC BLASTS!

WORRY NOT, DEFENDERS-- I SHALL PROTECT THEE FROM THIS SHOWER OF ICE!

MAYBE MOM WAS RIGHT! MAYBE I SHOULD'VE BEEN A CPA!

HELLO DOWN THERE!

I'M AFRAID TO LOOK!

HOT DOG, HANK! I NEVER REALIZED JUST HOW TOUGH THIS OLD GARGOYLE'S BODY IS! WHY, THAT BEASTIE WHOMPED ME FROM HERE TO SUNDAY--

--AND I HARDLY FELT A THING!

THANK HEAVEN FOR SMALL MIRACLES!

5

CORRECT ME IF I'M WRONG, BUT WE'RE SUPPOSED TO BE A TEAM, RIGHT?

WELL, WE SURE DON'T *FUNCTION* AS A TEAM! WHY, IF THE *X-MEN* OR *AVENGERS* HAD BEEN AS SLOPPY AS THIS BUNCH, WE'D ALL HAVE BEEN--

BEAST-- WE DO NOT NEED YOUR... WHAT IS THE PHRASE?... "PEP TALK!" THE DEFENDERS HAVE MANAGED TO WIN MANY A BATTLE WITHOUT RULES, REGULATIONS, CHARTERS ...OR *LEADERS!*

AND IF WE HAVE NEED OF A LEADER--DO YOU NOT THINK *BRUNNHILDA* WOULD BE MORE APPROPRIATE CHOICE --THAN YOU?

HEY! I WAS ONLY TRYING TO--

MY FRIENDS, WE HAVE NO TIME FOR SUCH PETTY BICKERING! OUR MINDS HAVE PINPOINTED THE SOURCE OF THE PSYCHIC EMANATIONS THAT LED US HERE!

BOTH DAIMON HELLSTROM -- AND THE DARK FORCE THAT HAS ENSNARED HIM --CAN BE FOUND--

--THERE!

BUT--THAT LOOKS LIKE SOME KIND OF MONASTERY!

MAYBE SO-- BUT I'M PICKING UP THE SAME VIBRATIONS OVER-MIND IS! DAIMON'S DOWN THERE, ALL RIGHT--AND HE'S IN TROUBLE!

Y'KNOW, PATSY-- I'VE BEEN MEANING TO *ASK* YOU ABOUT THESE MIND-POWERS OF YOURS! I KNOW YOU DIDN'T PICK THEM UP WITH THAT *CAT-SUIT* YOU'RE WEARING, SO--

--WHERE *DID* THEY COME FROM, HANK?

I THOUGHT I'D LOST THE ABILITY TO DO THAT FOR A WHILE, BUT--

UH...AM I CRAZY? OR DID THAT DOOR JUST OPEN...*BY ITSELF!*

I GUESS THAT MEANS WE'RE SUPPOSED TO GO *IN*, HUH?

THEN WE WOULD SUGGEST WE DO PRECISELY *THAT* --AND SEE WHAT AWAITS US...

BELIEVE IT OR NOT, FROM INSIDE *MYSELF!* WHEN I WAS ON TITAN, WITH MOONDRAGON, SHE TAUGHT ME HOW TO TAP THE VAST MENTAL ENERGIES WE *ALL* POSSESS!

6

"...ON THE OTHER SIDE!"

GREETINGS, MY FRIENDS! GREETINGS!

I COULD SENSE YOUR COMING --AND SO PREPARED A PROPER FETE IN YOUR HONOR!

WELL, DON'T JUST STAND THERE-- COME IN! COME IN!

WE FEEL WAVES OF INCREDIBLE POWER RADIATING FROM THIS ONE! HE IS THE SOURCE OF EVIL; THE FOCAL POINT WE HAVE BEEN SEARCHING FOR!

THEN WHY DO WE DALLY? LET US ATTACK... NOW!

VAL--WILL YOU RELAX! WE'RE DEALING WITH UNKNOWNS HERE! LET'S TAKE THINGS ONE STEP AT A TIME!

A SPLENDID IDEA, MISTER MCCOY! OR DO YOU PREFER ... BEAST? AH, YES! I KNOW YOU ALL! AND YOU-- SHALL KNOW ME!

FOR I AM-- THE MIRACLE MAN!

MIRACLE MAN?! HANK--I READ UP ON HIM BACK IN MY AVENGERS DAYS! HE'S AN ALL-POWERFUL LUNATIC WHO NEARLY TROUNCED THE FANTASTIC FOUR A COUPLE OF TIMES!

YEAH...I REMEMBER THE THING TELLING ME ABOUT HIM ONCE --AT A POKER GAME!

7

AND NO DOUBT WHAT HE TOLD YOU WAS *TRUE!* BUT THAT WAS THE MAN I ONCE *WAS...* A DELUDED MEGALOMANIAC WHOSE FRAGILE EGO COULD NOT HANDLE THE EARTH-SHATTERING POWERS BESTOWED UPON HIM BY THE INDIAN MYSTICS CALLED *THE CHEEMUZWA!*

THAT MAN -- IS NO MORE! FOR HERE, IN THIS MONASTERY, I HAVE BEEN... *REBORN!*

GLAD T'HEAR IT. NOW DO YOU MIND TELLING US WHERE IN BLAZES *DAIMON HELLSTROM* IS?

YOU MEAN THE SO-CALLED *SON OF SATAN?* STEP THIS WAY -- AND I'LL GLADLY TAKE YOU TO HIM!

NO, NO -- AFTER *YOU!*

HANK....?

VALKYRIE-- THOSE *MONKS--!*

I SEE, OVER-MIND! THEY SIT, BLANK-EYED, OPEN-MOUTHED, AS IF... ENTRANCED!

IT'S *HIS* GAME, PAT-- SO, FOR NOW, WE PLAY BY HIS *RULES!*

I BELIEVE THE ONE YOU'RE SEARCHING FOR IS RIGHT HERE!

BUT THAT -- IS A STATUE!

INDEED! I'M AFRAID I HAD NO RECOURSE BUT TO CHANGE HIM *INTO* ONE!

YOU *WHAT??* *!!!*

THERE, THERE, BEAST -- NO NEED TO GET SO EXCITED!

8

FOR I HAVE ONLY TO SNAP MY FINGERS--

SNAP

--AND HE IS RETURNED TO ANIMATE LIFE-- AS IS THE PIOUS ONE *BESIDE* HIM!

...OH...

...DEAR LORD...

DAIMON! ARE YOU ALL RIGHT?

NO! I AM *NOT* ALL RIGHT?

SO LONG AS THIS... MONSTER IS PERMITTED TO LIVE--I CAN *NEVER* BE ALL RIGHT!

"I CAME TO THIS MONASTERY A BROKEN MAN, SEEKING THE SOLACE OF ITS ABBOT, MY OLD MENTOR, *FATHER GOSSET.* INSTEAD, I ENCOUNTERED AN ENIGMA NAMED *BROTHER JOSHUA:* A SOFT-SPOKEN SOUL WHOSE GENTLE EYES HID AN AWFUL SECRET! A MAN WITHOUT A MEMORY--WHOSE MIDNIGHT MEDITATIONS PRODUCED STRANGE AND WONDROUS MANIFESTIONS!

"THOSE MANIFESTATIONS TOOK A DARK TURN WHEN JOSHUA SPOKE THE ORDER'S HOLY VOWS --AND WAS TRANSFORMED INTO THE CREATURE THAT STANDS BEFORE YOU!"*

*IT ALL HAPPENED LAST ISSUE-- EDITORI-AL.

THE CHEEMUZWA HAD PLACED A VEIL OF IGNORANCE OVER HIM, IN HOPES OF SPARING THE WORLD FROM HIS WRETCHED EVIL! BUT--

DAIMON, JOSHUA IS NOT EVIL... BUT MIS- GUIDED! HE--

MY DEAR ABBOT, I AM NEITHER EVIL *NOR* MIS- GUIDED!

9

OH, I FREELY ADMIT THAT--UPON REAWAKENING--THE SUDDEN SURGE OF MY RETURNING POWERS RESULTED IN A MOMENTARY MENTAL IMBALANCE! THUS, MY ATTACKS ON THE BROTHERS-- *AND* ON YOU DEFENDERS!

BUT I SWEAR TO YOU-- I HAVE *FOUND* AN INNER BALANCE! I SEE NOW THAT I HAVE BEEN HANDED THE ABILITY TO MOLD THIS WORLD TO MY WILL!

H-HEY! WH-WHAT'S HAPPENING?

BUT, DESPITE WHAT THE SATAN-SPAWN WOULD HAVE YOU BELIEVE, MY INTENT IS NOT TO *SUBJUGATE* THE EARTH!

"OH, NO, MY DEAR DEFENDERS! *I* INTEND--"

--TO *LIBERATE* IT!

HELA'S GHOST! WHERE *ARE* WE?

YOU'RE RIGHT THERE WITH THE SHARP QUESTIONS TO-DAY--AREN'T YOU, VAL?

WAIT...LET US PROBE THE PSYCHIC ETHERS... LET US...YES!

MY FRIENDS, WE ARE IN INDONESIA! ON THE ISLAND CALLED-- *JAVA!*

10

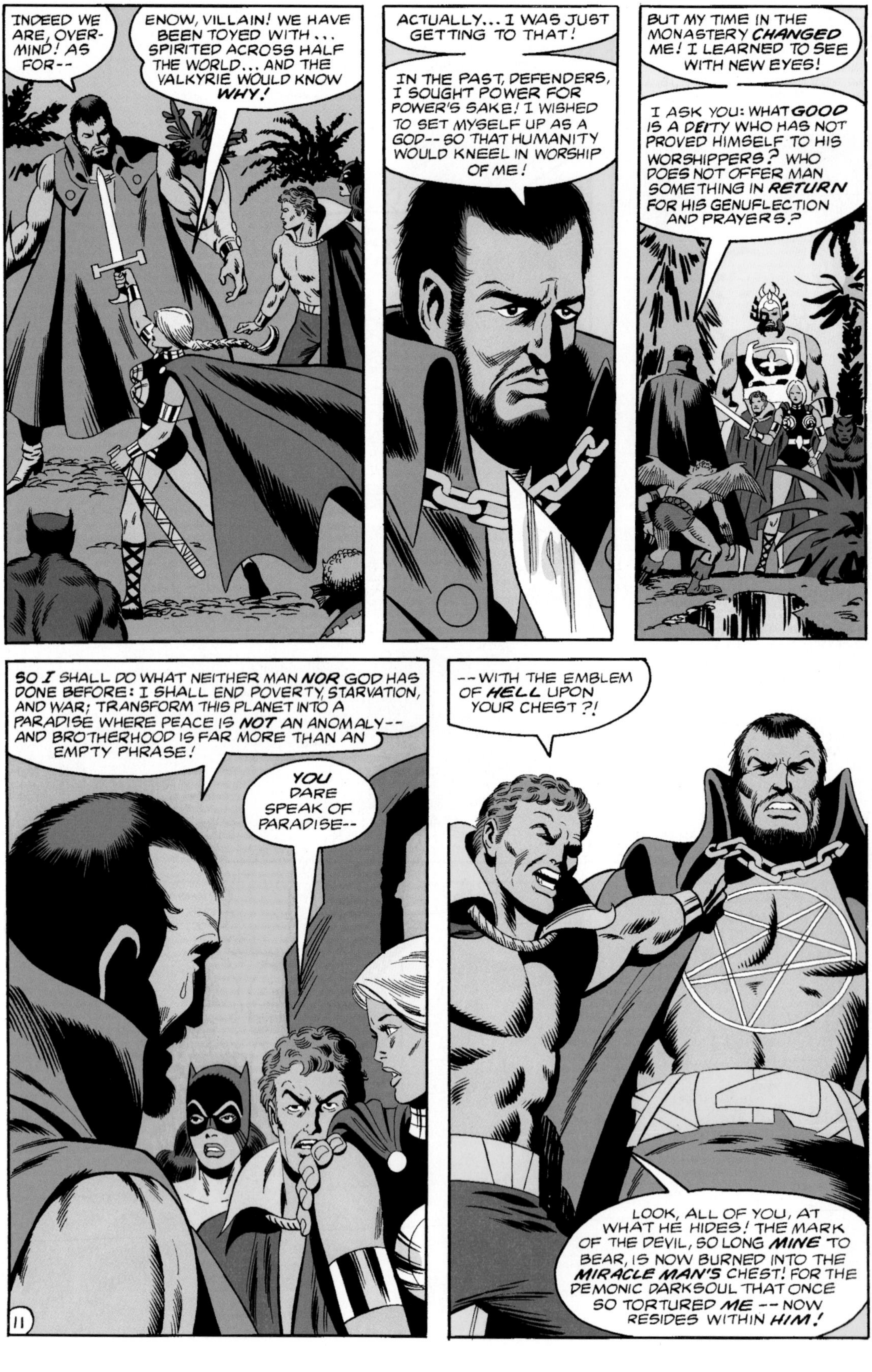
INDEED WE ARE, OVER-MIND! AS FOR--
ENOW, VILLAIN! WE HAVE BEEN TOYED WITH... SPIRITED ACROSS HALF THE WORLD... AND THE VALKYRIE WOULD KNOW WHY!
ACTUALLY... I WAS JUST GETTING TO THAT!
IN THE PAST, DEFENDERS, I SOUGHT POWER FOR POWER'S SAKE! I WISHED TO SET MYSELF UP AS A GOD-- SO THAT HUMANITY WOULD KNEEL IN WORSHIP OF ME!
BUT MY TIME IN THE MONASTERY CHANGED ME! I LEARNED TO SEE WITH NEW EYES!
I ASK YOU: WHAT GOOD IS A DEITY WHO HAS NOT PROVED HIMSELF TO HIS WORSHIPPERS? WHO DOES NOT OFFER MAN SOMETHING IN RETURN FOR HIS GENUFLECTION AND PRAYERS?
SO I SHALL DO WHAT NEITHER MAN NOR GOD HAS DONE BEFORE: I SHALL END POVERTY, STARVATION, AND WAR; TRANSFORM THIS PLANET INTO A PARADISE WHERE PEACE IS NOT AN ANOMALY-- AND BROTHERHOOD IS FAR MORE THAN AN EMPTY PHRASE!
YOU DARE SPEAK OF PARADISE--
11
--WITH THE EMBLEM OF HELL UPON YOUR CHEST?!
LOOK, ALL OF YOU, AT WHAT HE HIDES! THE MARK OF THE DEVIL, SO LONG MINE TO BEAR, IS NOW BURNED INTO THE MIRACLE MAN'S CHEST! FOR THE DEMONIC DARKSOUL THAT ONCE SO TORTURED ME -- NOW RESIDES WITHIN HIM!

I DO NOT DENY THAT I HAVE USURPED YOUR DARKSOUL, HELLSTROM-- **OR** THAT ITS ENERGIES HELPED BREAK THROUGH THE CHEEMUZWA'S VEIL AND RETURN MY SUPPRESSED MEMORIES AND POWERS!

BUT UNDERSTAND THIS: I AM **NOT** YOU! I CAN **CONTROL** THIS RAGING ENTITY WITHIN ME -- AND BEND IT TO MY WILL!

WHY DO WE STAND HERE LISTENING TO THIS PARADE OF LIES? DEFENDERS -- WE MUST BRING THIS ANIMAL DOWN!

BUT, HELLSTROM-- HE HAS NOT COMMITTED ANY TRUE CRIME!

WHAT.?!

I'M WITH OVER-MIND. WE WAIT. **FOR NOW.**

EXCELLENT! THEN PLEASE JOIN ME FOR A TOUR OF THIS SMALL SECTION OF POOR, BELEAGUERED JAVA--AND SEE THE PURGATORY I SHALL SOON... TRANSFORM!

WE WALK, DEFENDERS, THROUGH **RANNGKASBITUNG**: A COLLECTION OF VILLAGES SOME 150 MILES WEST OF JAKARTA.

THESE PEOPLE SUFFER FROM OVERPOPULATION... MALNUTRITION...LACK OF HOUSING! UP TO THREE FAMILIES ARE OFTEN CROWDED INTO ONE PATHETIC THATCHED HUT!

THEY HAVE NO ELECTRICITY! NO RUNNING WATER! THERE ARE ONLY 32 LATRINES TO PROVIDE FOR THE NEEDS OF 9,000 PEOPLE!

"IN SHORT: IT IS THE PERFECT TESTING GROUND FOR ME TO PROVE BOTH MY INTENTIONS --**AND** MY ABILITIES!"

WE WHO HAVE KNOWN SIMILAR AGONIES IN OUR FORMER LIVES--CANNOT HELP BUT BE DEEPLY **MOVED** BY THIS!

HANK--DO YOU REALLY THINK HE **COULD** CHANGE THINGS HERE?

I DON'T KNOW, PATS. I JUST DON'T KNOW!

12

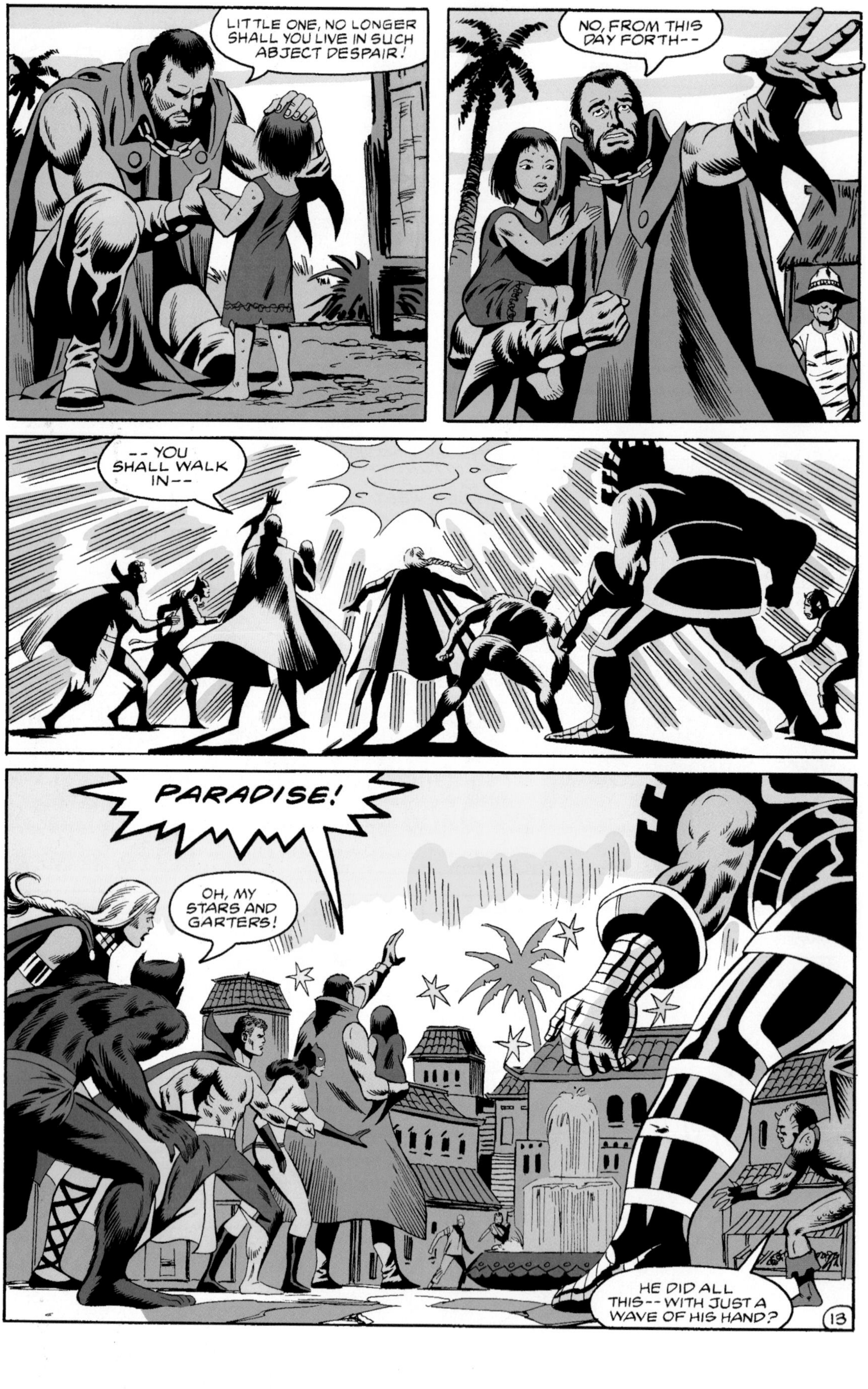
LITTLE ONE, NO LONGER SHALL YOU LIVE IN SUCH ABJECT DESPAIR!
NO, FROM THIS DAY FORTH--
--YOU SHALL WALK IN--
PARADISE!
OH, MY STARS AND GARTERS!
HE DID ALL THIS--WITH JUST A WAVE OF HIS HAND?
13

VALKYRIE--LISTEN TO THE JOYOUS CRIES OF THE PEOPLE! THEY SENSE THAT THE DOORS OF AN EARTHLY HEAVEN HAVE BEEN OPENED WIDE TO THEM; THAT THEY WILL NEVER AGAIN KNOW HUNGER...OR FEAR!

IF THE MIRACLE MAN COULD WORK SUCH WONDERMENT ALL ACROSS THE GLOBE-- IT COULD BE THE BEGINNING OF A VERITABLE... GOLDEN AGE!

OVER-MIND, YOU ARE YOUNG IN MANY WAYS! DO YOU NOT THINK ASGARD'S LORD ODIN COULD BRING SUCH A..."MIRACLE" ABOUT IF HE SO DESIRED? IT IS WELL WITHIN HIS REACH --BUT HE REFRAINS!

FOR WE GODS LEARNED LONG AGO THAT MAN MUST MAKE HIS OWN HEAVEN! TO HAVE IT IMPOSED UPON HIM FROM WITHOUT RESULTS ONLY IN CHAOS-- AND IN DEATH!

THE VALKYRIE SPEAKS WISELY! WE CAN'T ALLOW THIS TRAVESTY TO CONTINUE!

DAIMON, LOOK AROUND! LOOK AT THE HAPPINESS REFLECTED ON ALL THOSE FACES! DO WE HAVE THE RIGHT TO TAKE THIS AWAY FROM THEM--BECAUSE OF A VAGUE MORAL QUESTION?

I DON'T THINK IT'S SO VAGUE, PATSY! WHO ARE WE TO GO MUCKING AROUND WITH THE DIVINE PLAN?

I DON'T KNOW IF I EVEN BELIEVE IN ANY DIVINE PLAN, ISAAC-- BUT THERE'S SOMETHING ABOUT THIS THAT DOESN'T SIT RIGHT WITH ME!

SAVE YOUR DEBATES, DEFENDERS! THERE IS WORK YET TO BE DONE!

AN IMPERIOUS CLAP OF THE HANDS...

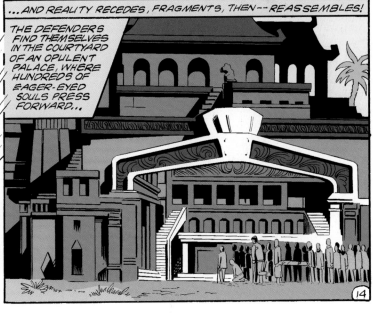

...AND REALITY RECEDES, FRAGMENTS, THEN-- REASSEMBLES!

THE DEFENDERS FIND THEMSELVES IN THE COURTYARD OF AN OPULENT PALACE, WHERE HUNDREDS OF EAGER-EYED SOULS PRESS FORWARD...

14

...SEEKING THE TOUCH OF A NEW-BORN GOD!

THESE ARE THE DISEASED, THE UNBALANCED, THE CRIPPLED, AND DEFORMED. ONE BY ONE THEY ARE CALLED BEFORE THE MIRACLE MAN, AND, ONE BY ONE...

...THEY ARE CURED!

⟨DON'T BE AFRAID, OLD ONE. I HAVE BUT TO PLACE MY HANDS UPON YOUR BROW-- AND YOUR BLINDNESS SHALL BE LIFTED.⟩*

⟨I-I AM SORRY, GOOD SIR--⟩

*TRANSLATED FROM THE SUDANESE--AL.

⟨--BUT I CANNOT ACCEPT YOUR GRACIOUS GIFT.⟩

⟨SURELY, YOU'RE JOKING!⟩

⟨NO. I HAVE EMBRACED THE FATE THE GODS HAVE BESTOWED UPON ME. TO TAKE YOUR HEALING WOULD BE TO DENY THEIR WILL.⟩

SNAP

⟨THEIR WILL?!⟩

⟨M-MY LEGS! I...CANNOT WALK!⟩

⟨NOW YOU MUST BEG FOR MY TOUCH!⟩

⟨I...CAN-NOT...⟩

⟨BEG!!⟩

⟨I...CAN... NOT...!⟩

⟨BEG!!!⟩

15

UH...GROUP WE SEEM TO HAVE A MAJOR PROBLEM ON OUR HANDS!

INDEED. IT IS THE *DARKSOUL'S* INFLUENCE, FURTHER CORRUPTING HIM.

COULD BE. OR MAYBE IT'S JUST THAT OUT-OF-CONTROL *EGO* HE SAID HE'D TRANSCENDED!

GNAT! WHY DO YOU JUST LIE THERE? DOES YOUR LIFE MEAN SO *LITTLE* TO YOU?!

WE'RE WAY PAST THE POINT OF DISCUSSING DELICATE *MORAL* QUESTIONS! THIS GUY'S GONE OVER THE EDGE--AND WE'VE GOT TO STOP HIM BEFORE HE TAKES THIS WHOLE ISLAND WITH HIM!

BEAST...OUR OWN DESIRE FOR EASY ANSWERS DROVE US TO TAKE THE MIRACLE MAN AT FACE VALUE. NOW WE ASK THAT WE MAY BE THE ONES TO PUT A SWIFT END TO HIS *INSANITY*.

MAKES SENSE, O.M.! MIRACLE MAN'S POWER COMES FROM HIS MIND... AND YOU'RE THE BEST MIND-ZAPPER WE'VE GOT, *SO*...

...GO GET 'IM!

THE UNITED MINDS OF SIX OF EARTH'S MOST POWERFUL TELEPATHS CALL UP PSIONIC ENERGIES THAT COULD LAY WASTE A MOUNTAIN...

SHRAKKKK

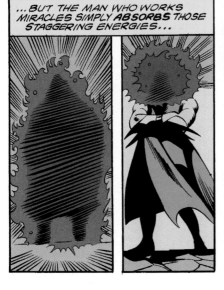

...BUT THE MAN WHO WORKS MIRACLES SIMPLY *ABSORBS* THOSE STAGGERING ENERGIES...

...AND SPITS THEM *BACK* IN THE OVER-MIND'S *FACE*!

SHOOOM!

16

OVER-MIND'S DOWN! WE'VE GOT TO TRY A MORE COORDINATED ATTACK! START WORKING LIKE A TEAM!

VILLAIN!

OH, NO! THERE SHE GOES AGAIN!

MISCREANTS! I COULD KILL YOU! ALL WITH A SINGLE THOUGHT! BUT I PREFER INSTEAD TO HUMBLE YOU--

--IN MY MOST INIMITABLE STYLE!

SHANGG

A DUEL, VALKYRIE-- AS IN DAYS OF OLD!

IF YOU THINK TO STOP ME WITH ONE FECKLESS BLADE CREATED FROM AIR AND DUST, MIRACLE MAN, YOU ARE SADLY--

--MISTAKEN...?

ODIN'S EYE!

NOT EVEN MISS VALKYRIE CAN FIGHT HER WAY THROUGH THAT WALL OF STEEL! SHE'S TRAPPED!

WHY THAT THICK-HEADED ASGARDIAN A--

WHY NOT SKIP THE NAME CALLING, BEAST--AND CONCENTRATE ON YOUR ORIGINAL IDEA! IF WE'RE A TEAM--

-- THEN LET'S START *ACTING* LIKE ONE.

ISAAC! WHILE PATS AND I KNOCK HIM OFF-BALANCE -- YOU HIT 'IM... *HARD!*

GOTCHA!

ISAAC! STOP! CAN'T YOU SEE WHAT YOU'RE *DOING?*

BY THE SEVEN CIRCLES! I SPEAK-- BUT THERE IS NO SOUND!

THE MIRACLE MAN HAS ROBBED ME OF MY VOICE!

WELL, HOW DO YOU LIKE THAT? WE DID IT! HE'S DOWN! AND, JUST AS SOON AS I SIPHON OFF A WEE BIT MORE OF HIS LIFE-FORCE--

--HE'S GONNA BE--

HA-HA HA-HA!

--OUT...?!

YOU LUDICROUS, BAT-WINGED GROTESQUERY! DO YOU THINK I CAN BE SO EASILY BESTED? ALL YOU'VE "DEFEATED" IS AN ILLUSION THAT I PLACED IN YOUR MIND!

HANK! PATSY!

WH-WHAT HAVE YOU *DONE* TO THEM?

I HAVE DONE NOTHING! *YOU*, ON THE OTHER HAND, RENDERED THEM UN- CONSCIOUS WITH YOUR BIO-MYSTIC ENERGIES!

THAT *DOES* IT!!

YOU JUST MADE ME

18

183

MAD!!!

WHAMM!!

I WAS NEVER MUCH FOR FISTICUFFS—AND I'M ONLY *BEGINNING* TO FIGURE OUT *JUST* HOW STRONG THIS GARGOYLE'S BODY REALLY *IS*—

BASSSH!

—BUT I'M BETTING IT'S STRONG ENOUGH TO BELT YOU CLEAN BACK TO MASSACHUSSETS!

YOU... *HURT*... ME!

AND, FOR SUCH AN UNFORGIVABLE TRANSGRESSION—

"—YOU MUST PAY THE PRICE OF THE DAMNED!"

HIS VOICE RETURNED, DAIMON HELLSTROM CALLS OUT TO HIS FRIEND...

...BUT THERE IS NO REPLY.

FOR WHEN DID *STONE* EVER SPEAK?

"HEAVEN HELP US," HELLSTROM THINKS. "THE DARKSOUL HAS RISEN COMPLETELY TO THE FORE! THE MIRACLE MAN'S VERY FEATURES HAVE BEEN TWISTED INTO A DAEMONIC MASK!

"HE BELLOWS AND RAGES—AND THIS... PARADISE OF HIS—*ERUPTS!*"

SO IT DOES.

THE EARTH SHAKES AND SPLITS WIDE. THE SKIES DARKEN AND SPIT LIGHTNING.

BUT PERHAPS MOST CURIOUS OF ALL IS THE MOMENTARY *CONFUSION* THAT SEEMS TO COME OVER THE MIRACLE MAN.

FOR AN INSTANT, DAIMON HELLSTROM SWEARS HE CAN SEE THE PAINED, PLEADING EYES OF *BROTHER JOSHUA*, STARING OUT AT HIM; THE EYES OF A MAN TRAPPED IN A HELL OF HIS OWN MAKING.

19

AND HE KNOWS WHAT MUST BE DONE!

MY DARKSOUL--*HEAR* ME! COME FORTH AND FACE YOUR OTHER SELF!

...UHHH...

I AM HERE, DAIMON HELLSTROM! SAY WHAT YOU WILL AND THEN... I SHALL *SLAY* YOU!

AND, EVEN AS THOSE EYES ARE ONCE MORE FIRED WITH SATANIC FURY, DAIMON HELLSTROM COMES TO GRIPS WITH AN AWFUL TRUTH.

I MAKE YOU AN OFFER, DARKSOUL! ABANDON THE MIRACLE MAN'S BODY AND RETURN HERE TO ME! I--

HA-HA-HA! RETURN TO *YOU*? TO THE ONE WHOSE REJECTION OF ALL HE TRULY *IS* NEARLY OBLITERATED ME? DO YOU THINK ME AN IDIOT, DAIMON?

NO. BUT I THINK YOU ARE UNAWARE OF WHAT ULTIMATE FATE AWAITS YOU!

UNLIKE ME, THE MIRACLE MAN IS HUMAN-- FULLY, *PURELY* HUMAN-- AND WITHIN *ALL* INHUMANS ARE THE SEEDS OF A DIVINE GOODNESS THAT IS ANATHEMA TO YOU!

AS BROTHER JOSHUA, THE MIRACLE MAN MADE *CONTACT* WITH THAT PART OF HIMSELF AND, ONCE TOUCHED, IT WILL NEVER DIE!

IT MAY TAKE TIME, BUT HE WILL INEVITABLY RISE UP-- AND *DESTROY* YOU!

FOR YOU WERE BORN TO INHABIT A SPAWN OF THE DEVIL-- NOT A SON OF MAN!

AND WHAT DO YOU PROMISE ...IN *EXCHANGE* FOR MY RETURN?

I GIVE YOU MY INVIOLABLE WORD THAT I SHALL *NEVER DENY YOU AGAIN!* I SHALL EMBRACE YOUR WICKED PATH-- GRANT YOU FREE REIGN-- AND, TOGETHER, WE SHALL SIT BESIDE MY FATHER ...ON THE THRONE OF HELL!

THERE IS WISDOM IN YOUR WORDS, DAIMON! I ACCEPT YOUR OFFER! PREPARE TO WELCOME ME... *HOME!*

DAIMON ... NO!

20

I CAN'T LET HIM *DO* THIS! I LOVE HIM! *I LOVE HIM!!*

OVER-MIND? C-CAN YOU *READ* MY *THOUGHTS?*

YES, PATSY...

THEN YOU *KNOW* WHAT WE HAVE TO DO!

B-BUT WE ARE...*TOO DRAINED!* WE DO NOT HAVE THE POWER TO--

DON'T GIVE ME *EXCUSES!* JUST LINK YOUR MINDS UP TO MINE AND--

--LET'S *DO* IT!

WE MAY *BOTH* BE WEAK AS *KITTENS,* BUT TOGETHER, THERE'S A *CHANCE* THAT WE CAN--

PATSY! *LOOK!* IT IS *HAPPENING* ALREADY!

THE *DARKSOUL*--IS *RISING!*

SSSSS

THEN WE CAN'T *WAIT!* NOW, OVER-MIND!

NOW!

NOW.

21

186

NO! WHAT IS HAPPENING TO ME?

STOP!

STOPPPPPP

THE INHUMAN SHRIEK FADES INTO A SIBILANT HISS. THEN COMES A SILENCE, DEEP AS ETERNITY.

AND THEN...

SHA-KOOOM!

...THE WORLD EXPLODES!

WH-WHERE ARE WE?

APPARENTLY --BACK AT THE MONASTERY!

BUT-- HOW?

WITH THE DARKSOUL TORN FROM HIS BODY, JOSHUA'S MIND COLLAPSED INWARDS --AND THE EFFECTS OF ALL HIS ..."MIRACLES" REVERSED!

BUT THE DARKSOUL, PATSY! WHAT DID YOU AND THE OVER-MIND DO? WHERE IS IT?

WHERE IT BELONGS, DAIMON.

"WHERE IT BELONGS."

FINIS?

 NEXT

AMONG OTHER THINGS: THE ICEMAN!

THE ORIGINAL PAGE 12 FOR *SON OF SATAN #8*, SEEN HERE, WAS REJECTED BY THE COMICS CODE AUTHORITY. THE REPLACEMENT PAGE IN THE PRINTED COMIC WAS SCRIPTED BY **ARCHIE GOODWIN** AND PENCILED BY **JOHN ROMITA SR.**

ORIGINAL *GHOST RIDER #10* REPRINTED *MARVEL SPOTLIGHT #12*.
COVER BY **MICHAEL BAIR**

SON OF SATAN CLASSIC TPB COVER BY **JOHN ROMITA SR.** & **VERONICA GANDINI**

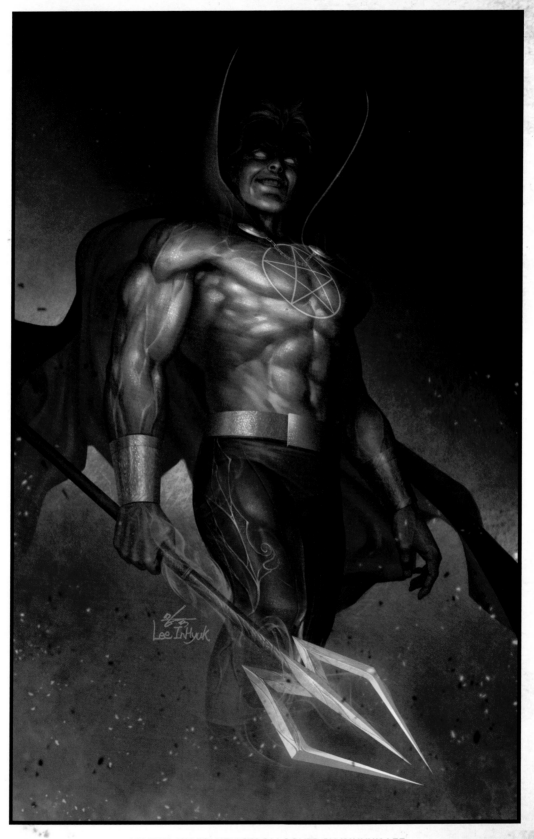

MARVEL TALES: HELLSTROM COVER BY **INHYUK LEE**

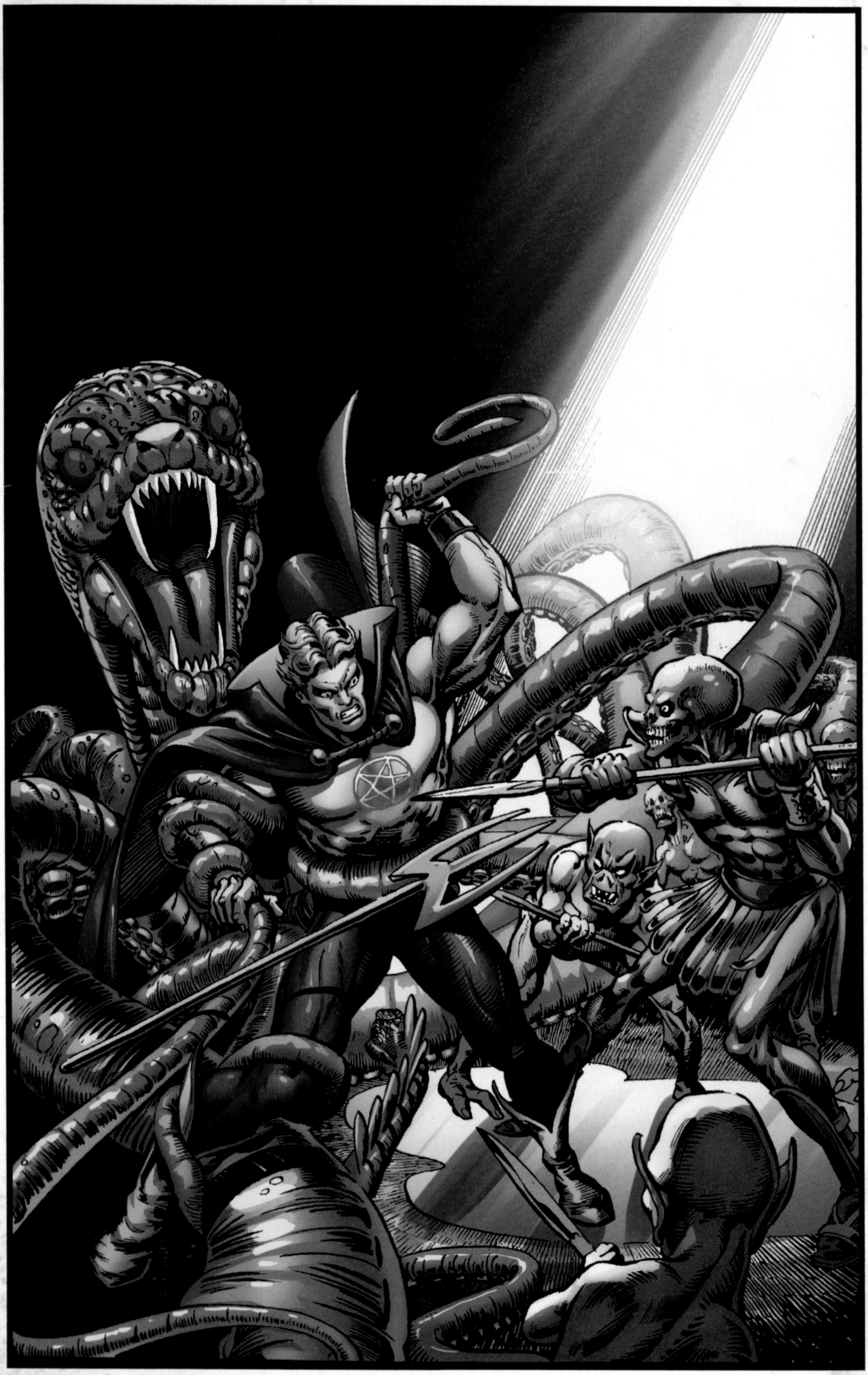